Everyday Playfulness

of related interest

Supporting Toddlers' Wellbeing in Early Years Settings
Strategies and Tools for Practitioners and Teachers
Edited by Helen Sutherland and Yasmin Mukadam
ISBN 978 1 78592 262 6
eISBN 978 1 78450 552 3

Exercising Muscles and Minds, Second Edition
Outdoor Play and the Early Years Curriculum
Marjorie Ouvry and Amanda Furtado
ISBN 978 1 78592 266 4
eISBN 978 1 78450 557 8

Learning through Movement and Active Play in the Early Years
A Practical Resource for Professionals and Teachers
Tania Swift
ISBN 978 1 78592 085 1
eISBN 978 1 78450 346 8

Listening to Young Children in Early Years Settings
A Practical Guide
Sonia Mainstone-Cotton
ISBN 978 1 78592 469 9
eISBN 978 1 78450 855 5

Create, Perform, Teach!
An Early Years Practitioner's Guide to Developing
Your Creativity and Performance Skills
Nikky Smedley
Illustrated by Sam Greaves
ISBN 978 1 78592 431 6
eISBN 978 1 78450 799 2

EVERYDAY PLAYFULNESS

A New Approach to Children's Play
and Adult Responses to It

STUART LESTER

Edited by Wendy Russell and Jeremy Lester

Jessica Kingsley *Publishers*
London and Philadelphia

First published in 2020
by Jessica Kingsley Publishers
73 Collier Street
London N1 9BE, UK
and
400 Market Street, Suite 400
Philadelphia, PA 19106, USA

www.jkp.com

Library of Congress Cataloging in Publication Data
A CIP catalog record for this book is available from the Library of Congress

British Library Cataloguing in Publication Data
A CIP catalogue record for this book is available from the British Library

ISBN 978 1 78592 064 6
eISBN 978 1 78450 326 0

Printed and bound in Great Britain

Contents

Foreword: *Jeremy Lester* 9

Foreword: *Wendy Russell* 15

Acknowledgements 17

Front Cover Image – Unburdened Children: Just off to Play 21

Preamble 25
The bedroom scenario 26
Setting the scene for what follows 29

1. **An Introduction** 35
   Setting the scene 35
   Perspectives on play: an introductory overview 37
   Play in a wider context: the individualisation of life 41
   Playing in an even wider context: a neoliberal life 44
   The power of binaries 48
   Beyond binary thinking 50
   Summary: going beyond what we know about play 52

2. **Play: A Different Line of Enquiry** 55
   Introduction 55
   Everyday acts of playing 57
   The value of the example 61
   Bringing play to life 63
   Play lines of movement 73
   Summary 84

3. Some Thoughts on Play and 'Well-Being'   87
    Introduction   87
    Well-being and policy   88
    Children's well-being   89
    Playing and being well   94
    Playing and resilience   99
    Children's right to play: a right to life   105
    Summary   111

4. Play and Space   115
    Introduction   115
    Co-creating play spaces   118
    What is 'space'?   121
    The production of children's 'play spaces'   125
    A brief genealogy of children's playgrounds   127
    The natural playground   130
    The adventure playground: a counter movement?   135
    Playgrounds on a plane of organisation   140
    Summary   145

5. The Micro-Politics of Playing   147
    Introduction   147
    Playing as political action   148
    Playing and 'becoming democratic'   156
    Play, spatial justice and a right to the city   163
    Summary   169

6. Cartography and Account-Ability   171
    Introduction   171
    Taking account of the everyday   174
    Mapping as process   176
    Towards a cartography of play   181
    A nomadic approach: mobile methods   182
    Summary   189

7. Critical Cartography and Response-Ability   191

    Introduction   191

    Towards a critical cartography of play   192

    Plugging in: theory, research and practice   197

    Navigation and negotiation revisited: lessons from resilience
    scholarship   199

    Amin's four registers of the good city   199

    Planning for play   209

    Summary: enchantment and practice account-ability and
    response-ability   216

8. An Ending that is Not an Ending   219

    Another line of becoming   219

    Retracing lines   221

    Plugging in again (and again and...)   221

    Moments and movements of hope   224

    References   227

    Index   245

Figures

Figure 1.1: A line of development   42

Figure 1.2: A self-enclosed organism   43

Figure 1.3: A plane of organisation   45

Figure 2.1: A (life)line of movement   74

Figure 2.2: A child's drawing of a body   74

Figure 2.3: Moving lines at the bus stop   78

Figure 3.1: Lines of flight on a plane of organisation   103

Figure 4.1: Becoming trees   119

Figure 4.2: Cutting play from movement   121

Foreword: Jeremy Lester

*Man only plays when in the full meaning of the word he is
a man, and he is only completely a man when he plays.*

Friedrich Schiller 1909–14, Letter *XV*

'When I use a word,' said Humpty Dumpty, 'it means
just what I choose it to mean – neither more nor less...
The question is...which is to be master – that's all.'

'*The question is,*' said Alice, '*whether you can
make words mean so many different things.*'

Lewis Carroll 1903, p.212

Each epoch, to paraphrase the words of Walter Benjamin (1999, pp.838 and 863), has a side turned toward dreams, the child's side. If only we could liberate the enormous energies of history that are slumbering in these dreams and, by implication the 'what if...', together with the realm of play that accompanies and stimulates them, then just imagine what energies would be released. To a large extent, this is what the present work by Stuart Lester seeks to do, in terms of liberating not only the child's perspective of dreams and play, but the adult's perspective as well. The book takes us on a series of marvellous adventures and explorations, but the terrain covered cannot be expressed in normal geographical terms. Instead, one is guided along a route that is more akin to the Situationist notion of 'psychogeography', one which constantly relishes the unpredictable, the unexpected, the provocative. After all, is it not by this means that one can best escape – better still, *subvert* – many of the conventional forms of conformist control that are intrinsic to normal life? At the end of the journey, one's mind, and even more so one's creative imagination, is a whirligig, a merry-go-round, a helter-skelter of ideas spinning, rotating, faster and faster, some jumping off here to shoot down new paths, others jumping off there. And just as the mind begins to settle down and rest a little bit, it is then that we are treated to a marvellous ending – one whose intention was never to be closed but always, forever open. It comes in the form of a simple statement, yet it almost sounds like a confession (for which, of course, no penance, no amount of 'Hail Marys' is either expected or required): 'If I ask myself what is it that I have been doing all my life, the best response I can give would be to say, I have quite simply been playing.' Oh, how this statement resounds with the echoes of another great advocate of play as a subversive parable in life, and one who we know exerted great influence on all who knew him – Colin Ward.[1]

Yes, I am aware that I have broken a golden rule here. Here we are at the beginning of a foreword, and I have already revealed the ending. How many times have we been told that one must never prematurely reveal the ending? Indeed, how many times have we ourselves told others this when, for example, we watch a film with someone who has already seen it? Yet, you see, I couldn't resist. It is such a charming, enchanting and so appropriate an ending. And I couldn't resist because I also know – as perhaps you the reader already know – that this particular ending of a book masks and hides a very different type of ending – one that I wish I did not have to reveal; one that I wish had remained hidden and unrevealed for a long time to come; one that came so abruptly, so harshly, so cruelly, so unexpectedly.

'Once a coincidence was taking a walk with a little accident, and they met an explanation' (Carroll 1889, cited in Deleuze 2004, p.66).[2] As fate or destiny would have it, a book dedicated to celebrating play and opening its remit out to so many other dimensions of life would also turn out to mark a closure of the book of the author's own life. What should have been his 'latest' book, therefore, has now sadly been transformed into his last. But what a celebration of life it is, a celebration of Stuart's

---

[1] For a wonderful appreciation of Colin Ward's work and influence, see Stuart Lester (2014a).

[2] Deleuze is referring to a couple of passages taken from Lewis Carroll's work, *Sylvie and Bruno*.

own life and the enormous practical and theoretical contributions he made to the realm of play.

History is full of unfinished works – of literature, art and so on – that can often lead to something happening to that work that was not originally intended. Fortunately, in this case, the manuscript that Stuart bequeathed us was so near to being complete that it has been a relatively straightforward, if nevertheless very sad and painful, task of finishing it off. The division of labour between us was very easy to determine. After all, only one of us possesses the in-depth knowledge and understanding of the role and capacity of play, and who thus became Stuart's principal collaborator on so many of his projects. Over the course of time, there have been many great pairings in all intellectual domains. Well, in the realm of 'play' – and its whole broader significance in all aspects of our lives – there are few pairings that can match the visionary approach of 'Lester and Russell'. The only other task, meanwhile, was the responsibility of simply checking over some of the more general details of the manuscript. In doing this, it gave us both the wonderful chance to *continue* a long-standing dialogue and series of exchanges that we have had with Stuart over the potential contributions and input that some philosophers have had, or might have, on the realm of play. And we have used the word 'continue' here deliberately. As the great Palestinian poet, Mahmoud Darwish (2009, p.29), put it: 'No one exactly dies. Rather souls change their looks and address.' Stuart's death takes us from one meaning of our contact and relationship with him to another meaning. And although the 'herald of the invisible' struck him down, hasn't he also defeated death by the permanent things and creative ideas that he left behind?

When it comes to his philosophical influences, needless to say, for Stuart this meant principally his long-standing – and often playful – use of key ideas and concepts associated first and foremost with Gilles Deleuze (and Félix Guattari). To say that Deleuze in particular became a guiding influence on Stuart, leading and directing him down all kinds of creative and innovative paths, is something well known to all his colleagues. I have often wondered how Stuart actually first came into contact with Deleuze's work. I never did ask him outright about this and now – like so many questions that I have – I wish fervently that I had asked. If no definite response can now be given, I would like to think or imagine – call it one of those small examples of 'what if…' – that his first encounter was by coming across, perhaps even accidentally, Deleuze's constant fascination for the *Alice* stories by Lewis Carroll. This would strike me as a wonderful and truly enchanting place for Stuart to have met Deleuze for the very first time.

As Deleuze (2004, p.ix) emphasises (and eulogises) right at the outset of his study dedicated to the logic of sense, the world of Lewis Carroll has everything required to please:

> splendidly bizarre and esoteric words; grids; codes and decodings; drawings and photographs; a profound psychoanalytic content; and an exemplary logical and linguistic formalism. Over and above the immediate pleasure, though, there is something else, a play of sense and nonsense [and] a chaos-cosmos.

A meeting of creative minds and playful imagination between Deleuze and Stuart would have been immediately on the cards from this moment on. And as Deleuze develops, expands and deepens his reading of Carroll, the merger of sympathies in a shared 'adventure playground' would have likewise increased. By accompanying Alice on her adventures, Deleuze, and we too, can enchantingly explore 'the secret of events and of the becoming unlimited which they imply, in the depths of the earth, in dug out shafts and holes which plunge beneath, and in the mixture of bodies which interpenetrate and coexist' (Deleuze 2004, p.9). In other words, it is almost as though the world itself has become a veritable adventure playground in its entirety. Finally, a point would have been reached of mutual harmony between Deleuze and Stuart. This is the point at which brand new games can be invented of the most bizarre kind, and in which existing known games can be completely transformed, games which have no fixed rules, regulations or functions, but where simply one begins when one wishes and stops at will. These are games, notes Deleuze, which have in common a great deal of movement and which permit neither winner nor loser. Of course, we are not under normal circumstances of play acquainted with such games which seem to contradict themselves. They are determined 'by hypotheses which divide and apportion chance, that is, hypotheses of loss or gain' (Deleuze 2004, p.69); what Deleuze himself refers to as the spatial domain where the '*what happens if...*' rules the roost. Such games and forms of play, he goes on, are like thoughts which emit a distribution of singularities:

All of these thoughts communicate in one long thought, causing all the forms or figures of the nomadic distribution to correspond to its own displacement, everywhere insinuating chance and ramifying each thought, linking the 'once and for all' to 'each time' for the sake of 'all time'. For only thought finds it possible *to affirm all chance and to make chance into an object of affirmation*... In it there is nothing but victories for those who know how to play, that is, how to affirm and ramify chance, instead of dividing it *in order to* dominate it, *in order to* wager, *in order to* win. This game, which can only exist in thought and which has no other result than the work of art, is also that by which thought and art are real and disturbing reality, morality, and the economy of the world. (Deleuze 2004, p.60)

One aspect of Carroll's story that particularly fascinated and enchanted Deleuze – and what reader hasn't been fascinated and enchanted by it, we ask ourselves – was, needless to say, the smile of the Cheshire cat; that wonderful smile which remained hanging, floating, in the air long after the material incarnation of the cat had gone away. It has traditionally been thought that smiles are ontologically dependent on faces, that a smile lies in the face, that it can only exist as part of the face. But perhaps this relationship needs to be rethought. To use a Spinozian term, a smile can be a 'substance in itself'. It truly can be ontologically and conceptually independent of anything else; completely autonomous in its own right. It was undoubtedly with this image in mind that another philosopher, and one who likewise greatly inspired Stuart's work, Jacques Derrida, wrote a note shortly before his own death in 2004, with strict instructions that it only be opened and read (by his eldest son, Pierre), during the celebratory wake of his own funeral. As was disclosed at the appropriate time, the note contained the following handwritten cryptic message:

Jacques wanted no rites and no orations. He knows from experience what an ordeal it is for the friend who takes on this task. He asks me to thank you for coming and to bless you. He beseeches you not to be sad, to think only of the many happy moments you gave him the chance to share with him.

Smile for me, he says, as I will have smiled for you until the end.
Always prefer life and constantly affirm survival....
I love you and am smiling at you from wherever I am.
(Derrida 2007, p.462)

Some deaths, and the absence that accompanies death, are, as Derrida himself often reminded us in his body of work on mourning, *unthinkable*. This, for us at least, and we know for so many others as well, is definitely the case with Stuart. His death, just over a year ago, has been mourned (like that of Derrida's) without the usual rites and artificial ovations. His death is still mourned. But one must not let that continued mourning dominate the thoughts that precede and accompany the reading of this book. As stressed above, it is – and deserves – to be read as a true celebration of Stuart's life, work, impact and achievements. As we read it, let us therefore reflect his own smile on to us from wherever he is at present *playing*. After all, isn't our intrinsic relationship with death a form of play, a variant of the game of hide-and-seek? And even when the eternal victor in this game eventually captures us – or embraces us, some might even prefer – in its arms, who is to say that this marks the veritable end of the time for play? Consequently, as we read this book and contemplate Stuart's smile shining down on us, let us recall as well a sentiment beautifully expressed by Jorge Luis Borges (Borges 1999), whenever he gave advice on how his stories, poems and other writings should be approached and read, which seems so appropriate here. For Borges, it is as though everything in life (and literature) happens for the first time, but in an uncanny way that makes it seem as though it is eternal. Words may have been written by him (or by any author) but it is always each and every individual reader who *invents* those words.

Jeremy Lester, May 2018

Foreword: Wendy Russell

As adults, we have lost our way when it comes to children's play. We have over-coded it, superimposed adult desires and anxieties onto it, colonised it, turned it into something other than play. For too long, we have felt the need to show just how useful it is for things other than play. This book offers a radically different way of thinking about play and our adult responses to it:

> This is how it should be done: lodge yourself on a stratum, experiment with the opportunities it offers, find an advantageous place on it, find potential movements of deterritorialization, possible lines of flight, experience them, produce flow conjunctions here and there, try out continuums of intensities segment by segment, have a small plot of new land at all times. (Deleuze and Guattari 1988, p.178)

It was pure chance that I ended up working in children's play, but I knew straight away it was the stratum on which I wanted to lodge myself. In true nomadic and rhizomatic fashion, I experimented: the pathways I have wandered have not been planned with any great deliberation but have emerged from mostly chance encounters. One such encounter was with Stuart Lester, whose playfulness, great intellect, integrity and commitment to children's play I found inspiring. We were both seeking ways of thinking and doing 'children's play' differently. Neither of us knew it at the time, but we were both following Deleuze's advice; it was Stuart who discovered his work and has indeed 'plugged into' it to disturb our habits of thought and practice regarding children's play – performing what Deleuze and Guattari (1988) term acts of deterritorialisation and lines of flight from the molar assemblages that constrain children's right to play.

Having spent the best part of the last two decades working collaboratively with Stuart, I have been his editor more times than I can count. But I didn't think that I would be in the position of having to edit and complete this book. It is a task that has been both a privilege and a sorrow. Stuart's sudden and unexpected passing in May 2017 left us all bereft, but I was heartened to find the manuscript sufficiently worked up to make me think it could be published without too much distortion. I am so grateful to have been able to work with Jeremy, Stuart's philosopher brother, in this endeavour. Our collaboration has made the task less overwhelming, less lonely. We have been able to have some excellent discussions with each other and with Stuart in the process. The shared desire to bring this legacy into print has kept me going. It has also given me a reassurance in some areas of philosophy where my own knowledge has been lacking.

This work would probably be 'old hat' for Stuart were he still with us. He was always looking for the next 'small plot of new land'. However, I am still living with this land, shifting as it does, wandering it and being open to new encounters. I am grateful to Stuart for leaving such a comprehensive legacy of a method for supporting children's play that does not colonise it for adult ends. This book illustrates richly what Stuart was so good at: it is deeply philosophical, radically different, embedded in ideas of justice and yet highly practical. Stuart weaves obscure concepts and mundane moments of nonsense with ease, showing us different ways of thinking and working with children's play. I hope that what Jeremy and I have done to complete it retains a fidelity to his intention for it, and that you too can take from it a different way of thinking about and working with adults' account-ability and response-ability regarding children's right to play.

Wendy Russell, August 2018

Acknowledgements

True to the central concepts developed throughout this book, this is not a single-authored work but assembled with a cast of thousands. Given one of the central themes which runs through this account, how could it be otherwise: life and its continuation through playing is never an individual affair. To attempt to list performers in order of appearance or significance would require more time and space than this format affords and still fall considerably short in accounting for their immense contributions. I have been fortunate to spend a lifetime working with play (which may appear as a paradox) and even more fortunate to have encountered so many other people who have shared this fascination. The countless children and playwork practitioners whom I have had the privilege to work with in a variety of spacetimes remain an important part of this refrain. Encounters with committed and passionate 'play people', friends and colleagues across this territory continue to challenge and inspire. I hope, in some way, you will find yourselves in this piece.

Of course, children are central to this, people who spend very little time 'thinking' about play but expend incredible energy and skill in continuing to navigate and negotiate time and space for playing. Some of the practical ways this occurs are included in this book – drawn from experiences of working at adventure playgrounds, after-school clubs, holiday playschemes, school playtimes and museums. But this is not limited to environments that appear to have some specific responsibility for working with children. As Colin Ward notes, children will play anywhere and everywhere, and some of these occasions are drawn on as examples of the multiple and generally minor ways that children enliven the practicalities of everyday life.

These personal observations are mixed with other examples of children's play drawn from a variety of sources. Thanks to all those who have shared observations, directly and indirectly, in particular Emma-Louise Simpson for the detailed account of children making worlds out of poo – a moment of wonder and nonsense illuminated by the phrase 'what if...' that has become a significant part of my refrain and influenced and extended thinking over the past several years. This also includes, but is not limited to, playwork settings in Manchester (notably Barlow Moor Community Association and the Anson Cabin project) and Homerton Grove Adventure Playground in Hackney, London, for their participation in an action research project which worked with emerging ideas around play and space. Outside dedicated environments for play, Manchester Museum was a significant entry into thinking about playful institutional spaces. Its desire to enable the entire museum environment to be 'playful' contributed to refining ideas from playwork practice into approaches designed to enhance the possibility of playful moments to emerge in these environments – subsequently developed in work with Eureka, English Heritage and Chester Zoo. Play Wales supported our research into the Welsh Government's innovative Play Sufficiency Duty, which offered the opportunity to think about adult response-ability regarding the conditions that support children's capacity to take timespace for playing in their everyday lives.

There are many significant conceptual influences in this writing, a cast of unusual suspects that rarely find their way into traditional accounts of play. As will be apparent, some of these characters have a more prominent role than others and I am forever grateful for their inspiration and insight that collectively offer ways of getting out of oneself.

I am indebted to co-script writers who have contributed to many of the ideas on show here, notably Wendy Russell, for accompanying me into new territories to see what more might be possible. I also would like to thank Professor Andrew Parker and Doctor Malcolm MacLean for their ongoing attention to production values and editing of my PhD thesis, on which this book is based, and to Hilary Smith who has worked tirelessly to maintain a stage for play within the University of Gloucestershire.

And of course, a special thanks to my wife Mary, the starring role in this production, although 'thanks' is hardly adequate in expressing the deep gratitude I feel for all the ways in which she has contributed to creating this piece, both backstage, behind the scenes and in the wings, prompting, supporting and encouraging and taking centre stage by performing all the unseen, intangible practices and routines that enabled lives to go on while this was in production. Also, thoroughly entangled in this are the two best-supporting actors, Tom and Ben: thanks for the innumerable shared moments of playfulness and enchantment that permeate our lives.

Stuart Lester, April 2017

Front Cover Image – Unburdened Children: Just off to Play

This simple child-like composition has been motivated and inspired by an equally simple graphite, crayon and ink drawing composed by Paul Klee in 1930, entitled *Burdened Children* (*Belastete Kinder*: 650 x 458 mm), which now forms part of the Tate collection of works by the Swiss artist. Often accompanied by Klee's well-known statements in his Notebooks that 'drawing is like taking a line for a walk' which begins 'with a point that sets itself in motion' (Spiller 1961, p.105), this is what the new composition has precisely attempted to do: take lines – those most primitive of elements – for a playful walk with the intention in this case of 'liberating' the burdens so often placed on children in the modern world. In this way, it seems a very fitting tribute to what Stuart did throughout his working life, particularly in those years in which he worked with some of the most poverty-stricken children in Liverpool and Manchester on various self-constructed adventure playgrounds.

Klee's original drawing was well known to Stuart (as it is to his long-time colleague, Wendy Russell). Moreover, of all the artists that he greatly admired, Paul Klee ranked among the highest, not least because of his capacity to create microcosmic worlds of the imagination in such simple and direct ways, which were nevertheless rooted and inspired by the most acute, and often critical, observations of everyday life, particularly as they impacted on children. It was an attribute, of course, that he shared with many of his contemporaries, not least Kandinsky, Matisse, Picasso, Miró and Dubuffet, all of whom possessed the deep desire to recover the spontaneous innocence of the eye and to represent nature with the freshness, vitality and emotional rawness of a child, or of a blind person suddenly restored to sight. Although designed to illustrate the dreadful burdens so often placed on young children, as the poet Linda France has rightly noted[1] (in a short tribute which accompanies the original drawing on the Tate's website), there remains the prospect and desire for liberation in Klee's work (see also France 2010, p.35):

> But still they walk together, in the same direction, eyes on the horizon [so that they] might keep from vanishing, if they can only leave the squares that have grown on the rough angles of their shoulders… How many catastrophes must a child be burdened by while the rest of us reconcile the distance between what we want and where we've been? Gather hand, heart and eye by degrees into some sort of a future no one will need to fear.

One can also relate this drawing to the philosophical writings of Gilles Deleuze and Félix Guattari, which underpin so much of Stuart's work and which lie at the heart of this particular book of his. For Deleuze and Guattari, the drawings of Klee are invariably like 'nomadic' lines invested with abstraction; ones that have the innovative, creative power of expression and not of form or, to use Klee's own terms, they are lines that promote essence and quality, not appearance and quantity. One also recalls here Henri Bergson's notion that this kind of drawing is a form of autogenesis stretching out across time on an unshrinkable duration which is one with the original essence. As for the attempt to transform the original into something related but essentially with a different meaning, was it not Klee himself who insisted that the viewer must journey through his work so as to make novel associations and to create new, strange resemblances between the scattered signs scribbled across the canvas? In short, one must *perform*, rather than *conform*. Such is the 'magic of experience' so crucial to all of Klee's *oeuvre*.

There is one additional connection that one can make here with another thinker whose work Stuart admired greatly – that of the contemporary anthropologist, Tim Ingold. For Ingold, drawing a line on a piece of paper or other material has an intrinsic relationship with telling a story, and telling a story is likewise related to a line or a path

---

1   https://www.tate.org.uk/art/artworks/klee-burdened-children-t06796

that marks out (traces) the terrain of lived experience. Each of these relations, meanwhile, is a meshwork of interwoven trails and threads. Most significant of all, there is a never a fixed point in these lines and woven threads where one can categorically say that the story is complete or that life has begun. As with Klee's line that goes out for a walk, so in the story as well as in life – one might say, the story of our life – there is always a line, connected to a thread, that can take us further (see Ingold 2007, p.90).

Finally, we finish with a story that the great Uruguayan writer, Eduardo Galeano, would invariably tell people whenever they had the great fortune to meet him and to talk to him. For Galeano, stories were like memories of fire, and each memory, stretching into the past – and each memory likewise stretching into the future – was (and will be) connected by a series of non-linear lines and threads linking us all together. Here, then, is one of his own most favourite stories. It is a true story (as are most of his stories) told to him by the person who experienced the event in question. It is included here not least because Stuart (and, indeed, Paul Klee) would have loved it:

The…political prisoner may not talk without permission, or whistle, smile, sing, walk fast, or greet other prisoners; nor may they make or receive drawings of pregnant women, couples, butterflies, stars, or birds.

One Sunday, Didaskó Pérez, school teacher, tortured and jailed *for having ideological ideas*, is visited by his daughter Milay, age five. She brings him a drawing of birds. The guards destroy it at the entrance to the jail.

On the following Sunday, Milay brings him a drawing of trees. Trees are not forbidden, and the drawing gets through. Didaskó praises her work and asks about the coloured circles scattered in the treetops, many small circles half-hidden among the branches: *"Are they oranges? What fruit is it?"*

The child puts a finger on his mouth. *"Sssssssshhhh."*

And she whispers in his ear: *"Silly. Don't you see they're eyes? They're the eyes of the birds that I've smuggled in for you."*

Jeremy Lester

Preamble

As Burghardt (2005, p.xii) states:

> The problem of defining play and its role is one of the greatest challenges facing neuroscience, behavioral biology, psychology, education and the social sciences generally…only when we understand the nature of play will we be able to understand how to better shape the destinies of human societies in a mutually dependent world, the future of our species, and perhaps even the fate of the biosphere itself.

For me, after working with and studying play for over four decades, and of course an even longer period of playing, the meanings of play are more elusive now than ever. This position may lead the reader to question 'well, if you don't know what it all means then how can you possibly write a book about it?' A good question indeed, but one that perhaps misses the essential feature about playing: we, as adults, seem to be so obsessed with trying to work out *why* we play, what it *is* and what it all *means* that we perhaps lose sight of the *movements* of play and the pleasure and joy that moments of play produce.

This preamble is a preparatory state before moving off to pursue a different line of enquiry, one that is not normally followed in play studies. I have become increasingly accustomed to, and embrace, a state of not knowing, because it continually discourages the temptation to try and overcome a condition of presumed ignorance to get to the point. There is no point or end destination to playing; if this is accepted, then one stops searching for it and can start to look differently at this form of behaviour. This shift persistently and continuously uncovers the possibility of an open and wandering concept of play. It provokes a nomadic 'quiet restlessness' that has created relationships with a multitude of concepts situated in diverse landscapes and territories as will, I hope, become apparent through this account.

And so, as far as possible, this book avoids seeking to arrive at a conclusive definition of play and defers the attribution of meanings concerning what children might 'get' from playing – meanings which generally say more about adult desires, designs and intentions for children than what children themselves value about playing. That is not to disparage the vast volume of studies that have wrestled with these questions and contributed so much to recognising the importance of play to human and non-human life and well-being. Indeed, many of these works have helped shape my thinking about this subject at various stages and continue to be a source of inspiration and frustration in varying degrees. For the most part, play scholarship adopts a stance that highlights the value of playing for individual lives, predominantly for psychological or physical development. Encounters with these studies will appear at various times throughout this book and there may be occasions when it drifts into making claims about playing that appear to fall back into cause–effect relationships. The important point to stress from the start is that this should not be read as a definitive position that establishes a series of inclusions and exclusions. If something is defined once and for all it fixes an identity that inevitably positions it in a relationship to other things (ideas, behaviours, feelings and so on): either it resembles other definitions and categorisations or opposes them. Thus, everything gets reduced to what already exists and it becomes very difficult to think the 'new' and create conceptual transformations that unsettle and reconfigure the limitations of existing frameworks of theory and practice.

The bedroom scenario

A brief example is introduced here to play with this approach:

> A child (aged 9) has some friends staying overnight for a 'sleep-over'. When it comes to bedtime, a parent helps settle the children down into beds and sleeping bags before saying 'goodnight', turning off the bedroom light and going downstairs.

When asked to consider what might happen next, a whole series of possibilities may come to mind, generally expressions of playing or messing about that are often drawn from personal experiences of being both a child and parent in similar situations. Each of these possibilities will be a singular example that emerges in an indeterminate manner and according to the unique set of circumstances that prevail at the time. While there may be some environmental conditions that might limit playful movements (for example, a situation which may have led to children having to share a room together), it is commonly accepted that the atmosphere of the bedroom is conducive to moments of play emerging in an unpredictable manner. But not just anything can happen: there are some framing limitations in place that will inhibit some forms of behaviour while supporting others. From the perspective of one strand of play studies, these moments can be classified into specific types of play, with meanings attached to these forms. Such an approach employs the term 'is' to fullest effect: this *is* play by definition, it *is* this type of play, and from this it *is* possible to suggest children are learning to…or acquiring important skills of… (complete the sentence according to which disciplinary perspective you wish to apply to the study). Using this application of theory, play is revealed and valued through what is already known; these are the foundational gestures by which we can give meaning to the world.

This process is significant and has some merit in helping practitioners who work to support children's play make sense of complex behaviours. As the discussion progresses in this book, it will at times necessarily present an overview of 'is' positions, both in terms of play and the wider production of childhood, while recognising the inherent dangers in reducing complex ideas to superficial generalisations that belie the subtlety, heterogeneity and power of these concepts. A key argument offered in this book is that application of these concepts carries limitations; they are poorly suited to the study of the fleeting, ephemeral and irregular movements that are inherent qualities of playing. Rather than seeking to fix the movement of play by 'is' classifications, the intention here is to wander elsewhere to see what more might be offered to thinking and practice. It is less concerned with the validity and applicability of existing concepts and more drawn towards *how* playing might emerge from the prevailing conditions. As such, interest lies with the ways in which moments of playing come about, or are actualised, from a virtual field of potential (for example, a bedroom with lighting *and* bodies *and* materials *and* imaginations *and* movements *and...*). The key difference here is the use of the conjunction 'and' which always extends relationships beyond fixed limits of either/or; the use of 'and' brings another dimension and direction by bringing more and more things into play (Deleuze and Parnet 2002).

The focus of attention is not to account for play by reducing highly novel behaviour to more of the same and inferring meanings but to extend thinking through multiple readings and producing more and more descriptions of events to discern patterns and potentials. We might call this a 'critical cartography' of children's play, a methodology discussed throughout the book and in more detail in Chapters 6 and 7. As with playing itself, it draws in all sorts of uninhibited and speculative possibilities that generate more and more questions, challenges and paradoxes that lead off to who knows where. Playfulness and the very combination of contingent enjoyment, uncertainty and hope would seem to thread and sustain its way throughout daily life for children and adults alike yet often becomes deadened when fixed to words on paper. Playing has a vitality that exceeds the representation of the event.

In pursuing this quest, the book draws on a selection of my published materials about play, playwork, childhood, movements and space. These, in turn, are informed by my practice experiences and contributions to what may be referred to as the 'field of play' through a variety of small-scale research projects, conference presentations, workshops, and training and education programmes. And of course, my experiences (of being a parent, relation, friend, neighbour and someone who moves through an environment that always contains possibilities for playing to emerge) are influential in shaping the direction and content of this book. However, this is not an attempt to reflect, justify, or produce a coherent autobiographical account: life and play simply don't work like that! It takes inspiration from a variety of diverse sources, brought in to work with the movements of playing and indeed of the process of life itself. The work of Gilles Deleuze and his collaborations with Félix Guattari permeate everything (concepts and practice) and offer a significant point of departure by injecting awkwardness into common-sense and orthodox thought, making things stutter and opening them out to new ways of theorising. It is also a response to Robert Fagen's (2011) illuminating chapter in which, after a lifetime of studying play, he asserts the need for new ways of thinking about this form of behaviour as novel and bold as play itself. Fagen (2011) raises concerns about the domination of biological/psychological accounts of play and the continued search for definitive meanings and utility. Tellingly, in terms of this account, Fagen (2011) suggests that prior to fully appreciating ludic behaviour there needs to be a different understanding of the universe itself and it may be fruitful to turn to philosophy, quantum physics, children's geographies and dance performance – a somewhat esoteric collection, but a line of enquiry that is tentatively pursued here.

From Deleuze's philosophical foundations, which in turn can be mapped through Nietzsche, Bergson and Spinoza, further lines of movement extend into contemporary physical and biological sciences, complexity studies and non-anthropomorphic accounts of life. It will engage with, for example, (post)human geography, critical early years writings, the growing field of children's geographies, what might be loosely termed political and cultural studies, childhood studies, and natural and physical sciences. But it is not an attempt at synthesis, consilience, or the development of a grand unifying theory about playing. The multiple concepts of play have irregular contours that do not correspond to each other; they are not jigsaw pieces that neatly interlock. Neither is this merely playing with abstract concepts or a work solely intended for academic audiences; there is a desire to challenge existing ways of thinking and acting with children's play that might reconfigure adult practices to create more just and equitable relationships and environments for children.

Moments of 'just playing', as previously noted, are generally dismissed as unimportant and to a certain degree this *should* be the case; the ways in which children can produce play spaces is ordinary and should not be over-stated in adult play evangelists' zeal to highlight the importance of play as a panacea for all that is presumed wrong with children.

Setting the scene for what follows

I hope you already have a sense that this is a departure from standard accounts of play and professional practice. This book starts in a different place from standard texts by recognising that playing is an act of co-creation between bodies and things in motion, imbued with a pleasurable mood; a play space does not pre-exist but is always dynamically constituted. Rather than considering why play might be important and what it might mean in terms of learning and development, attention is drawn to *how* moments of play coalesce and fall apart. This is different from trying to rationalise events after they have occurred and make judgements about the efficacy of individual practice against predetermined concepts, standards and performance criteria. Such a process of abstraction (distancing oneself from practice) is overcome by becoming more attentive to the ways in which moments of play emerge from the materials at hand. In developing this, a range of practice methods are introduced that are attuned to the process of playing and the ways in which they emerge from the rhythms, relationships and routines of the environment. These critical cartographic methods, at the same time, cultivate a practice disposition that continually seeks to foster conditions in which the environment remains open to further playful movements.

In line with Deleuze and Guattari (1988) it may be read as a long-playing record (LP); some tracks might appeal and get repeated plays while others are skipped. But the format also requires some structure, so these different lines of enquiry are presented in distinct chapters. As the book (or LP) unfolds, you will find that a series of persistent refrains come into being to produce an open territory of exploration and wandering; there are times it repeats but this is always repetition with difference to compose a score that offers a generous account of playing. It will invariably raise many objections and questions, and in fact invites these disturbances as a way of reconfiguring what we already know. At the same time, I would invoke Deleuze's (Deleuze and Parnet 2002, p.1) comment, 'Every time someone puts an objection to me, I want to say "OK, OK, let's go on to something else. Objections have never contributed anything". This is not an act of arrogance or indifference but a way of getting out of turning in circles, to invent one's own questions rather than have others create them for you.

Chapter 1 sets the scene by considering the 'common-sense' understanding of the nature and value of play, most predominantly as a key instrument that is useful for supporting children's learning and development. This orthodox way of thinking about play, rooted in developmental psychology and neoliberalism, has powerful effects in shaping adult practices and productions on behalf of children.

Countering this has been the emergence of the social studies of childhood, which emphasise children's agency in constructing their own lives and present playing as a vital component of children's culture. These broad social perspectives are entangled in wider viewpoints about childhood – and by inference adulthood – and perpetuate dichotomous distinctions between adult/child, nature/nurture, structure/agency and so on. While these two major viewpoints are rooted in contrasting disciplinary fields, they share a common feature in presenting a viewpoint of the 'child' as an individual, more or less competent to acquire the skills to become a fully functional adult. They also perpetuate binary positions of, for example, adult/child, culture/nature. The final section of this chapter introduces alternative perspectives, setting the challenge for the rest of the book of looking for ways out of this binary bind to see what more can be said about play and where this might lead practitioners.

Chapter 2 starts to respond to some of the challenges established in the introduction by developing a different line of enquiry. It draws on a range of published material (Lester 2013a, 2014a, 2016b, 2017) that presents ideas from materialist philosophy, life and physical sciences, and key readings from the field of children's geographies to situate playing in the wider forces and processes of life going on. In particular, it draws on the writings of Gilles Deleuze to present a different perspective on playing that brings attention not simply to the reality of play but the points about which this reality is actualised from an ever-present field of virtuality. With this switch in focus, movement and sensations become the driving force for a life, a pre-individual and impersonal force that flows in-between stuff. The chapter introduces the value of examples as a significant methodology for the study of playing, and this approach is maintained across all chapters.

Chapter 3 sets Deleuzian concepts to work to present a perspective on the relationship between playing and being well. Again, it draws on ideas developed in a series of published materials (Lester 2013a, 2016b; Lester and Russell 2008a, 2010a) to briefly explore ways in which the somewhat contested concept and rhetoric of well-being now pervades policy formulation and implementation in minority world contexts. It then turns to consider playing as a collective expression of 'being well' and a health-enabling process. This extends thinking about the concept of 'resilience' – generally applied in policy and practice terms as an individual capability – to a self-organising capacity: children can co-create play timespace that will enhance their health.

These ideas are further developed through a discussion on children's rights, notably children's right to life (Article 6 of the United Nations Convention on the Rights of the Child – UNCRC) and the expression of this as a right to play (Article 31). The main thrust of the argument here is that playing, as a form of self-protection (self is applied here as mutual, reciprocal and relational rather than individual), is an expression of resourcefulness – not simply coping with the uncertainties of everyday life but challenging the underpinning conditions that lead to such uncertainty. From a playing perspective, this means having a right to co-create beneficial health conditions – in other words, time and space for playing – while at the same time local communities should ensure that children can fully participate in the production of play spaces. This presents playing as a political movement, concerned with the equitable distribution of resources, something that is considered in more detail in Chapter 4. It concludes with an introduction to a practical form of ethical account-ability and response-ability as the foundation for thinking about policy and practice implications in Chapter 5.

Chapter 4 builds on the foundations established so far and draws on a volume of published materials (Lester 2014a, 2015a, 2016b, 2018) to explore the meaning of a 'play space' both from traditional accounts that seek to situate playing in a specific physical location, performed at certain times with standard play things, and from alternative perspectives that see a play space as contingent, indeterminate and emergent, recognising that 'where children are is where they play' (Opie and Opie 1969, p.11). The history of adult planning for play is marked by a troublesome understanding of childhood and space that finds form in adult-designed playgrounds in various guises. The contemporary version of this relationship is exemplified in the play, childhood and nature discourse and its concrete expression in the 'natural playground' movement. While well intentioned, the rhetoric of the child in nature perpetuates a romantic account of childhood and the need to situate children in spaces that preserve their innocence. Such approaches seek to appropriate playing to a plane of organisation where segments (school, family, nursery, playground, health centres and so on) work in concert to produce the future citizen that neoliberal economies demand.

Chapter 5: If playing and 'spacing' are relational achievements, it is possible to note that playful movements co-create a 'play space'. This also opens up the possibility for sensing play as a form of micro-politics, the opportunity to reconfigure, or deterritorialise, the macro-structures that seek to stabilise and fix life. This chapter establishes some central principles for starting to think about practice in supporting children's right to play with specific reference to UNCRC (2013) General Comment 17 and associated concepts that bring a critical approach to issues of spatial justice and equitable distribution of resources, namely space and time, for children's play.

Chapter 6 marks the beginning of an attempt to consider possible implications for professional practice in supporting children's play. In particular, it draws on research studies (Lester, Fitzpatrick and Russell 2014; Lester and Russell 2013a, 2014b) to introduce cartography as an approach to accounting for children's play. This is a Deleuzian approach to mapping that works not with fixed and accurate representations but with process and possibility. The chapter introduces a range of 'more-than-representational' practice-based research methods that can be used to document the co-production of play spaces as relational achievements. The aim here is to work with singular examples to develop ways of paying attention to and documenting how play emerges from whatever is to hand. It works not only with words but with a range of sensual methods that can work with affective atmospheres.

Chapter 7: While Chapter 6 explores approaches to account-ability – the ability to take account of children's ability to find timespace for playing – Chapter 7 discusses the partner concept of response-ability. If the cartography of account-ability works towards a sense of what contributes to the conditions for play to emerge, then response-ability is the move towards a *critical* cartography that holds up the habits of spatial productions to critical scrutiny in order to work towards a more equitable spatial justice for children. The two processes of account-ability and response-ability are not separate but entangled, given that the process of documentation itself also gives rise to changes in practices. The chapter uses two key sensitising concepts: Ungar's (2008) notion of navigation and negotiation and Amin's (2006) four registers of the 'good city' (repair and maintenance, relatedness, rights and re-enchantment). It also considers the inseparability of theory, research and practice, using Deleuze's concept of 'plugging in', where research and practice can work with concepts to produce new concepts and practices. This approach offers an alternative to traditional ideas of planning for play that takes account of the ways in which play emerges from current conditions, presenting this as an ethical move concerned with spatial justice for children.

Chapter 8 offers some thoughts on the material introduced in the book, not to neatly tie everything up and summarise approaches to good practice in supporting children's right to play, but as ongoing, open-ended, nomadic wanderings and wonderings. It offers up the idea of play as life itself, as moments and movements of hope that can counter a sense of alienation with the modern technocratic and rational ways of conceptualising childhood and play. It is a move towards re-enchantment. What if…?

■ CHAPTER 1 ■

An Introduction

Setting the scene

This book began life primarily addressing practitioner roles that have specific responsibility for supporting children's play, notably in playwork and early years. But as it developed it became clear that the ideas presented here are also highly relevant for other adult roles that directly influence the conditions under which playfulness thrives (for example, schools, museums and other cultural institutions) and also for those which may be perceived as having a more remote responsibility but in fact have considerable influence in shaping conditions for children's play, including planners, landscape architects, police and politicians. And of course, while this is directed to professional practitioners, the opening claim would be that all adults affect children's opportunity to play from near and afar. Furthermore, this is not limited to adults: children have considerable power in negotiating conditions for playing and the material environment is not passive in this process. And herein lies a challenging dilemma which this book seeks to take up: playing is emergent, indeterminate, spontaneous, improvised and so on. Its appearance cannot be predicted in any direct cause–effect relationship. As Colin Ward (1979, p.86) observed, children will 'play anywhere and with anything' and adults' attempts to plan for play exist on one plane, but children's playful expressions exist on another. Similarly, Iona and Peter Opie (1969, p.11) remark that 'where children are is where they play'. So how can adults begin to consider working with this apparent paradox?

This fundamental dilemma has significant implications for starting to think about supporting children's right to play and these will be considered as the book develops. But a note of warning: some readers may be expecting a practical guide and tips on how to plan play environments for children or ways to 'provide play' (a notion which has always struck me as a well-intentioned but misguided statement that presumes play is within the gift of adults and something that can be 'provided'). This is entirely understandable in the current policy and practice climate in which practitioners are expected to adopt quick-fix solutions to a range of perceived childhood problems and success is measured against predetermined outcomes. However, rather than seeking to establish a series of guidelines and 'how to...' prescriptions, the overall aim here is to explore ways in which professional practitioners may take account of and act responsibly and responsively with moments of children's play and playfulness.

The terms 'account-ability' and 'response-ability' permeate all chapters and will be discussed in more detail later. Nonetheless, a brief and basic introduction is offered here. The ability to take account of, or 'account-ability', refers to the ways in which adults perceive and sense moments of children's playfulness. Sensing is an embodied pre-personal and pre-conscious state that resists fact and meaning-based analysis. If the focus moves away from the imposition of meaning and its significance, it becomes possible to explore the production of children's playful thinking, talking, doing, in more open and mobile ways (Olsson 2009). Account-ability is the basis for 'response-ability', an ethical position that seeks, as far as possible, to maintain favourable conditions for children's play as a matter of spatial justice. This suggests that adults are alert to what unfolds as children are playing without prescription or projection of where it might go, which requires considerable sensitivity and restraint.

A starting position in responding to this challenge is to develop an opening consideration of 'playing' while as far as possible avoiding definitive statements. For the purposes of the discussion, play will be understood and presented intransitively, that is, as a verb that doesn't need a direct object to complete its meaning; playing exists 'alongside other intransitive verbs such as to hope, to grow and to dwell' (Ingold 2011a, p.6) rather than as a transitive verb that is identified by a specific and definable product or activity. This establishes *playing as process* over the identification of a distinct and final form. For play scholars, discontinuous, contingent and multiple forms of playful expression that pervade and persist across life present a constant challenge to the production of conclusive and universal accounts.

Perspectives on play: an introductory overview

The primary focus for this publication is the by now well-rehearsed and indisputable argument that playing is an important and vital force of life (for children and adults alike). While most adults would appreciate the importance of playing to some degree, the value and associated benefits attributed to this form of behaviour for children are less straightforward. It is fair to state that academic interest and research in play and the subsequent application of this into policy and practice are dominated by a minority world perspective that inextricably links understandings with the wider matter of the nature and purpose of childhood. Increasingly, such perspectives are being 'exported' to majority world contexts as global economic and social aid programmes superimpose minority world development goals onto indigenous cultures (for a detailed examination of this process and the impact on children's lives see, for example, Katz 2004). The terms 'minority' and 'majority' are used in this context to refer to so-called 'developed' and 'developing' countries. The terms recognise that economic, political and cultural power lies with a minority of countries and these directly and indirectly affect the majority of countries across the globe. These macro-terms are representative of ways in which children's lives, in multiple locations, are shaped by broad-ranging political-economic and social-cultural forces (Philo 2000). And at the same time, it is acknowledged that adults and children are intimately connected near and afar as 'embodied, perceiving, acting, expressing, connected with other humans and with objects, both natural and social beings' (Ansell 2009, p.199).

Most societies use the concept of childhood to distinguish children from adults, a reflection of the presumed physiological and psychological differences of children. However, the cultural, political and social value of what these differences may mean for the everyday lives of children and adults varies considerably across the globe (James 2010). While play may be a ubiquitous feature of childhood, an understanding of the underlying relationship between play and culture is far from complete (Roopnarine 2011). Often the complexity of cultural practices is overshadowed by universal accounts of childhood and play based on minority world perspectives:

A fundamental problem with universal claims about play is that they basically ignore the contrasting realities of childhood experiences and the cultural forces that may shape caregivers' ideas about play and early learning, and children's role in their own play. Across human societies, even under difficult social and economic circumstances, cultural beliefs and practices, family structural arrangements and modes of production have a tremendous influence on the expression of play, the determination of play partners, the settings in which play occurs, time allocated to play and work and the links between play and cognitive and socio-cultural skills. (Roopnarine 2011, p.20)

Across a range of studies, the primary concern is not so much with playing, per se, but what it adds to children's development. For the most part, common sense assigns an instrumental or utilitarian worth to play. It is a well-established and dominant position that proposes playing is an important tool that can be used to support children's learning and development, matters which are deemed to be most important in ensuring children grow up to become fully functioning adults. From this perspective, play has acquired value for what happens outside playing or what Burghardt (2005) refers to as 'deferred benefits'. This belief in progress (Sutton-Smith 1997) or advancement through play is a 'cherished ideal that maintains considerable status...and influences the ways in which adults seek to organise and structure children's play experiences' (Lester 2009, p.535). A significant consequence of this dominant belief is that playing is cut off from everyday life, compartmentalised and situated in segregated times and spaces and furnished with specific play materials. The progress orthodoxy not only shapes the physical environments designed for play but also has a significant influence on adult practices which are largely directed to progressing children by ensuring the right kinds of play are taking place. Provision for children's play becomes caught up in technological systems of governance in which quality standards, outcome measures, tight performance management, pseudo-scientific impact assessments and cost–benefit analyses are just some examples employed to maintain an accent on children's futures.

Given the increasing emphasis on future-based outcomes for children and their 'well-becomings', there is almost a universal resistance in policy, funding and practice terms to articulate the value of playing.

These seemingly trivial acts must have some purpose beyond apparently pointless moments of 'messing about'. The material-discursive[1] effects of this are profound, as evidenced by a review of promotional literature and policies at three play centres in Manchester, which for the most part suggest that children are engaged in purposeful play, such as 'elemental play to learn about nature' or 'cooking activities that promote practical skills' (Lester 2016a).

However, this does not align neatly with observations in these settings that show how practices establish or co-create environments in which moments of playing, or messing about, continually emerge from the prevailing conditions, typified by the following observation:

> …rolls of tape offered a central point around which children improvised a range of playful actions, starting off with a small group of girls sticking strips of tape to their arms before peeling it off (with accompanying conversations about 'waxing'). One child then places tape over their mouth with sounds of 'mmmm' and gesticulations. Other children copied this and ran outside to perform a dance routine before returning indoors to dance to the music playing in the background. There are more exaggerated sounds of 'mmmm' as children attempt to talk to each other when a playworker offers a challenge 'let's see who can scream the loudest' (with one particular child producing a piercing scream). Shortly afterwards children started to also tape hands and legs together before shuffling outside. (Lester 2016a, pp.32–33)

When interviewed about this apparent incongruence between what happens in the setting (valued by practitioners and children as a place for 'just chilling out') and the articulation of value to the outside world, practitioners generally comment that funders would not consider supporting time and space for messing about worthy of consideration. This, to a certain degree, is understandable in the current policy and funding climate where the state of childhood and children's futures is of overwhelming concern. But to invest such political, social and

---

1   'Material-discursive' is a term, explored in more detail throughout the book, from the work of Karen Barad (2007) and refers to the dynamic and ongoing entanglements of meanings, language, practices, matter and so on, in ways that produce 'common-sense' understandings and practices. Ideas and language do not exist separately from everyday practices and relations; thus, dominant narratives have powerful effects on the way we live our lives and relate to each other.

economic 'hope' in children as redemptive agents to secure a better tomorrow may unwittingly be harmful to children's present lives. And the cycle continues: funding demands outcomes, practice supplies supposed evidence of meeting these. The aim here is to reposition these moments of messing about as vital life-enhancing processes for the time of playing.

Bearing in mind the principle of and/and, there is no great desire to fully dismiss the 'play as progress' rhetoric. Undoubtedly what occurs in play will trickle down into what happens in the near future (Sutton-Smith 1997). Yet in reviewing the evidence, Smith (2010) acknowledges that the numerous experimental attempts to connect play with learning, so often carried out in the laboratories of natural science or developmental psychology, have been largely flawed in design and implementation. The firm belief in the efficacy of play for development marks what Smith refers to as the 'play ethos', a cherished assertion of play's importance and a justification for campaigns that seek to demand a greater share of resource allocation (money, time and space) for largely adult-designed children's play. Equally, Sutton-Smith (1997) suggests that much of this belief is based on assumption and self-referential presupposition rather than empirical evidence. When subject to critical examination, ideas that play behaviour may replicate real-world skills necessary for progress and survival are found largely unsubstantiated, tenuous and often misleading. Closer examination of the claim that play is rehearsal for adult life reveals, for example, that playful movements are exaggerated, incomplete and de-contextualised. Children's imaginations and playful plots and storylines are often irrational and unpredictable and accepted conventions are subverted and inverted (Lester and Russell 2010a). All of which would suggest that playing runs counter to the necessary skills and qualities associated with being adult.

A different but complementary reading can be found from proponents of play as an expression of children's culture. The concept of a natural childhood as a period of biological growth and teleological development has been challenged from numerous disciplinary perspectives, most notably from the broad field of the social studies of childhood (see, for example, James and Prout 1997; Lee 2001; Mayall 2002; Prout 2005). The promotion of childhood as a social construction contests grand narratives (Lyotard 1984) by pointing to the multiplicity of childhoods (Holt and Holloway 2006; Katz 2004; Punch 2003; Tisdall and Punch 2012), questioning the presumed immaturity of children and the limitations of developmental psychology (Burman 2008; Mayall 2002), and adopting a sceptical stance towards adult understandings of and value given to play (Lester 2013b; Lester and Russell 2008a). This multi-disciplinary field has established both the contingency and agency of childhood; children are no longer seen as passive in their own development and playing is portrayed as the outcome of children's agency, self-expression and creativity (Tisdall and Punch 2012). This repositions children's play in time and space as something that children can create anywhere and everywhere when conditions are favourable. From this perspective, playing is less about progression and the 'becoming-child' and more about children being children in the here and now of their childhoods. Undoubtedly, this offers a contrasting perspective, but as discussed later in this chapter, this move is also beset by its own limitations.

Play in a wider context: the individualisation of life

Play as progress (a universal and natural biological/psychological perspective on life and development) and play as cultural expression come from fundamentally different disciplinary perspectives. However, both have emerged from what Henricks (2015, p.7) describes as: 'Modernizing societies with strong middle classes [who] endorse commitments to self-control, the future, social mobility, material and cultural acquisition, procedural fairness and education as a pathway to success.'

Much has been said and written about the influence of developmental psychology in shaping understandings and practices in regard to the period of childhood. A summary of this position is presented at this stage, sufficient to develop the discussion while also mindful of making over-simplistic generalisations.

The predominant mode in western thought is the assumption that human development follows a pre-existing design pattern. Growth is presented as the phenotypic materialisation of this inner design, the observable characteristics of the interaction of genes and environment

(Jablonka and Lamb 2005; Lewontin 2000; Oyama 2000). Models of development (largely from a minority world perspective but increasingly exported to the majority world) present the period of childhood as a universal unfolding of biological material accompanied by the acquisition of the appropriate cognitive, social and cultural skills required to become a fully functioning and contributing member of society. Ideas and ideals of development presume and assume a maturation process achieved by progression through universal 'ages and stages', categories that mark a journey from simple to increasingly complex, to become 'an ideal-typical citizen-subject who is knowable, known, docile and productive' (Burman 2008, p.26).

At this point, a cursory introduction to *life lines* is offered, a concept which is further developed later in this chapter. The standard model of development is often presented as a single straight line, representative of a known and predictable future. In this sense, development is a regular movement that pre-exists the unfolding of life, as shown in Figure 1.1.

Figure 1.1: A line of development

A review of developmental psychology textbooks notes the almost universal application of a chronological timeline spanning birth to death, often specifying age limits to distinguish separate time and developmental periods (Burman 2008). Undoubtedly, there is far greater interest in the period of childhood than the remainder of the life span, a measure of adult concern to both understand the purpose of childhood and ensure that appropriate actions are taken to progress children along the line.

Such texts pay little regard or sensitivity to cultural, class or other variations in life. Development becomes a process of 'achieving full potential' or becoming filled with what a child needs to become an adult. Life from this perspective begins with possibility but progresses towards a final, fixed and self-enclosed state in which possibilities are closed off (Ingold 2011a). Tracing this process of development produces an organism, or what Ingold (2015) refers to as a 'blob', an individual body of mass and volume that is solid and enclosed (see Figure 1.2).

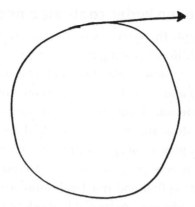

Figure 1.2: A self-enclosed organism

This simple act of inversion of a life line illustrates the ways bodies are turned in on themselves and so separated from 'the environment'. Bodies become closed off; the organism is 'in here' and the environment 'out there' (Ingold 2011a). Individuals are constructed as autonomous agents, atomised and insulated from an external world. A further act of inversion takes place by situating the mind as a self-enclosed organ within the body, producing a clear inside and outside, with an inside in the inside that assumes the role of command centre. This act of enclosure follows a wider philosophical movement from the time of Plato onwards that distinguishes between nature and culture (Lester 2015a) and can be seen in the traditional Cartesian dualism where the mind is made of matter that is distinctive from the body. Further, not only is the mind separate from the body, it assumes a favoured position in creating and giving meaning to the world. The seemingly rational mind is of a higher order to the irrational and base body. Such an abysmal yet powerful separation lingers today (Damasio 1994) and the privilege afforded to this binary and hierarchical thinking has profound influence on minority world thought and practices; the mind is something to be cultivated and enriched, the body and its affects are to be kept in check and exercised. Given that the mind has transcended nature and biology, child development is presented as movement from an irrational, heteronomous and presumed natural state of neediness, unruliness and dependency to a rational and autonomous being. The closing of the circle masks any movement of the line – it appears static, folded back and closed off from the outside.

Playing in an even wider context: a neoliberal life

But this is not simply the workings of a single academic disciplinary perspective. Childhood is caught up in the struggle for future economic well-being (also understood in terms of progress, growth and development) and as such is an important site for intervention, a move that has intensified and diversified in modern times (Burman 2008; Dahlberg, Moss and Pence 2013). And as previously noted, understandings of play are shaped within this framework, hence the dominance of the play as progress rhetoric (Sutton-Smith 1997). The philosophical, conceptual and practical foundations of childhood, and by association playing, are rooted in modernity and a dominant neoliberal model of development that, I would claim, is detrimental to both children and adults. The concept of neoliberalism warrants a more expansive and critical investigation but within the limits of this book it is taken to refer to a form of capitalist governance based on principles of market liberalisation, privatisation, individualisation and deregulation. Harvey's (2005, p.2) oft-cited definition of neoliberalism provides a useful introduction:

> A theory of political economic practices that proposes that human wellbeing can best be advanced by liberating individual entrepreneurial freedoms and skills within an institutional framework characterized by strong private property rights, free market, and free trade. The role of the state is to create and preserve an institutional framework appropriate to such practices.

Neoliberalism is much more than a set of free-market economic policies; it operates a form of political rationality that coordinates the political realm, government practices and what it is to be a citizen. Free-market capitalism, combined with a dominant legacy of developmental psychology, constitutes the foundations for discourses, institutions, laws, policies, scientific approaches and measurements, and associated practices that produce a *dispositif* (Foucault 1980) of childhood. Foucault (1980, p.194) describes a *dispositif* as a:

> heterogeneous ensemble consisting of discourses, institutions, archi-tectural forms, regulatory decisions, laws, administrative measures, scientific statements, philosophical, moral and philanthropic propositions – in short, the said as much as the unsaid. Such are the

elements of apparatus. The apparatus itself is a system of relations that can be established between these elements.

Neoliberalism may be understood as historically and locally specific, unevenly developed, with hybrid and contingent patterns of organisation brought about by dominant structures of economic and political regulatory systems (Brenner, Peck and Theodore 2010). Although neoliberalism is mobilised in multiple ways, there may be commonalities across these diverse contexts without reducing important differences to universal and totalising accounts and to 'avoid imposing a monological, internally consistent, temporally linear, and systematic frame on that which is none of these things' (Brown 2006, p.690).

The neoliberal agenda is in part at least characterised by a constant and unrelenting desire to achieve hegemony over bodies and processes of life through the exercise of 'bio-power' that constructs and consolidates a coalition of the willing (Amin and Thrift 2013; Garrett 2009). It marks a strategic organisation of the multiplicity of forces that make up life in the service of global capitalism (Anderson 2012). As modern forms of neoliberal government have progressed, so too have the means to capture, entrain and foster biological capabilities and behavioural tendencies (Foucault 2008). States and other agents attempt to forge connections between forces of life processes, beliefs and values, and political legitimacy to secure a certain future (Lee and Motzkau 2011). The straight line of development introduced in Figure 1.1 is overlaid with a series of values, laws, beliefs, orthodox thought, practices, policies, institutions and so on that collectively operate to steer children to their destiny (see Figure 1.3).

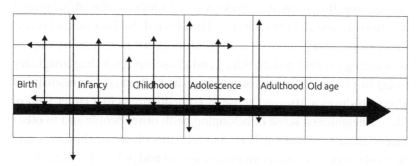

Figure 1.3: A plane of organisation

Clearly defined institutional segments operate in all kinds of directions to appropriate life (Deleuze and Parnet 2002). Each segment works in concert with adjacent territories to regulate movement and collectively establish a 'plane of organisation' (Deleuze and Guattari 1988) that concerns 'both forms and their development, subjects and their formations' (Deleuze and Parnet 2002, p.130). It builds an aggregate of systems that work together to construct an imaginary norm and organise the processes and relations that legitimise the power and associated status of that norm (Garland-Thompson 2002). In the desire to avoid uncertainty and stress, uncritical, accepted wisdom and conventions assume a 'taken-for-granted sense that harbours given solutions that correspond to given problems and given answers that correspond to given questions' (Olsson 2009, p.82). Categorical distinctions between right/wrong, true/false and safe/risky are carried out with good intentions and in the best interests of children. The plane of organisation establishes a variety of sophisticated identities (schoolchild, son/daughter, special needs, delinquent, at risk and so on), switching from one to another but always in line with the axiomatic of capitalism which requires everyone's compliance towards its ends (Mozère 2006).

In perpetuating and strengthening its hold, bio-politics features two interrelated characteristics. First, it produces particular forms of knowledge of the processes of circulation, exchange and transformation that make up life, increasingly recognised as a self-organising, affective process (Anderson 2012). These forms of knowledge are applied to powerfully over-code those elements which could be classified as potentially unruly (in this context, to include the period of childhood and play). The term 'affect' is often used to describe emotions, but throughout this book it is applied in a broader sense of 'relational reactions' or the ability to affect and be affected. In this sense, a body is never alone, always more than one (Manning 2013). Affects are ways of connecting to other bodies, things and situations (including imaginary ones) in processes that are larger than the individual. An intensity of affect produces a 'stronger sense of embeddedness in a larger field of life – a heightened sense of belonging, with other people and to other places' (Massumi 2002, p.214). As such, affect is about the forces and flows of encounters and is inherently spatial and political (Thrift 2008).

Affects can be 'engineered' by powerful designs on space (buildings, signs, codes, spatial arrangements), embedded in habits and routines, and cultivated through affective atmospheres. The concept and production of childhood is affective in that it shapes adult memories, desires and practices about children, and this is certainly in evidence in many of the ways adults now talk about childhood, play and space, particularly the desire to represent a 'lost childhood' (Horton and Kraftl 2006a). The principle of adult account-ability attends to the ways in which adults may shape affects through their actions, and the impact of this on children's affects and practices (recognising that this is not linear or predictable in any predetermined sense) and is something that will be looked at in more detail when considering attempts to plan 'play spaces' for children.

Second, bio-politics makes strategic interventions based on the value of certain forms of life over others, as the very existence of difference may be perceived to threaten order. Judgements are made about what constitutes normal development and what might fall outside this regime. For Foucault, both the disciplines of the body and the bio-politics of the population coalesce to form 'liberal mentalities of rule' (Miller and Rose 2008, p.203). Bio-power operates partly pre-consciously on bodies and their desires to create a humanist subject – an individual that is presumed to be free and have agency but something to be kept under external and self-control for fear of sprouting deviancy or getting out of joint (Mozère 2006). At the same time, neoliberalism demands creative forces to drive forward innovation without which capitalism would stagnate and suffocate. Processes of de- and reterritorialisation are encouraged and managed to keep such forces in check:

> So as soon as desire explodes – one could say, agency is empowered – there is a double movement for the axiomatic of capitalism. One aspect is the recuperation of that which has given life (or birth) to innovation, and the other is the recuperation of the excess of desire, channelling the overflow back into old or newly patterned identities, keeping them under control. (Mozère 2006, p.112)

Thus, children's desires and impulses are valued for the contribution they make to their progress and this becomes an overriding feature in the design of state systems (institutions, policies, environmental design and so on). Bodies become the object of political strategies and practices (Foucault 2008), to be controlled and regulated. Playing becomes a separate process, distinct from other forms of behaviour but equally the 'same' in that it contributes to progression along the straight line of development.

The power of binaries

As previously noted, childhood is produced as a movement from disorder to order with associated material-discursive effects that bind adults and children into certain forms of relationships. Adulthood and childhood are constructed through dichotomy; each side is attributed with opposing values such as rational/irrational, competent/not yet competent, independent/dependent. In these relationships, privilege is generally afforded to the first of these terms. Children are positioned as 'other' than adult, separated as a distinct group in need of special and exclusive attention. Separation arises from difference, used in this context as a relative measure of sameness, that is, children are different from the 'same' that they will become. Childhood, or the not-yet-adult, becomes a unitary and universal category. Distinctions of 'sameness but separate' (Dahlbeck 2012; Lee 2005) also imply that there is a teleological and transcendental trajectory between the inferior child and superior adult – a binary categorisation that reinforces the crucial distinctions between these states. But this is not merely a one-sided process, as adults are equally positioned as responsible for steering children to become the same.

Increasingly, this vitally important role is subject to more surveillance and measurement. Adults, as the protectors and educators of children, need to be scrutinised, made accountable and carefully regulated to avert any threat to children's presumed innocence (Fenech and Sumsion 2007). Regulation is enacted through a series of judgements and comparisons (policies and standards) and associated practices of symbolic and material rewards and sanctions that come to represent the worth and value of individuals and organisations (Lester and Russell 2014c), constraining and restricting human possibilities.

This is but one example of the ways in which life is cut into segments through classifications, oppositions and resemblances to determine the identity of subjects and objects; thus, the separation of mind/body, nature/nurture, structure/agency and so on works in concert to produce an ordered account of life and the world. Traditional accounts of childhood as purely nature or nurture, gene driven or environment shaped, give primacy to one set of foundational causes while accepting the secondary role of the other. Various interaction models suggest it is formed from a mixture of both elements thereby reinforcing the existence of the two foundational states. Natural and cultural properties in this interactionist mode are immutable; forms spring out from these two terms, yet the foundations remain unmoved in the process of interaction (Barad 2007; Hinchliffe 2007; Oyama 2000). Analysis revolves in a fruitless and self-defeating cycle of how much goes into the mixture rather than thinking differently about the ingredients that constitute life. All the action is passed backwards to pre-formed origins; children's development is framed by what has already been determined by foundational conditions and inversions (the biological form); 'the trouble is that in this account of the world, nothing new could actually happen...there's no time-space for difference' (Hinchliffe 2007, p.50).

The ways in which the human is cut apart from the non-human, animate from inanimate, cultural from natural and so on, produce crucial materialising effects. Play is commandeered into this regime as behaviour that can be utilised to fix the identity of the child. From this point of view, play is defined and classified as an ordered, structured activity situated in specific timespaces. It becomes fully implicated in the neoliberal project through a range of strategic promotions designed to inculcate values and norms of appropriate behaviours to support progress towards economically productive and healthy adults, evident in everyday terms such as 'play nicely' or 'play properly'. What this does is reduce complex and lively behaviour to narrow instrumental purpose, drawing on a normative biomedical developmental model that tolerates no deviation. There is little room for polyvocality: 'a child who runs around, plays, dances and draws cannot concentrate attention on language and writing, and it will never be a good subject' (Deleuze and Guattari 1988, p.81). The idea of a natural child produces a metanarrative that positions childhood as risky and needy, a condition defined by multiple and omnipresent threats to progress that are analysed with little regard for the multiple and complex ways in which children feel about, negotiate and act in their everyday lives (Lester and Russell 2014c).

Countering this movement, a social/cultural turn challenges the idea of a fixed universe subject to immutable scientific laws and rational explanations. Social constructivism acknowledges that the world is open to innumerable interpretations and contains an openness that is always socially produced. Each culture creates its own world and there is divergence between different constructions (DeLanda 2002). The general claim from a social constructivist view is that the world, rather than being fixed and objective, can only be revealed through human representation and intervention. While the turn to the social has rescued the child from universal truth claims about development, the identification of childhood as a social construction and children as active agents may well have served its purpose and indeed inhibit future study and analysis (Prout 2005). In the desire to overturn the privilege afforded to 'natural' accounts of life, the nature/culture binary is maintained, namely an autonomous material world that operates according to essential and rational laws against a relative world of human construction (Lester 2015a). It has resulted in a reversal or mirror image of the binary relationship between developmentalism (becoming and structure) and social constructivism (being and agency), reinforcing the hegemonic adult/child dualism rather than seeking other possibilities (Ryan 2012; Strandell 2005). The idea that everything is a representation of human making by privileging epistemological over ontological issues renders matter mute (Hinchliffe 2007), presenting it as merely a stable background on which humans construct their lives.

The intention of what follows is to consider other ways of thinking about life and play, to not get caught up in binary thinking but to adopt the principle and/and/and…

Beyond binary thinking

Thinking in terms of binaries is so engrained that they form 'inaugural gestures' (Massumi 2013, p.x) that establish and activate an orthodoxy of thought where it is impossible to think differently. What is offered here is an analysis that does not 'presume that the terms of either side of the equivalence relations are given' (Barad 2011, p.123).

Jack and the Beanstalk

Let's introduce an experiment here, drawn from Lester (2013a), which considers the folk tale of *Jack and the Beanstalk*. There are numerous versions of this story and for those not familiar with it there is a link at the bottom of this page.[2] Who would you say is the main character of the story? If you were given a character (for example, Jack, Jack's mother, the cow, the beans, the giant, the soil), could you develop a persuasive argument to position each one as the central character? In the traditional story, Jack is usually identified as the hero, the central character around which everything revolves. While he is often portrayed as simple, his brave deeds transform the fortunes of the family. But it may also be possible to position other characters, organic and inorganic, in the centre. For example, the magic beans are pivotal in changing fortunes, the cow has central value as the means of exchange to purchase the beans and so on.

This simple manoeuvre offers the possibility of thinking differently about the story, replacing one heroic figure with another. And while this opens up some interesting perspectives, the thinking process, or the inaugural gestures (Massumi 2002) that frame analysis, is consistent. The assumption is that a story requires a central individual. But what if we apply a fundamentally different starting position in which the idea of self-contained individuals acting on passive objects is set to one side and replaced by a viewpoint in which the juxtaposed materials which form the story collude to form the reality of the tale? The movement of the story is revealed through the conjunction 'and': Jack *and* mother *and* beans *and* cow *and* beanstalk *and*...; 'the constitutive assemblage of all the parts of the story cannot be reduced to a binary relationship and cannot be organised in terms of a fixed identity' (Lester 2013a, p.133). Given this liveliness of arrangement, there is always the possibility for becoming different. Rather than each character (organic or inorganic) being a fixed and separate entity, they are constantly changing through what Barad (2007) terms 'intra-actions'; the story emerges in the in-between.

This counter movement, what might be referred to as 'posthumanism', is characterised by a number of key interrelated principles that challenge the humanist tradition of human exceptionalism (that is, that humans are 'apart from' nature and can control it): the rejection of any central organising system that determines relationships (Jack and mother and cow and...); the rebuttal of any principle outside life that governs

2   www.dltk-teach.com/rhymes/beanstalk/story.htm

living systems (what happens emerges from the collusion of organic and inorganic materials rather than any predetermined destiny); and a challenge to the primacy given to cognition and calculation in favour of relations that are always contextual, contingent and specific (the affective encounters between materials and forces) and not determined by general and universal rules and patterns (Hayles 2005). In contrast to the straight line of progressive movement proposed by developmental psychology, a posthuman lens acknowledges that childhood is not a unitary phenomenon, but may be viewed as 'heterogeneous, complex and emergent, and because this is so, its understanding requires a broad set of intellectual resources, an interdisciplinary approach and an open-minded process of enquiry' (Prout 2005, p.2). However, there has been a general reluctance to date to engage with childhood as more than social processes (Kraftl 2013; Prout 2005; Ryan 2012), and studies of play rarely break out of their disciplinary boundaries. There is an intention in this book to move out of this state by drawing on a different set of conceptual tools, notably Deleuze and Guattari's philosophy of immanence introduced in the next chapter.

Summary: going beyond what we know about play

The themes introduced at this opening stage are developed in more detail throughout the remaining chapters and while it meanders rather than getting straight to the point, there is an overarching sense of direction, namely to reconfigure understandings of playing and by doing so to bring about the creation of more just and equitable worlds for children and adults alike.

Fagen (2011, pp.92–93) notes that 'play is still totally mysterious and intractable' but the legacy of scientific approaches has been the separation of playing from other behaviours and expressions through identification, resemblance and opposition with the purpose of conducting valid, objective and reliable research. It 'cuts' play in a specific way, excluding other possible cuts. What is presented here are formations that begin to consider these circumstances and how they might be differently enacted. It is a stuttering attempt to find a way out of worn-out binary productions and to rethink causality, agency, power and ethics in a way that 'undermines the metaphysics of individualism and calls for a rethinking of the very nature of knowledge and being' (Barad 2007, p.23). There is an exploratory movement to consider the possibilities of human and non-human relations and a way of engaging differently with life. This is not to idealise play as some mystical, meaningful and transcendental experience; far from it! Playing, as developed in this account, is an everyday ordinary occurrence that appears fleetingly in the most mundane circumstances. Yet there may be something in the process of playing and its very ordinariness that demands far greater attention, accountability and responsibility.

CHAPTER 2

Play: A Different Line of Enquiry

Introduction

Now we start to look in more detail at playing, but this also involves an excursion into the meaning of life itself, wandering into the realm of philosophy and physical and life sciences.

Worlds made of poo

This chapter opens with an example of playing, a casual moment recorded by a playworker in the UK.[1] It is a moment that may be familiar to some who have read my previous work or listened to conference presentations and it has taken a central role in the movement to thinking differently about playing (see, for example, Lester 2013b, 2014b; Lester and Russell 2014c). It involves a young boy and girl (about 6 years old) who are sitting and running their fingers through some 'gloop', when the boy turns to the girl and says:

> Boy: What about if everything was made out of gooey?
>
> Girl: Well, hmm, we would actually have all goo on our bums and stuff and we'd be all gooey and pooey and booey.
>
> *The boy laughs*
>
> Boy: What if everything was made out of poo? Eugh!

---

1   Thanks to Emma-Louise Simpson for sharing this observation.

Girl: Err, we would all have poo on our bums.

Boy: And what about poo people?

Girl: Yuck!

Boy: And what about poo willies?

Girl: No [boy's name], no!

Boy: What about poo trees?

Girl: Yuck!

Boy: What about, this is the worsest thing, what about poo leaves?

Girl: Why would you want to make poo leaves?

Boy: What if everything was made out of poo?

Girl: I dunno.

Imagining *worlds made of poo* is just one of the multiple ways in which children continuously question materials and bodies to see what more might be possible. Such 'imagining otherwise' appears in everyday life woven with and through the materials at hand. This fleeting moment is nothing extraordinary and it is likely that the children involved will not be able to recall this event, particularly if prompted by an adult to describe 'what have you been playing today'. The movements, perceptions, sensations and their affects are beyond representation in words; there is always an excess that escapes capture.

In general, adult explanations of what the children are doing seek to fit the material of everyday life into pre-existing frameworks (it is play or not play because it contains or is missing some or all the hallmarks of accepted definitions). Thus, the actuality of the event and the unique composition of *worlds made of poo* is reconstituted by installing it into a pre-existing system of thought and experience. In our desire to classify and categorise, we can easily gloss over the fine details of the example. Labelling this behaviour as play – or indeed not play – loses the particularity of the event by reducing it to more of the same. The desire in this account is to look for more rather than less and as such it is additive rather subtractive, generative rather than reductive. It is an attempt to work with the *intensive* movements that actualise such moments and the *extensive* connections that may spring from it. The significant feature in the playful example of making a world from poo is the notion of 'what if...' deployed by the children to continually problematise the given order of things, a speculative movement to co-create a timespace that is temporarily better and livelier by going beyond the limits, rationalities and sensibilities of the 'real' world. The playful phrase is also of great significance in this account as it invites a questioning stance: 'what if' different ideas, a conceptual toolset from a range of diverse fields and across disciplines, are brought to bear on playing, what more might be possible?

Everyday acts of playing

There is something of a dilemma here: the separation of play from other behaviours has significant consequences. Moments of co-creating *worlds made of poo* get lost within this atomising framework, yet they are occasions that show how the everyday, with its connotations of familiarity and mundane existence, is extremely lively and extraordinary (Bennett 2001). It is the context for minor acts of creativity and innovation that simply makes life worth living.

As we will see throughout this book, bodies have unlimited possibilities for experimenting with movement and rhythm in everyday contexts. Moments of playing are constituted through and with the sensations, textures, rhythms and intensities of everyday life (Stewart 2007). This is a central feature of what follows: it marks a practice approach that is conversant with the relationship or correspondence (Ingold 2015) between bodies, imaginations and the material environment and the ways in which they are always entangled in an indeterminate and unforeseen manner. Everyday life is never stationary; it is a dynamic and continually changing flow. Two children casually running fingers through gooey stuff is among the most ordinary elements of life. Moments like these largely go unnoticed, which is not a failing but simply an expression of the ways in which we get on with our daily lives. However, that is not to dismiss them as having little value; these things matter and bring more to the world.

Playing is an expression of desires that produce an intensive difference while at the same time hold the promise of keeping whole clusters of affects attracted to them (Stewart 2007); they are extensive in scope, maintaining an appetite, or anticipatory alertness and readiness (Bennett 2004) to the possibility of further moments of playing. This is perhaps the most important feature of play: it generates a desire for more of it and all that this offers is simply greater satisfaction in being alive (Sutton-Smith 2003). The very ordinariness of playing has immense affective and life-enhancing significance. This apparently straightforward claim is profound and on its own would suggest that any society that claimed to care for children should position play at the centre of policy-making and not something that is a luxury, to be considered after the serious business of growing up is completed.

Yet while the everyday is pervasive, it remains one of the most overlooked and misunderstood aspects of life (Gardiner 2000). It is simply taken as given and so often ignored because of its inherent messiness. Avoiding this apparent mystery, play research generally draws on conceptual tools that are designed to work with plots, to establish some universal meaning by application of rationality, a process diametrically opposed to the messy, plotless movements of playing (Sydnor and Fagen 2012). The indeterminacy and complexity of playful encounters escape accurate retelling: 'What is it we really saw?', 'How can we be certain it is play?' and so on are questions designed to assess what playing might mean or whether it is good or bad in the bigger scheme of things. They are questions grounded in traditional research assumptions that there is an eternally existing reality that can be discovered and represented in words.

A different movement switches attention from these questions of representation towards how moments of playing come about and where they might go. The focus shifts from adult imposition of meanings onto *post hoc* reconstructions of experience to the presentation of flows of practices and experience that precedes all thinking and representation. As such, and following a lead from Thrift's (2008) Non-Representational Theory (NRT), or perhaps Lorimer's (2005) notion of the more-than-representational, this account acknowledges the limitations of representation and thrives on this recognition to offer a more affirmative position that adopts a stance of life and play as 'more-than representation':

> To take the event-ness of the world and affect seriously requires a shift from an empirical mode that is driven by the imperative to denote, to

one oriented towards the work of description. The aim is no longer to seek after explanations that claim to go beyond the event being described, but simply to present descriptions that are infused with a certain fidelity to what they describe. (Latham 2003, p.1903)

One of the key features of adult account-ability is increasing attentiveness to the everyday mo(ve)ments[2] of children. As Bennett (2010) highlights, this ability can be developed with practice as a form of enchantment, not in a naive, idealised, over-optimistic or romantic sense, or a refusal to accept the intolerable cruelties that are present in the world, but rather an openness to the delights and wonders that the everyday contains. Being alert to this and the possibilities that are always present for reworking these conditions reveals the world to be a lively place, where matter is always animate, always has the potential to surprise beyond the world given by disciplinary power, rationality and scientific calculations. Even in the most mundane environment, moments of enchantment are ever-present, as the following observation at a railway station illustrates (Lester 2018, p.85–86).

Strawberry mermaids

An adult (male) with two young girls, one who appeared slightly older than the other, were making their way to the platform, the two girls each holding a bag of sweets. As the adult walked ahead, the two girls paused to look inside each other's bags and the older one said to the other, 'Wow, you have got pink mermaids. They can do magic', waving her arms in the air as though holding a magic wand and performing a pirouette. The younger girl held her bag open and peered closely into it, smelling the contents as the older girl continued, 'They are lovely and made from strawberries.' The other girl half smiled at this, faced the older child, but looked a little unsure and said, 'I don't think I like strawberries.' Her friend calmly said, 'Never mind, I'll have them,' and

---

2   As will be discussed later in more detail, playful movements are productive of moments of timespace which might be recognised as 'playing' – the shorthand for this, adopting from Curti and Moreno (2010), is the hybrid term 'mo(ve)ment' which highlights the interconnectedness and continuous dynamic relationship between perception, sensation and movement.

then quickly added, 'but I am not going to give you any of mine.' Both girls closed their bags and skipped to catch up with the adult.

Another shared moment of enchantment is taken from an observation/ encounter in a school playground. It was mid-winter and there had been a slight snowfall and freezing conditions. Children were sliding over playground tarmac, trying to make snowballs with the little snow available and shattering the icy puddles. One child approached me to say his hands were cold. I enquired whether he had gloves, but the child ignored this question and continued with a story of how he had found a 'beautiful ice-diamond', his eyes wide with wonder as he retold this discovery. He explained, 'I put it in my pocket for safe keeping but it has all gone now.'

The ability to slow down and unobtrusively witness requires suspending critical faculties and deferring attempts to impose meaning on what unfolds; one is simply caught up in the mo(ve)ment, an enjoyable experience that 'temporarily eclipses the anxiety endemic to critical awareness of the world's often tragic complexity' (Bennett 2001, p.10). The following two examples, offered by participants from a series of continuous professional development sessions to explore a Welsh local authority approach to 'play sufficiency', further highlight this process.

Walking blindfold

At the Bull Ring shopping centre in Birmingham on Sunday morning, full of Christmas shoppers and people going to and from the New Street Train station, I walked past a young girl wearing a red coat and a pink bobble hat. She was about 7 or 8 and was holding on to her mum's hand. They were walking towards us in the middle of the pedestrian traffic and the girl had her hat pulled down over her eyes. She had her free arm stuck out from her body a little way, as if helping her to balance a little and was keeping pace with her parents, not lagging behind.[3]

---

3   Thanks to Rebekah Jackson for sharing this observation.

Becoming dogs

My two bored children were helping with the supermarket shop. They had done the usual look at toys, pleaded for biscuits and crisps, picked out dinner and so on. When we entered the pet food aisle, Aled started with, 'When can we have a dog?" Before I could answer, Catrin had dropped on to her hands and knees to be a dog. She crawled up and down the aisle sniffing at the food on the shelves. Aled copied for a bit but soon gave up to be the owner. She let him pat her on the head and came when he called her. They were totally engrossed in their game. A dad and daughter came around the corner, the girl also dropped to her knees, but she did not acknowledge my two or them her. When she got to the end of the aisle she got back on to her feet. My two carried on the game until they got to the tills where it was much busier, and they then stopped to put the shopping on the conveyer belt, so they could race it to the till. The dog game was over.[4]

While seemingly insignificant, these examples not only reinforce Ward's (1979) observation that children will play anywhere and with anything, but also have implications for considering adult practices in supporting opportunities for children to play, something that will be explored in later chapters.

The value of the example

Before we proceed to explore the mo(ve)ments of playing and their affects and the potential this holds for transforming understandings and practices, there needs to be a brief discussion around the value and process of exemplification, that is, the significance of the example as an exemplar and the ways in which this is applied in this discussion. In traditional research terms, examples may be readily dismissed as insignificant, anecdotal and unscientific unless they can be used to prove a pre-existing theory or categorised into larger themes thereby generalising the specific instance. But the aim here is to treat an example differently and to defer as far as possible framing it by what is already known. In this context, and following Massumi's (2002) advice, examples are always singular and cannot be held to represent

---

4   Thanks to Mel Kearsley for this observation.

the general features of any system. Each observation of playing above signifies nothing other than itself; it is a small story that is important for its particularity and, in its singularity, it acts to create concepts that work with the specificity of the event. The challenge is to produce concepts that are sensitive to the prevailing conditions of the event rather than over-code it. As such, this account does not simply utilise disciplinary insights but questions the ways in which these establish and maintain boundaries – what might be termed 'material-discursive effects' (Barad 2007). Ideas and concepts are not innocent or neutral but actively engage in diffractive entanglements to produce conditions in which new concepts and practices may emerge or dissipate.

The emergence of *worlds made of poo* flows and coheres around the question 'what if...', and the self-organising movements of bodies, sensations, imaginations and materials activate the apparently mundane details of the event; each minor moment matters as it opens to more questions and digressions (MacLure 2010; Massumi 2002). It is not about isolating an event but seeing how it might work and where it might lead. And while each example is singular, together several examples can form a series of particularities that can make more of movement without reducing to universal claims. Thus, an exemplary approach has the potential to disturb, unsettle and enliven existing ideas to extend the possibility for thinking otherwise (McCormack 2013).

Each of the chapters in this book is littered with playful examples as a way of overcoming a form of writing that seeks to represent an externally existing reality in order to establish meanings and explanations. They are drawn from playwork practice, everyday life, research projects and more remote sources. The examples are not deliberately selected to prove this or that point, but are entangled with the very process of writing. The desire to create concepts rather than simply use what already exists brings to mind particular occasions that resonate prior to representation; they are felt and *sensed* moments before putting concepts into language, a 'Möbius strip between language and the world' (Deleuze 2004, p.23)[5] that cannot be situated according to either/or positions. And while positioned at specific points in the discussion, they are mobile and could be readily interchanged without

5   Deleuze used this notion of a 'Möbius strip' with specific reference to Lewis Carroll and his story of *Alice's Adventures in Wonderland*.

effacing their singularity. But above all, an exemplary methodology is an ethico-political manoeuvre, a tentative and modest experiment in (re)thinking and thinking anew what constitutes a 'good life' and how we might increase capacities to create a more just and equitable world in which all life can flourish.

Bringing play to life

As a first move in this new direction, it is necessary to step back from considering play as a recognisable activity to present a perspective on life itself and to briefly introduce some of the key concepts that underpin what follows. This is highly complex material, and ideas are introduced in sufficient detail alongside more examples to create a different reading of play before considering associated implications for practice. It should not be read as a definitive account nor a close reading and interpretation of a specific set of ideas.

There are numerous conceptual allies that accompany this movement, notably the philosophical productions of Gilles Deleuze and his collaborations with Félix Guattari that continue to stir an exploration of the possibilities of human and non-human relations and a way of engaging differently with life. I first encountered these ideas in Prout's (2005) proposal that the period of childhood cannot be viewed as an interaction between natural and cultural forces but needs a different approach that overcomes binary classifications. Supplementary lines of movement extend into contemporary physical and biological sciences, complexity studies and non-anthropomorphic accounts of life, particularly in the field of 'more-than-human' geography (Hinchliffe 2007; Whatmore 2002), new materialism and posthuman studies (Alaimo 2010; Barad 2007; Bennett 2010; Braidotti 2013; Haraway 1991) and anthropology (most notably in the work of Ingold 2007, 2011a, 2011b, 2015). Ideas from these diverse sources leak into everything that follows, with occasionally more explicit forays into key concepts.

It is a tentative movement to add more to critical studies by bringing life, as biological, physical and chemical process, back into play. But this is not an attempt to synthesise, elucidate and analyse the fine details of such disparate approaches. The appropriated concepts appear to employ similar terms (for example, matter, becoming, entanglement, assemblage) but these are specific to their relative ontological positions and not necessarily compatible. Thus, Deleuze's 'immanence' account of life is fundamentally different from Barad's (2007) concept of 'agential realism' (Hein 2016). To conflate these approaches would lead to accusations of lack of academic rigour and conceptual confusion. The intention is not to dwell on these arguments nor to falsify or justify specific materialist philosophies. Burghardt's (2005) comprehensive study into the genesis of animal play concludes with the recognition that definitions and meanings about play are still elusive and perhaps can only be approached through play itself. Thus, in play, strange juxtapositions and incongruities can appear without need to rationalise and justify their existence. Lester (2012, p.19) provides an exemplary illustration by drawing on a child's short story related by Loizou, Kyriakides and Hadjicharalambous (2011, p.72): 'Once upon a time, there was a clown who did tricks and an elephant ran over the clown and then the clown ran over the elephant.'

This is a minor example of seeing and representing the world differently through the inversion of the apparently natural state of things and conjuring up a picture of marvellous possibilities by a simple irrational connection. Rather than a stratified stable system of thought in which ideas are constrained and limited to faithful reproduction, with any slight disturbance quickly suppressed, playing can actualise different ideas by amplifying diversity and extending possibilities through positive and discrete iterations, phasings and dephasings that exhibit creative adaptation. While not wanting to reduce complex ideas to universal statements, there is a common theme across concepts introduced in this account in that they may be described as 'playful', concerned with getting out of tired binary relationships by attuning to the force and movement of life. These concepts are uprooted, or following Massumi (2002), shamelessly poached, from their original sources and set to work to create new ways of thinking about playing. As such, it is a process of abstraction to work with the materials and practices of everyday life rather than remaining in the abstract.

Deleuze and Guattari (1994) suggest that the purpose of philosophy is the art of forming, inventing and fabricating new concepts rather than repeating tried and tested ones; concepts do not pre-exist the act of creation. As such, as with playing, it is an exploration of the possible, a questioning 'what if…', that overcomes the limits imposed by dogmas and rules of representation and the ways in which language is used to present a truth that becomes set apart from the messiness of life. Imagine the following situations, an exercise often used in workshop situations with adults to explore ideas:

> What if your head is where your bottom is? What if you had a nose on the end of your hand? What if legs are where ears are?

Participants, working in small groups, are given a very short period to explore a range of possibilities these scenarios might offer. At the outset, it invariably provokes an outburst of laughter at the absurdity of such propositions before playing with the opportunities that they open up. This is much more than a cognitive exercise as bodies move to consider what the world might look like, generating a whole series of digressions, further questions and a multitude of 'what ifs'; the process is open-ended and extensive. Deleuze and Guattari's philosophy offers ways of working with the 'real' that precedes the creation of epistemology (theories of knowledge), overturning the habits of fitting experience into pre-existing modes of thought. Concepts are 'centres of vibrations' (Deleuze and Guattari 1994, p.23) that ripple and disturb each other rather than universal and uniform accounts of a stable life.

In the examples already introduced, anything could happen, but there is only one actuality: the reality of the event. For the most part in play studies, the actual is the primary focus of attention and attribution of meaning (the *is* of play). In this sense, reality becomes a stable foundation for forming stable concepts that can project into the future; if it *is* this form of play, this *is* what it does. With this certainty, it is possible for adults to steer and manage what happens in order to achieve the desired outcome, and this is often accompanied by habitual common-sense expressions. For example, in the bedroom sleep-over situation introduced in the preamble to the book, the actualised activity of pillow-fighting may often lead to adult projections that lead to sanctioning this form of playing because 'someone will get hurt and it will end in tears'. It is a reading of play that starts with the actuality as the origin, an inaugural gesture that treats irrational behaviour as if it is rational. But Deleuzian philosophy invites a different approach, attracting interest to the processes that bring about this moment by discerning three different but always entangled and dynamic realms of reality. This ontology (theory of being) is briefly introduced here with a focus on how it extends thinking about playing (bearing in mind the qualifications previously outlined):

1. *The actual or apparent reality of play.* In the bedroom scenario, the children might be in sleeping bags and decide to stand up and try to knock each other over. We can name this visible and concrete form of behaviour as, for example, rough-and-tumble play. While anything *could* happen in this scenario, there is only one actuality of playing – namely sleeping-bag fights. But this actuality is not pre-figured and always contains within it the potential for becoming different. And if one pays close attention to this, it is likely that this 'actuality' emerged from a series of indeterminate movements attuned to the unique conditions at that time – maybe, for example, a short period of stillness as the children anticipate the adult moving downstairs, followed by some initial testing that the coast is clear, slight movements and noises that gauge the possibility for more possibilities, perhaps leading to a child emitting a small farting-like noise with accompanying muffled laughter and so on before sleeping-bag knock-down emerges.

    The actual is comprised of stratified human and non-human entities; it appears as a steady state that is often reinforced through classificatory practices. Thus, the body is produced as individual, enclosed within a 'shell' that separates it from the outside world. This is a dominant account that produces a powerful cut on the world – while it does produce a stable state, it also excludes other ways of accounting, since it masks the processes that give rise to it, namely the 'virtual multiplicities' that are ever-present in a system and as such may be presented as 'actual' in themselves. Thus, for the most part, the focus for children's play is the actual product of playing rather than the processes that bring this form of behaviour to life. The exemplary account of producing *worlds made of poo* becomes both solidified and broken apart to classify and interpret individual behaviour at the expense of the processes (bodies, materials, movements and affects) that produce this moment of becoming different.

2. *The process of actualisation:* (the 'intensive') or the moment when something becomes 'real'. This is the moment of 'what if...' that brings form to the movements of the children as they casually run

their fingers through the gloopy stuff. Deleuze draws on Simondon's concept of individuation to distinguish this process and refers to the ever-present capacity for what might appear to be stable states to fall out of phase (dephase) or destabilise the given order by overflowing out of it (Simondon 1992). Dephasing is a non-linear and discontinuous process that unfolds through multiple phases (as suggested by the bedroom situation); there is not a single moment of dephasing but the instance when complex relations and flows cohere is a 'remarkable point' (Manning 2013), a momentary resolution 'into this or that singular event or discrete occasion of experience' (Manning 2013, p.18). As previously noted, the children and everything else in the bedroom are entangled in movements in-between, a sequence of 'remarkable points' emerges from a series of dephasings that may give some temporary form to what is happening (pillow-fighting) but always contains the potential for becoming something else.

3. *The virtual* (or the 'plane of immanence'): the impersonal and endless process of life in constant movement and flux. Forces and flows of material moving at different speeds and intensities collude to connect, disconnect and reconnect with each other in indeterminate ways to form 'reality'. On the plane of immanence there are only complex networks of forces, 'relations of movement and rest, speed and slowness between unformed elements, or at least between elements that are relatively unformed, molecules, and particles of all kinds' (Deleuze and Guattari 1988, pp.23–24).

The plane of immanence, or what Deleuze sometimes refers to as a plane of consistency, is fundamental to understanding his philosophy; it is the necessary condition for all of life (material and immaterial) but is always unformed and imperceptible and thus cannot be expressed in conceptual order or form. Simondon's (1992) concept of individuation is the process by which the 'real' is produced through intensive processes that move a state of virtuality across a threshold to actuality. It is a process of ontogenesis, or transformation, which brings forth forms in an emergent and discontinuous manner rather than forms being given in advance. It is from this plane that subjects and objects are produced, but the plane of immanence itself is non-productive.

Now, this may appear extremely alien to traditional ways of thinking about the unfolding of life as a presumed movement from simple to more complex behaviours, in which the pre-figured potential of bodies is actualised through experience. Growth proceeds along the line of development (Figure 1.1) and bodies become self-enclosed (Figure 1.2). From this perspective, life can be *differentiated* into pre-existing schemes through the application of binary concepts that situate and fix children to the line. And from this position, the purpose of childhood is to reinforce an individual sense of 'self' as a distinctive identity set apart from the external world and contained by an outer layer of skin, the limits of a body. Yet, as Manning (2009, p.34) suggests:

> To posit skin-as-container as the starting point for the notion of interactive self-sufficiency is to begin with the idea that the well-contained human is one who can actively (and protectively) take part in self–self interactions. Self–self interactions depend on a strict boundary between inside and outside. They occur within the realm of clear bounded selves. Interaction is understood here as the encounter between two self-contained entities (human/human or human/object).

But, as Manning (2009) questions, what if instead of placing self at the centre of development, we were to propose relation as key to the process of life going on? And, in response to this proposition, that a turn to Deleuzian ontology offers another way of approaching this by getting out of individual and teleological accounts of development to present life as an impersonal process of emergence through continuous and discontinuous self-organising connections and relations whose outcomes are not determined in advance by intrinsic properties of already formed matter (Colebrook 2005). There is no form or principle which guides life; 'all we have is the potential for difference and variation' (Colebrook 2005, p.2). It is this process of *differentiation*, dynamic and continuous change, that is at the heart of this analysis – rather than difference being a comparative state between pre-existing entities, every aspect of life is evidence of difference rather than sameness. From a Deleuzian standpoint, attention shifts from reducing life to its presumed separate parts to looking at the continuous process of things making a difference in unique and particular ways. Life is 'difference-in-itself', with each moment a singularity composed from heterogeneous materials; the production of difference is internal to this formation, 'implicit in being that particular' (Stagoll 2005).

Philosophy, for Deleuze and Guattari (1994), is not about representing ideas nor is it about deciphering meaning, but rather it is about paying attention to processes of individuation, the intertwining relationship in-between the actual and the virtual that is always an ever-present 'field of movement moving' (Manning 2014, p.164). The emphasis in this movement of difference is not the fixed essence of the real but how those processes of individuation are brought into being, how they might change over time to become different, and what they might do to affect and be affected by other beings. There is an ambition to explore how play might emerge from all the other possible behaviours that may occur at any given moment. Increasing awareness of the *process* of playing may help adults to better appreciate and work towards supporting conditions in which children can play.

One can begin to see how the prevailing conditions of children being left alone in a bedroom (and all that this contains) may produce an atmosphere conducive to playing and 'messing about' but this cannot be expressed in a deterministic manner; there is no original cause that effects what happens. Consideration is given to movements that give rise to the actuality of play (bearing in mind all the qualifications raised about this to date). Focus falls on the disturbance and ripples in the surface level of 'reality' with its accompanying and generally unquestioned common sense to see what more can be said and done to affect life in more just and equitable forms. Moments of play are diffractive, concerned with disturbing rather than reflecting present reality. As we saw with the example of *Jack and the Beanstalk* in Chapter 1, Barad's (2007) compelling concept of agential realism proposes that *all* matter *performs* and has agency; nothing (pre-)exists in isolation and everything affects, suggesting that agency is an enactment and not an individual possession – it is a matter of intra-acting. Everything is caught up by a collective force or power that is less specific and more indeterminate, overturning traditional attribution of agency as a matter of choice in liberal humanist terms. This immediately brings into question the idea of an autonomous child 'freely choosing' to play.

Walking the lines at the museum

The virtual field insinuates itself into all forms of what happens, which is always a partial and fleeting expression of what the movement has become (the reality). Another example is introduced at this stage, drawn from an observation of two children's playful movements:

> There are large square floor tiles in the main entrance to the museum. A young girl is carefully balancing along the grooves between the tiles in a seemingly random fashion. A short while later another girl joins in, setting her own pattern of movements. As they pass each other, the new arrival turns to the first child and says, 'What happens if you fall off?' (Lester 2015b, p.4)

This mo(ve)ment of coming together may or may not be classified as playing. We could apply any of the numerous definitions of play that exist to test this out. For example, much of the literature suggests key characteristics of play as being voluntary, intrinsically motivated and pleasurable, with a variety of other characteristics too (see, for example, Burghardt 2005; Garvey 1990; Krasnor and Pepler 1980; Playwork Principles Scrutiny Group 2005). It may be that we can attribute the development and refinement of some important 'skills' – calibration, balance, self–other awareness, communication and so on. But as previously noted, this is not the direction followed here.

In this example, the children rarely make eye contact with each other but somehow their bodies and movements resonate to produce a moment when things start to cohere. 'What happens…', as with 'what if…' is a step to coordinate a shared event or 'remarkable point' (Manning 2013) that always retains the potential for moving off elsewhere. So too with concepts: they are not immaterial and outside life but can resonate to produce temporary formations that work together to overcome dogmatic thought. Undoubtedly Deleuze's diverse writings and collaborations over the years produce unstable concepts. This is not simply to create an impression of difference but also to develop a series of different ideas around the same subject; they are concepts which rub up against each other while retaining enough connection to continue to work together in an extensive manner, forming new connections and possibilities (DeLanda 2002). And while Deleuze and Guattari's writings are expansive, they contain some central features that have considerable relevance for this discussion, notably a central proposition that differences of matter are brought about and emerge in dynamic, indeterminate and complex ways without any necessary foundational differences of being. Life does not merely operate at the level of an individual organism (a presumed stable *being*) but emerges from the self-organising capacities of organic and non-organic materials to co-create novel formations, a continuous and fluid state of *becoming* (another example of the principle and/and as opposed to either/or relationships).

Bodies are processes of movements and encounters. Life, from this perspective, is a condition for action and movement; beings are always in the process of becoming *with* other things in motion. As such, life takes place 'in-between', an important term that overcomes the idea that bodies pre-exist their relations. It differs significantly from 'between', which assumes that there are pre-existing states that come together to form temporary alliances but can always return to their original foundational condition. Life goes on, following Barad (2007), as processes of *intra-action* rather than interaction. Bodies are produced through a collective urge to compose relationships that enable life to flourish. Deleuze's (1988) reading of Spinoza suggests that life, as an impersonal force, continues through a vital desire to affect and be affected to produce the best possible state that conditions allow at any given moment. This notion of desire and affect is of central concern in reconfiguring understandings of play: bodies are porous, an assemblage of human, organic and inorganic processes, what Deleuze and Guattari (1988) refer to as a 'body without organs', or without internal organisation.

Worlds made of poo and *walking the lines at the museum* are lines of desire, entangled movements of bodies and things that co-create a more joyous state which is indicative of life going on in an affirmative manner, a phrase which appears frequently in this account. It is an 'ability to act and in acting to make oneself even as one is made by external forces' (Grosz 2011, p.62). Affirmation, following Manning's (2016) account, is a creative force within an event that can re-orientate experience. The ways in which children constantly question 'what if the world was made of poo' seek to go beyond what is known rather than make judgements about the possibilities using what is already known and given. It is tangential in that it seeks to go elsewhere; 'affirmation does not yet know what the field can do, and so it neither predicts nor (de)values it in advance of its coming to be' (Manning 2016, p.201). As with all examples to date, mo(ve)ments of play are speculative and experimental – they do not conform to existing rules of experience and work with the principle and/and to maintain co-existence for difference to emerge, 'the push, the pull that keeps things unsettled, a push that ungrounds, unmoors even as it propels' (Manning 2016, p.201).

If bodies, and the associated concepts that produce the idea of a body, are unstable, then we can no longer think in terms of a pre-figured and self-contained individual but rather bodies and ideas are temporarily and dynamically composed from processes in-between all sorts of things in motion. As Manning (2016, p.19) states, 'Volitional movement understood as movement belonging to the subject and fully directed by the subject is…impossible.' Deleuze and Guattari (1988) helpfully describe this feature by drawing a distinction between the games of Chess and Go. In Chess, the identity and the associated possibility for movement of each piece is preconfigured and seen as intrinsic to the character of the piece. And while collectively there are multiple arrangements and forms of complex manoeuvres and strategies within the game, each piece can only ever perform within its inscribed identity and interacting with other pieces on the board; movements are carried out according to the relative position of each of these pieces. But in the game of Go, the pieces contain no intrinsic features; their identity emerges through the relations that pieces enter. Thus, over the course of a game, the identity of the counters changes as they are perpetually becoming, composed of movement and rest across the entire board; each counter has the capacity to affect and be affected in a space of compossibility or heterogeneous formations (Deleuze and Guattari 1988). A Go counter, as indeed a stable body, is extremely short-lived; it is not something that holds together across space and time.

While the examples introduced to date are singular, they contain a series of arrangements and processes that are worth examining in detail by becoming attentive to the subtle movements as playing emerges. The example can be extended into more and more particularities to build concepts that might be more attuned (*account-ability*) to the ways in which playing emerges from the conditions of everyday life to act responsibly (to develop a *response-ability*) with these conditions. From this process, it is possible to deduce essential features that are highly significant for addressing issues of spatial justice and play.

Together, the chapters in this book bear witness to what Deleuze described as the guerrilla campaign against ourselves and established ways of thinking; as with playing, it is an inevitable consequence of the general desire to think and act differently. They amount to a renewed attempt to bring Deleuze's pragmatic philosophy into contact with the real, which is the only way to keep it alive.

There is hope that by resisting the arrival at fixed meanings one might develop an approach that recognises plenitude and not lack; as Derrida (1976) asserts, the play of difference creates meaning rather than destroys it. Contrary to the foundations of scientific research, this is not an attempt at rationalisation, but neither is it neutral, universal, apolitical, value and emotion free. The scale of this is considerable; it is a philosophical, ethical and political stance towards the world that ambitiously seeks to reposition play as the driving force of life itself. But the account is not simply performed at a level of abstraction; what is under discussion – namely playing – is an everyday, mundane and banal way of being in the world. Studies of play need to be extended to re-find or re-search the wonder of the perfectly ordinary (Laurier and Philo 2006). Yet at the same time it is a modest endeavour. If one is to consider the possibility of a better future, it is important to overcome arrogant ideas of certainty and finite knowledge. In this sense, modesty is not a meek or weak position but simply a constant challenge to ourselves (Cilliers 2005).

Play lines of movement

We are all made of lines of different intensities, speeds, flows and force; a somewhat obscure concept but a central idea to what follows. Life, suggests Deleuze, may be presented as a permeation and permutation of lines; 'we have as many tangled lines as a hand' but complicated in different ways (Deleuze and Parnet 2002, p.5). The endeavour here is to follow these lines of enquiry and to give more attention to the ways in which bodies, symbols and materials are always entwined in a trajectory of becoming that 'comprises the texture of the world' (Ingold 2011a, p.14); indeed, such lines have the power to change the world (Ingold 2007). What all lines have in common is movement; 'only movement concerns me' (Deleuze and Parnet 2002, p.127). Following Ingold (2011a, 2015), and in contrast to the combined straight lines of Figures 1.1 and 1.3, the movement of life may be represented as in Figure 2.1.

Figure 2.1: A (life)line of movement

This line contains no inside/outside but only a continuous flow of movement, pushing from the point with a desire to affect and be affected with the bodies/materials at hand, a productive force that co-composes favourable conditions for an impersonal life to continue. Each trail reveals a relation 'not between one thing and another – between the organism "here" and the environment "there"…it is a trail *along* which life is lived' (Ingold 2011a, p.69). When we look at the ways in which young children may draw human and animal figures (see Figure 2.2), they invariably contain a 'body' or an enclosed blob, but this is enhanced by limbs that have a stick-like quality (Ingold 2015). Here the 'blob' is extended through the lines of arms and legs, an expression of movement rather than fixity and enclosure. These lines of movement are significant: the mobile limbs of the body and their lines of movement are what Deleuze and Guattari (1988) refer to as lines of flight, a break away from the immobile body that a plane of organisation seeks to order.

Figure 2.2: A child's drawing of a body

The idea of life as a single line, while escaping enclosure and adding movement, remains isolated from everything else in the environment. Given that life is not an individual affair, it is possible to present a more complex and relational picture by attempting to 'map' the flows and encounters between bodies and things. The idea of making a map is another key concept from Deleuze and Guattari (1988) and the practice implications of this are discussed in more detail in Chapter 6.

A map is as an open landscape in which movements are possible in all directions, fostering connections between multiple locations and overcoming impediments that delimit the formation of ideas; 'the map is open and connectable in all of its dimensions, it is detachable, reversible, susceptible to constant modification' (Deleuze and Guattari 1988, p.13). The process of mapping is nomadic and rhizomatic, two more concepts which permeate Deleuze and Guattari's later work. A rhizome is flat and extensive with many growing points (for example, bamboo, ginger, iris and the dreaded couch grass). It has the potential to connect any point with any other and cross heterogeneous domains (physical, organic, chemical) and modes of expression (speed and slowness, movement and rest). There are no positions in a rhizome that fix multiples to a central point of origin, only lines of movement. Each movement is a unique event and not a copy or model of a presumed original. As such, rhizomatic thinking counters arborescent thought which fixes everything to a root in hierarchical formations: branch, leaf and trunk are multiples of tree, many parts of one and all connected and traceable to a point of origin.

Returning to the story of *Jack and the Beanstalk*, arborescence would place Jack as the central character, and the multiple characters and materials act to serve Jack's position as hero. It may be possible to substitute one hero for another (Jack's mother, beanstalk, cow and so on) but the thinking/movement remains arborescent. So too with the study of play which produces 'tracings' rather than maps by applying 'scientific' methods to establish cause–effect, teleological relationships and certain outcomes. A tracing is a rigid line that regulates and orders bodies, materials, spaces and relationships through 'either-or logic of value-laden binary oppositions' (Tarulli and Skott-Myhre 2006, p.190).

There is a significant distinction between making a map and a tracing: a map is the privilege of sensing and movement, while a tracing simply outlines a route between two points thereby seeking to secure everything in relation to these predetermined positions (Deleuze and Guattari 1988). Tracings are the mark of adult rationality in which children's movement is fixed to the line of becoming adult; anything that deviates from this is either marginalised or a matter for professional intervention to effect a return to universal developmental trajectories. The everyday act of adults walking along pavements with children illustrates this marginalisation through the ways in which children may be 'dragged along like a suitcase on wheels' (l'Anson 2013, p.105). In contrast, rhizome thinking is concerned with movement, sensation and connection, marked by the conjunction and/and rather than either/or; as such it 'has neither subject or object, only determinations, magnitudes, and dimensions which cannot increase in number without the multiplicity changing in nature' (Deleuze and Guattari 1988, p.9). It may be broken apart, but it will start up again on one of its old lines or start a new line. Mapping is a process of paying critical attention to the lively, performative, participatory, ethical and political movements of everyday life (Crampton 2009). As with all Deleuzian concepts, it is entangled with notions of hybridity, assemblages, intra-activity, desire, bodies without organs, and other concepts that will appear at various points in the discussion to replace immobile accounts of life and development and associated fixed beginnings, terminal end points and clearly determinable trajectories.

Of all these Deleuzian terms, the concept of assemblages merits particular attention at this point, as it is a refrain throughout the book. Assemblages are dynamic formations in which organisms use their capabilities and capacities to form extensive connections with other bodies and materials (Bonta and Protevi 2004; Dewsbury 2011). As Dewsbury (2011, p.149) comments:

> Less epochal, more affirming an alternative, assemblage thinking promises to be an antidote to [the] foreclosure of other questions, issues, interventions and politics through understanding the make-up and organization of the social in more inventive and experimental ways.

Assemblages are formed through acts of deterritorialisation or the intensive ways in which new connections are formed with other assemblages (what if…). Deterritorialisation marks a movement or escape from a given territory (whether it be a social, linguistic, conceptual or affective one). This contrasts with and is related to the process of reterritorialisation, which refers to the ways in which movements of deterritorialisation coalesce to form a new system of relations or bring about changes in the previous assemblage. The two processes, as Deleuze and Guattari (1988) consistently emphasise, are not separate from each other: deterritorialisation is always present within a system and 'in turn inseparable from correlative reterritorialisations' (Deleuze and Guattari 1988, p.509). It is never an escape from or return to the old territory. What happens is indeterminate and often deterritorialisation is subject to forces of reterritorialisation that obstruct and suppress further movement and a new set of transcendent laws is applied (Bonta and Protevi 2004).

In the exemplary account of *strawberry mermaids*, the attendant adult might say to the two children, 'If you can't share your sweets nicely, I will take them off you', or children making *worlds made of poo* are admonished by an adult and told to 'go and wash your hands immediately' or even more severely, as a workshop with education professionals illustrated, the scenario might be read as a 'safeguarding issue'. But there are always opportunities for further acts of deterritorialisation within the system. At other times, there may be more positive and affirmative movements where lines of deterritorialisation connect with others' movements in mutually supportive ways and escape capture. Acts of deterritorialisation can be presented as important ethico-political manoeuvres and of primary consideration as ways in which bodies collectively increase their power to act, to 'create new becomings and joyous affects' (Bonta and Protevi 2004, p.55).

It is here, then, that we can now locate the connections between mapping and assemblages. Mapping is much more than an attempt to produce accurate representations of a so-called reality; it is an embodied way of coping with and navigating through uncertain and complex terrains (Laurier and Brown 2008). It focuses attention to broader and often imperceptible forces that flow across the landscape by locating the excesses, reverberations and perturbations that escape order and rationality. It attends to ways in which organisms and things intensively co-exist and co-create; everything does something, and nothing can be delineated as separate and apart from everything else (Barad 2007). It inevitably opposes an anthropocentric account of life;

everything (matter and meaning, object and subject, nature and culture) is mutually entangled through the ongoing formation of assemblages.

Moving lines at the bus stop

Another example is introduced at this stage to exemplify the process of mapping over tracing (see Figure 2.3). It was an initial experiment to produce a diagram of children's playful lines of movement at a bus stop.

Figure 2.3: Moving lines at the bus stop

This is a form of composition in which my feeling body produces a diagrammatic movement imbued with its own emotionality and action without immediate recourse to words; it is an embodied replay of lines as an entanglement of objects, habits, surprises, landscape features and generally unthought sensations and movements. It is, after Klee (1960), lines going for a walk, a performance full of openness and possibility. They are movements that compose an entanglement, assemblage or meshwork in intra-acting lines that at times become tightly knotted to form a metastable state before unravelling and moving off elsewhere. Accompanying this diagram is the rendition of movement into a text that flows along the lines (Lester 2017, p.317):

> Two children (boys, about 6/7 years old) are standing at a bus stop with an adult. One child starts to walk around the adult, lightly holding her coat as he moves slowly in an anti-clockwise direction; the other boy follows slightly behind, holding on to the child's anorak sleeve. As the coat becomes twisted around the woman, she shrugs the child off – he lets go, but the other boy continues to hold his coat. The first child moves slightly away from the adult and begins to pivot on one leg; the increasing speed of this movement also spins the other child around.

As the speed increases so too does the volume of laughter and giggles before the child releases the sleeve and makes a grab for the hood of the anorak. The child dodges the lunge of the other child and spins away in an almost balletic movement. At this moment, another person arrives at the bus stop and stands close to the first adult, slightly apart from the children. There is a brief pause as both children become stationary before the second child starts to balance along a very faint line/crack in the pavement tracing a move away from the adults, walking with one foot in front of the other, and arms outstretched. The first child follows this movement but then stops and turns his body so he is standing sideways on the line. He traces a semicircle on the floor out from the crack with his right foot and returns to the line, at which point his feet/legs are crossed; he lifts his left foot and traces a semicircle to the rear and back to the line to uncross his legs and carries on along the line, repeating this sequence – after a couple of moves he is joined by the other child, who follows this pattern; again the tempo increases and on a couple of occasions they lose balance and brush against each other which provokes further bouts of giggling. Throughout this period the children have not spoken directly to each other, but seem to communicate through giggles, look, nudges and so on. A short while later the woman calls to the children that the bus is coming and they meander over to where she is standing, and the child resumes a position of holding on to the adult's coat as they climb on board.

Children rarely walk in straight lines to move from A to B. There are all kinds of deviations and experiments that take place as they wander through their environments; shopping with parents in supermarkets, *walking the lines at the museum,* walking through the Bullring in Birmingham, and dancing along the line at the bus stop are minor disturbances to the order of space. You may recall similar experiences by revisiting the various locations of your childhood as an exercise in embodied memory work that attempts to move through what was once a familiar landscape, not in a child-like way but as a 'becoming-child' or what Deleuze and Guattari (1988) refer to as becoming-minoritarian, surrendering to sensations of movement. This is an innovative experiment of 'being (t)here again' and 're-doing' childhood to see new things (Horton and Kraftl 2006b, p.261). This is a method that brings about small moments of transformation and change; they are not specialist techniques but ways of reconfiguring awareness of movement and encounters with other bodies and materials that may reveal the fine and significant detail of once intimate and familiar settings and the various topographical features that afford such movements. For example, this could be the hollow in the path used for playing marbles, the feel of the uneven concrete block wall in the front garden, with its castellated effect as we balanced along the precarious surface, the bollard that we would attempt to leap-frog but at the last minute swerve to avoid as the nearer we came, the taller it seemed, until one day we actually did it and it soon became a matter of routine to jump over this on the way to school.

These are movements that may start pre-consciously before coming to mind, as children meander to points that appeal and attract; powerful things call out to them. Walls, kerb stones, paving slabs, bollards, cracks and dents in pathways, the general detritus of consumption (cans, bottles, paper, sticks) and street furniture affect and are affected by the movements of life. Even when there are few landscape features, children will find creative and imaginative ways to use bodies ('How far can you walk with one breath?', 'What is the fastest time you can reach...?'). They also find expression in various jostling, pushing, chasing and dodging movements. Bodies and things are always in motion. Thus, for example, the laws of gravity and biology clearly prohibit any attempt by humans to fly (unaided by forms of technological intervention). Yet children know that by putting their coat around their neck cape-style (perhaps fixing it with the hood), by making appropriate noises, and imagining, they can indeed fly. The virtual individuates into rational laws of probability and by doing so poses the Deleuzian question, who knows what a body can become? It is a reminder that bodies are restless and always in motion, even when they appear stationary. The following four-minute observation follows a child seated at an 'arts and crafts' table in an evening playcentre. A passing glance at the child would suggest she is sedentary and concentrating on painting lines on a piece of paper but there is much more happening than first appears:

> Young girl (aged 5/6?) walks around the arts and crafts area, stepping sideways as if dancing and then sits down, reaches to the centre of the table and picks up paintbrush – gets off her seat as another child arrives at the table and walks over to her, sitting alongside the child chatting

– then moves to a kneeling position on the chair for about 30 seconds. Then gets off chair and walks round to the bottom of the table, standing to wash her brush and then returns to her original seat where she sits and paints on the paper for a very short period before getting up and carrying the picture with her – at this point the other children at the table move away and she is left on her own – she stands still and looks (somewhat anxiously) at where they are going – after about 10 seconds some of the children return to the table and she carries on painting/chatting and looking at what other children are doing. (Lester 2016a, pp.26–27)

As noted, the linguistic representation of movement always falls short in describing all that is taking place in this short period. While recognising these limitations, it is suggested that the child's movement and affective energies are characteristic of 'bodies without organs', a Deleuzian concept which proposes a body is an assemblage or composition rather that a single, self-contained organism. The body of the child at and around the table is ever-restless, moving, sensing and responsive to local environmental conditions, an environment in which she is in-between and not outside. Ideas from, for example, developmental systems theory, epigenetics and enactivism highlight that development, rather than being fixed and pre-figured, must be viewed as an assemblage of genetic, chemical and physical processes, forces that operate across multiple scales of analysis. Beings are always in a state of becoming-with, not passively adapting to an external environment, but the environment seeps into the body. The taken-for-granted distinctions between nature and nurture are being obliterated; the body is always changeable and influenced by bio-socio-chemical pathways operating across multiple locations from the cell nucleus to the global atmosphere.

The extensive elements that make up a complex body are constantly forming differential relations with other bodies, materials and forces, getting out of its organisation (Bennett 2001). The relational restlessness of the child's movements around the table or *walking the lines at the museum* highlight the ways in which bodies must be open to their environment, or 'what surrounds', and that includes the human, inhuman, inorganic and the imaginary. Bodies are leaky things (Manning 2014) and emerge through these contingent and continuous movements. And if the skin is not a boundary between an enclosed self and the outside then all sorts of possibilities for thinking differently about life emerge; bodies can compose themselves in a manner that cannot be contained by the plane of organisation, they can twist and tweak habits and routines (Deleuze and Guattari 1988). Children are a generative force, moving lines of affect, or productive 'desiring machines' (Deleuze and Guattari 1984) that bring about transformations in the possibility of relationships with other bodies and things that always have the potential for becoming different: 'gestural, mimetic, ludic and other semiotic systems regain their freedom and extricate themselves from the "tracing"…a microscopic event upsets the local balance of power' (Deleuze and Guattari 1988, p.16).

From this point of view, rather than considering bodies as closed physiological and biological systems, we see bodies as open, participating in the flow or passage of affect, characterised more by reciprocity and co-participation than boundary and constraint (Seigworth and Gregg 2010). Returning to the children balancing on the lines at the museum, there is resonance as the children's bodies co-join in action, as if attached by invisible threads. Bodies, lines between tiles, the general ambience and so on are attuned and sensitive to subtle vibrations, colluding to produce an event that is always open to further possibilities for movement, continuing to sense the potential disorder present at this moment of time/space for becoming different. The moment of walking the lines can only emerge from the free association or correspondence in-between materials; there is no single individual leading this spontaneous and unpredictable movement, nothing has prepared them for it and the 'individual' is put to one side as the mo(ve)ment continues (Ingold 2015).

The girls *walking the lines at the museum* and boys dancing at the bus stop are examples of walking and resting, speed and slowness. It is a mode of being that is generally taken for granted. But when one pauses to think about this everyday action, it is possible to discern a subtle line of movement; the capacity to walk (and use feet in countless other ways) emerges as a property of systems of relations, from micro- to macro-scales of organisation and interpenetration. Walking is always contingent and situated, a largely pre-conscious movement that is exquisitely shaped and virtually imbued with all previous steps directed towards the almost future (Manning 2013). It requires an embodied activation of a degree of instability to propel oneself forward that at the same time requires movements to maintain a degree of stability and regain balance:

> We walk in a future-pastness whose virtual plenitude of experience and experimentation assures a metastability of balance. It's not exactly that we remember how the ground touches the foot and the weight shifts as the body transfers from step to step. It's that stepping recalls itself in the act... *The memory of having walked is in the walking.* This is a memory on the edge of perception, a memory in-act that activates in the moving the multiple metastabilities that make this singular choreographed movement possible. (Manning 2013, p.85, my italics)

The walking practices of moving bodies-in-relation are composed from infinite micro-movements that for the most part remain pre-conscious. But while habitual, walking is always repetition with difference, and no single step can be the same as another. It is the ongoing production of assemblages between bodily and environmental properties with all their complexities, as the above examples suggests. These movements may come to mind when the pattern is disturbed and bodies become more deliberate in their movements – a greater alertness to the assemblage of feet, body, mind, sensations, ground, air and everything else redistributes what has already happened with what might come.

In walking, the forward foot's movement through the air and contact with the ground mark the propulsion of life going on; it is a momentary point of the flowing line, all the while balancing, sensing and moving, not as a self-contained unit but in an intra-active state of constant flow and flux. The point of the line in Figure 2.2 may be the present 'reality' and appears to be relatively stable but it always carries with it a susceptibility to becoming unstable at any moment, as the following observation suggests:

> Three girls are in the corner of the hall and have assembled a range of materials that were lying around (black foam pieces, plastic bricks, small cable reels and other bits of stuff); two girls balance lengths of the black foam between the cable drums and then carefully support this by placing the plastic bricks underneath. One of the girls then positions herself at the end of the bridge, preparing to step on to the foam.

Close observation of movement reveals she is already positioning herself to fall, arms outstretched, body alert to the possible movements that will occur once she leaves the ground. She carefully lifts a foot and lays it very gently on to the foam, feeling the movement, body adjusting… The structure collapses almost immediately as the girl steps onto it. There are shrieks of laughter and the girls start to rebuild it – this time it is even more precarious, with a similar outcome as the girl tries to walk along it and more fits of laughter as it once again collapses before the girls move into the adjacent area. (Lester 2016a, p.25)

The details of this singular moment contain both the unique quality of this formation and a prospective movement; who knows where this might lead? The preparation and positioning of the body is inclined to be responsive to the movement of the assembled materials, generating a sense of anticipation and heightened awareness of the body's relationship with these supposedly 'inert' materials. And of course, it is fun to try it out and to let oneself go into a fall to regain balance. It is a minor example, a co-creation of bodies, sensations and materials as an act of affective participation in everyday life. The use of the term affective in this sense does not simply refer to emotions but forces that arise in such encounters or entanglements as 'walking the bridge'. Affects dispose a body to engage with the world in a certain style – every moment of an encounter shapes and orientates a body's affective disposition either by enhancing or diminishing the power to act.

Summary

This intensive and complex chapter has attempted to generate different ways of thinking about play. It performs a different cut, and, as with all concepts, it supports the formation of some inferences and disables other possibilities (Patton 2000). The ideas developed in this chapter are intended as an ethical move. They establish concepts that raise serious questions about the positive or negative capabilities of life: do they lead to greater freedom or do they perpetuate ideas of capture and of the individual, and how might we act responsibly to overcome these enclosures? This is revisited in more detail in Chapters 6 and 7. But for now, it is worthwhile restating these central concepts as a conclusion to this chapter:

- Life is not an individual affair: life, and the ways it goes on, is not a process of individual organisms striving for survival but is the ever-present and ongoing potential for change that exists in the relationship *in-between* bodies and things. Each of the playful examples offered here may be viewed not so much as an individual act of deliberation and exercising 'choice' but as largely pre-conscious and affective movements that intra-actively compose relationships *in-between* bodies and things. Such a perspective inevitably repositions a 'body' as thoroughly interconnected with the material world and not a self-contained unit.

- Life goes on through a desire to form arrangements or *assemblages* that are conducive to being well; bodies and things co-compose situations in which life can flourish. The examples of playing introduced to date are nothing special, but are fairly mundane and everyday movements fashioned in-between materials and bodies to produce states that simply for the time of playing generate a more pleasurable state: a state of 'being well'.

- From this, the primary force and desire of life is movement – the ability to move towards things that support flourishing and to move away from those things that reduce or limit this capability. As a body moves, it perceives and senses, while at the same time what it perceives and senses affects movement. Thus, minute by minute there are dynamic qualitative changes taking place within and in-between bodies and environment (Massumi 2002). This is how life goes on (human and non-human). For the most part, these movements are taken for granted. The argument developed here would suggest that greater attention needs to be given to the everyday ways in which children negotiate conditions for playing as the basis for adult response-ability.

While this is gross over-simplification of complex ideas, it is sufficient to begin to present playing as a process of life taking place, flourishing and going on in an affirmative manner, maintaining a healthy relationship between bodies, movements, materials and so on. Playful moments emerge from an unlimited field of potentiality (the virtual); what happens (the real) is a specific form that is actualised by fortuitous arrangements, diffractions and deviations that are beyond the control of a single author.

Playing as process defers end states through the creation of 'always-moving-on' practices. As with life itself, it always exceeds attempts to capture it in language. The challenge is to develop more mobile ways of paying attention to process rather than products, to pursue life lines rather than points.

This requires a different vocabulary (including cartography, lines, play space, assemblages, affects, planes of organisation, lines of flight, entanglements and the value of the example), one that can think/do differently. While seemingly abstract, the concepts are grounded in everyday life and practices; they help to bring a different focus to adult account-ability by paying closer attention to the detail and movements of children's encounters, a position of enchantment with the world.

Playing can appear anywhere and everywhere, generating moments in which life is temporarily more vibrant, simply producing greater satisfaction in being alive (Sutton-Smith 2003). This by itself would warrant the importance of paying more careful attention to establishing favourable conditions in which children's (and adults') playfulness thrives. For playwork settings, this is the prime purpose of practice; for other professions, playing may be perceived as peripheral to the overall intention of their role. Yet, given the claims made here, the argument would be that every adult has some influence in shaping an environment for playing and simply enlivening the practicalities of everyday life and by doing so making a significant contribution to children's well-being. This will be explored in more detail in the next chapter.

■ CHAPTER 3 ■

Some Thoughts on Play and 'Well-Being'

Introduction

There is a long-standing recognition of the relationship between play and well-being for human and non-human life. The interconnected principles previously introduced suggest that rather than following a pre-existing script, life and playing unfold in a dynamic flux of movements and encounters between bodies, imaginations, histories, materials and so on. While there is an overall intention to avoid adding to the long-standing debate about what play *is* and the associated benefits of playing, this brief interlude examines the concept of well-being in general circulation and presents a different reading in terms of the ideas developed to date. As Sutton-Smith (2003) asserts, the opposite of play is not work but depression of vital life systems. Given this, a repositioning of play-as-process firmly situates it as the co-creation of a zone of being well in which there is greater satisfaction in being alive. Yet the relationship between play and well-being is underplayed in policy and practice; support for playing is often framed in instrumental terms and as an investment for the future, with the assertion that playing builds specific skills and qualities that have value in terms of social, cultural or economic capital.

This chapter critically explores the relationship between play and well-being and offers another way of thinking that moves away from a discourse of children as discrete individuals with a range of potential deficits that necessitate health interventions (including play) and towards a spatial consideration of play and well-being that provides

Children as effect

87

the foundations for a more detailed exploration in Chapter 4. Again, it should be highlighted that the relationship between well-being and play is presented from a minority world perspective and the qualifications and complexity of this position presented in Chapter 1 equally apply to what follows.

Well-being and policy

Perspectives on well-being are wide ranging and draw on diverse disciplinary foundations such as economics, education, health studies, developmental psychology, neuroscience and more recently such specialist subject areas as positive psychology and happiness studies. It currently pervades many areas of policy-making and implementation in minority world countries and is articulated in specific well-being outcomes and measurements for major aspects of public policy in the UK and beyond (see, for example, Bradshaw 2016; UNICEF 2013). Increasingly, public-funded programmes are required to demonstrate how they contribute to overall, or a specific aspect of, well-being (Rowlands 2011).

Yet for the most part the term 'well-being' is poorly defined, and the various terms such as well-being, quality of life, happiness and so on are often conflated, vague, lacking definition, and used inconsistently in the literature. The origins of well-being can be traced to the health and economic sectors and each brings its own understanding and specific area of interest to the field. This is further confounded as other areas of public service have been caught up in the well-being agenda. As may be already evident, the notion is not without problems and along with other all-embracing concepts (resilience, social capital, for example) has become widely criticised (Camfield, Streuli and Woodhead 2009) for being 'conceptually muddy, but pervasive' (Morrow and Mayall 2009, p.221). Morrow and Mayall continue:

> the use of terms such as well-being should be critically considered, because if it is a kind of unit of exchange that works across cultures and nations, this is in itself politically loaded and problematic. Is well-being (simply) a word that economists can work with and understand? In the arguments for inter-disciplinarity, there is no mention made of critical sociology, political or social theory or philosophy, and no consideration

of the risks involved in transferring concepts between disciplines, cultures and languages, which we suggest should be acknowledged when concepts such as 'well-being' are studied. (Morrow and Mayall 2009, p.221)

As such, well-being is a highly political concept, and policy formulation and evaluation somewhat inevitably seek to adopt an objective, normalising and totalising account of what it is to be 'well'. Measures of 'well-being' say more about the priorities and ideology of political parties than lived experiences, and general definitions of well-being and happiness elide the cultural context of people's lives. This somewhat chequered history suggests that the concept of well-being should be approached with a degree of caution. Yet it may be that the very openness and vagueness of the concept has value for beginning to adopt a critical position to understandings and applications of policy designed to improve the conditions of people's lives. It is this critical stance that is adopted in this chapter by considering the ways in which children are positioned in well-being studies and policy, before turning to a closer examination of what the approach offered in this book can contribute to ways of thinking about the relationship between play, well-being and resilience. The chapter ends with an exploration of what a relational perspective might offer for the consideration of children's right to play and to life itself.

Children's well-being

As may be evident from the previous section, well-being does not have a coherent or unitary research tradition. Also, until recently, the field has largely focused on measuring adult well-being. The presumption here is that children's well-being is invariably tied to that of their adult caregivers. Yet what children value in their everyday lives may be considerably different from adults. In line with the surge to capture and utilise the concept of well-being, children's lives are increasingly subject to measuring and monitoring against an aggregation of beneficial outcomes across a series of presumed objective and subjective indicators. These metric devices over-code interactions and reduce complex relationships to standardised accounts. Thus, gross domestic product, educational achievement, body mass index and so on produce a norm that cannot accommodate the diverse ways in which these, and other variables, may produce more or less healthy childhoods:

> In the end, no metric can escape the conditions of its production and the partiality and incompleteness of its view on the world. In other words, if a metric is being applied, this is a sign that someone, at some point, has lost an argument. Zealous application of body mass index, for example, can be criticized in view of that metric's insensitivity to differences in the shape of healthy bodies. (Facer, Holmes and Lee 2012, p.171)

These calculations assume a relationship between children's health and development (generally measured in terms of educational achievement) and are conflated in such terms as 'healthy development', which acts as a shorthand for normative measurements of children's well-being. While research has become increasingly sophisticated in the collection and analysis of data, there is a continued underlying assumption and application of a deficit approach: children's well-being is measured by a 'lack of' something. Such a stance reinforces the dominance of a 'needs' agenda in which the identity of children is pre-ordained and applied to determine what may be missing from being and becoming 'normal'. It is ultimately an individualistic and highly subjective approach that depoliticises children's lives (Morrow and Mayall 2009) by isolating children from their everyday worlds and experiences. Measures of children's health and well-being are largely dominated by individual attainment of developmental milestones, largely expressed in terms of educational achievement and good states of physical and mental health. The emphasis is clearly on children as 'well-becomings'; the period of childhood is viewed as preparation for becoming 'grown up' rather than as something to consider of value in the here and now.

One consequence of this increasing attention to children's progress is the rise in surveillance of children, to such an extent that they have become the target of disempowering social, political, educational and legal regulations that constitute children as dependent in relation to adults in society (Robinson 2013). Measures collected through this process also establish the framework for making judgements about the possible interventions needed to ensure healthy development. Children's play is invariably caught up in this process; it becomes a form of health promotion whereby children are encouraged to be active

Good vs bad play (handwritten annotation)

in their play. This has a powerful normalising effect on what constitutes beneficial play, and by inference forms of play that are 'unhealthy':

> While playing simply for fun (that is, frivolous pleasure) is considered a common experience of childhood, it appears to be less important than the more productive and explicitly active play for health. (Alexander, Frohlich and Fusco 2014, p.1201)

This is not to deny that treatments for specific conditions lead to improved health, but broader outcomes, as identified in the increasing proliferation of indicators that seek to measure 'happiness' or general health and attainment, are complex and multi-variable, defying the certainty of specific cause–effect relationships. Certainly, the literature on resilience suggests that what may be deleterious conditions for one child may not be so for another. Well-being may be seen to be the result of a highly complex entanglement of context, environment, genetics and 'chance occurrences' (Ungar 2008). Recent attempts to acknowledge the subjective experience of well-being, especially with children, recognise that children are active agents in their lives and communities and seek to represent children's voices, aspirations and their position within local cultures and social structures. However, although well-intentioned, these attempts to capture and represent subjective experiences are inevitably frustrated by the very nature of representation, the limitations of articulating what it is one 'feels' about life. As Jackson and Mazzei (2013 p.262) say, the stories children (as with all research participants) tell are 'partial, incomplete, and… [are] always in a process of a retelling and remembering'. In addition, the assemblage of adult researcher, child interviewee and everything else at that time affects what is said. Thus, children's 'voices' become disembodied in adult agendas and participation systems, and there is always an excess of affect that cannot be represented in language alone.

Health (and by inference ill-health) are not states but processes, a becoming-other that fluctuates with the intensity of relations that impinge on the body (Fox 2012). The body always has some 'health' in it while alive, and most likely also contains some 'ill-health'. Thus, the health of a body is not an absolute or idealised state but continually negotiated and produced through a process of becoming-with and in-between relations with what is available in the environment at any given moment. This reinforces a central concept developed in Chapter 2, namely that well-being/being well, as a process of life going on in an affirmative manner, occurs as a dynamic, indeterminate relational process co-composed through desire and affect; that is, the ability of the mind/body to affect and be affected in relationships with others.

The concept of 'desire' becomes important in this discussion. Generally, 'desire' in its modern sense and application implies a negative need to acquire what one fantasises about. Yet having acquired the object of fascination, one no longer desires it; the need has been fulfilled, or indeed frustrated because the reality of the object does not match the fantasy. This version of desire assumes an important condition in capitalist consumption that rests on the continuous creation of a 'market' for desires. Thus, body shape and condition are created and fashioned as desire, an aspiration to achieve the ideal. But for Deleuze, drawing on the work of Spinoza, desire or *conatus* is the affirming force of production (not consumption) and a creative lifeforce to become something more, freed from a sense of lack to see what more bodies might do. The desire to be well permeates life: children (and adults) constantly move towards that which offers the chance of life being better. This can be very small, mundane mo(ve)ments such as, when entering a playground, seeking out people and things to engage with or avoid.

A moving bodily relationship in-between the environment, composed from memories, imagination, daydreams, emotions and representation of these as feelings, sensations, perceptions and materials and so on contributes to being able to cope with the messy 'ongoingness' of life. This is the 'body without organs' (Deleuze and Guattari 1988), an assemblage or multiplicity, including of the virtual/possible (remember the 'what if...' story about *worlds made of poo*) that by its very nature is open to its surroundings. As previously noted, the extensive parts that make up the complex body establish differential relations with other bodies and emerge through these contingent and continuous relationships.

Such an approach acknowledges that human existence is based on 'value' (i.e. the extent to which any situation affects the viability of a self-organising and precarious network of processes that constitutes a body without organs). This is not a fixed state but operates within certain parameters. When an organism/assemblage reaches the extreme of these limitations, integrity is threatened (generally manifest through illness and disease) and action needs to be taken to move away from this formation. Equally there is a range where the organism flourishes, a zone that may be described as 'being well'. The notion of value, in this context, relates not simply to survival, but to the quality of survival, a desire to seek the best possible position, that is, a state of joy. Playing is a pleasurable expression of 'being well' arising from the actualisation of desire. As has been said, bodies have an incentive to be restless, gravitating towards the things that will increase well-being and avoiding those that decrease this state. They are movements that seek a joyful union with other 'things' and to avoid assembly with things that lessen the capability to act. It marks an 'accretion of feelings, capacities, opportunities and interactions' (Duff 2011, p.149) in a singular mo(ve)-ment/event.

The concepts introduced so far can work with the playful examples to present an alternative reading of the contribution that playing may make to well-being while retaining a fidelity to children's movements. The entanglements of bodies *walking the lines at the museum*, stepping on to a precarious bridge or momentarily wondering at the discovery of an ice-diamond (and the subsequent loss of this precious item) are just minor formations in which children's bodies and materials collude to become different and by doing so fully participate, as children, in shaping local conditions to their advantage. This immediately throws a different light on the notion of the competent child – no longer can a child be identified by a store or lack of competences, and there is no predetermined map of individual development by which one can measure progress. It also suggests a different perspective on agency, which can no longer be presented as the individual freedom to make choices and act on these.

The 'locus of agency is always a human-non-human working group' (Bennett 2010, p.xvii). There is no individual autonomous 'agent' but rather agency is distributed between bodies and things that congregate to form a temporary 'identity', a metastable state which may temporarily hold together and always contain within it the tendency to get out of itself: who knows what else a body can do? From this point of view, a child (as indeed all forms of organic life) is a perpetual movement of becoming and not a being defined once and for all. This marks a significant conceptual movement by refocusing emphasis from what is happening inside individual children's minds to what passes within and in-between children's minds/bodies and everything else that constitutes the spaces of their childhoods. Thus, conditions of being well are situated and relational; there is always a spatial element. They are also co-composed rather than given, and each production contains within it the potential to increase or decrease the possibility of beneficial encounters that will enhance or reduce a sense of well-being.

Playing and being well

The playful production of space is explored further in Chapter 4, but for now the discussion moves to considering how playing might be understood as a health-enabling movement, extending understanding beyond the current instrumental value generally attributed to children's play. Another example is introduced here, an excerpt from a BBC (1994) production *Playing Out*, which follows a group of children making their way to and from school and playing out in the evening.

Tell your mum I saved your life

The following mo(ve)ment occurs as the group go to school in the morning (Lester and Russell 2008b, p.4):

> Two children are balancing along a dry-stone wall, one in front of the other. As they teeter precariously along the wall, the child at the rear grabs the shoulders of the child in front, shakes the child, causing a temporary loss of balance, and says, 'Tell your mum I saved your life'.

Working with the concepts and examples introduced to date, the question is not so much 'what does this mean?' but 'how does it work?' What are the prevailing conditions that enable this playful movement? At first glance, this looks to be a dangerous manoeuvre with every possibility that the child at the front may fall off the wall. But closer attention to the movement and the context offers a different reading. It is evident as the documentary progresses that the children are friends – the casual conversations, banter, teasing and name-calling as the children make their way through the environment are indications of bodies at ease with each other and they maximise the opportunities the environment presents for moving differently. For example, as they walk along the pavement, one child finds an empty can, stands on it to shape it to the bottom of his shoe and continues click-clacking along the street while rhythmically teasing his friend over a football result ('Easy! Easy! Easy!'). This would suggest that the motivation for jostling on the wall is not designed to cause injury but to inject an element of surprise and disturbance into what may be a habitual routine. What is noticeable from close observation of the movement in-between is the way in which the child at the rear holds on to the shoulders of the boy in front as he recites the traditional chant 'tell your mum...' as if he was ensuring that the child would not fall – and once he is reassured that the child has regained balance he lets go and receives an abusive riposte from this friend as they continue along the wall, laughing as they go.

A further question comes to mind: why would children put themselves in this position? Perhaps the most straightforward response, although one that drifts back into attributing meaning and motivation which is generally avoided in this account, might be that this is fun and better than simply walking directly to school. The entanglement of bodies, sensations, movements, shared history and routines, the wall and so on collude to produce this unique moment of enchantment with life. Balancing and jostling across the wall is the actualisation of playful dispositions: bodies and materials are alert to the possibilities and virtualities that are ever present to generate states of excitement, enjoyment and comradeship through tentative experiments with what bodies can do ('what if ...'). As with other examples, it is a meshwork of movements and affects, a *milieu* formed from the middle with its own conditions, forces, flows and time structure.

The adoption of the French term *milieu* is useful in that it conveys both 'middle' and 'surroundings' and by doing so overcomes the binary of inside and outside (Massumi 2013). It has neither unity nor totality but is composed of a set of lines and movements which are irreducible to some presumed original parts and much more complex than surface appearance. This is Deleuze and Guattari's body without organs that can generate events in all kinds of promiscuous ways and all of them equally (or com-)possible.

Such *milieux* are important sources of emergent capabilities (Duff 2011) and the accumulation of a repertoire of wide-ranging affective and relational resources (Lester and Russell 2014c). While they are ordinary and everyday events, these moments have properties which can increase the collective power to act and maintain an appetite to co-create more playful movements in the near future by being open to the possibilities that the world presents. It is the very ordinariness and ubiquity of playing which is significant – what Lester and Russell (2008a), drawing on Masten's (2001) study of resilience, refer to as 'ordinary magic'. The term 'magic' does not intend some mystical quality, rather that playing is produced out of the ordinary, it is composed from and transforms everyday stuff.

While we have to be wary of signification and reduction of singular examples to universal accounts, it is possible to discern some pattern and rhythm to the movements, notably through the questioning 'what if…' stance to the world as a way of creating situations in which the immediate future is uncertain and requires some temporary resolution, if only to inject further disturbance (playing as the phasings and dephasings of a metastable state discussed earlier). But this is not to completely surrender to forces of chaos; playful assemblages increase a collective power to act and thus retain a certain degree of control over the direction of movement. As Deleuze comments, bodies must keep a degree of identity simply to prevent falling into despair, while at the same time preserve the ability to continue to be open to the environment and the possibility of becoming different. If playing is tipping over into negative and constraining power, then it is possible to regroup through adjustments in response to perceptions, sensations, movements and their affects (for example, as if connected by invisible threads that coordinate movement in-between bodies in *walking the lines at the museum*) or more explicit tactical moves and expressions such as 'we are only playing' or 'I'm not playing, it's not fair'. These act as reminders that what they are doing is 'play', but of course things do not always work out and the assemblage falls apart or is reconfigured into a less favourable arrangement. The following observation (Lester 2015d, p.13) from an after-school club is an example of this precarious negotiation process:

> Two children, a girl aged 8 and a boy aged 6, are playing a make-believe domestic game in which the girl, evidently taking the dominant role in deciding the play, is the 'mother' and the boy plays her 'husband'. The girl issues a series of instructions to her husband – time to get up,

come and eat your breakfast, now you go off to work – and the boy follows these leads (a shared desire to affect and be affected). But as the 'husband' walks off the girl shouts to him, 'And then you die', which provokes a look of astonishment on the boy's face accompanied by a plea, 'Do I have to?' At this point the girl responds, 'Alright then, you just have an accident and you have to go to hospital.' The boy is happier with this instruction and falls to the floor, screaming in pain and holding his leg at which point the game has changed from domestic roles to a surgeon/patient scenario as the girl prepares to saw off his leg.

Lester and Russell (2008a) suggest the ability to generate uncertainty and regain balance, following the hypothesis established by Spinka, Newberry and Bekoff (2001), enables life to flourish. The sudden injection of disturbance as the two boys balance along the wall on the way to school causes a rush of mind/body responses to being surprised. This is more than an internal process: the space in-between is a relational field that ripples with intensive movements, counter-movements, continuous adjustments, an affective encounter with a force or desire to become different. It is a largely pre-conscious collusion of bodies and materials to co-produce playful entanglements imbued with an affirmative mood and style. The generation of moderately stressful situations, in which there is a greater power to act and increased capability to retain a collective sense of control over what is happening initiates, among multiple entangled processes, a flow of neurochemicals, increases heart rate, produces novel movement patterns, heightens alertness and responsiveness to movement and generates a range of vivid emotions. Playing may exercise these complex arrangements and prime stress response systems so there are some foundational capabilities to draw on later should the situation demand – as noted in Sutton-Smith's (1997) trickle-down effect. It is an intensive affect that can lead to extensive connections and more possibilities for action, as the BBC documentary illustrates.

Acknowledging the material manipulations of the editing process, the programme portrays a continuous sequence of playful mo(ve)ments along the route to school including sliding down snowy slopes, swinging across the outside of a bridge, racing each other across a road to reach a bus stop, where teasing and jostling takes place, and setting off a car alarm and running away. Alongside this there are other less energetic movements. A noticeable example is when three children are silently standing on a footpath under a low railway bridge, hands holding the roof of the tunnel and sensing the vibrations of an oncoming train. As it nears, one of the children whispers a countdown – 3, 2, 1 – while at the same time counting on his fingers. As the train passes overhead the children scream loudly and run out of the tunnel, laughing as they go on their way. One can imagine, in a becoming-minoritarian way rather than seeking to interpret and give meaning to this example, the resonance in-between bodies, histories, imaginations and movements that creates the atmosphere of this *milieu* and its affects. While this may have become something of a daily habit, it is always repetition with difference as the routine always contains the possibility for further deviations. And so, at various times on their travels, children will engage in forms of verbal sparring, playing with disgust as two children seek to outdo each other with claims of eating food and 'throwing up' and daring each other to do what might appear to be quite dangerous tasks (I dare you to put your hand in the fire).

These playful states are desirable and pleasurable: it is enjoyable and better than the routine and order of being a child in a world largely designed and controlled by adults. The production of joyful states creates a sense of optimism to the present and near future; life is worth living (Sutton-Smith 2003). Following Deleuze's (1988) reading of Spinoza, the intensive state of joy is an active mode which continues and extends as long as a body's powers increase; it pursues new possibilities that expand imaginations, refine an ability to feel and be affected, and extend capacities for action and passion (Hardt and Negri 2009).

What is evident as the children walk to and from school, and in the other examples included to date, is the generation of moments of laughter as a response to unexpected changes in non-serious events. It is possible to laugh in the face of incongruity and surprise, as the following observation of two schoolchildren following routines at break-time exemplifies:

> During hand washing before lunch, A. walks up behind R., who is waiting to use the sink, tugs the elastic waistband of his pants, and snaps it. A. screams loudly and laughs. R. turns to him and laughs. He reaches to grab A.'s waistband to retaliate, but A. steps away from him. Both children continue laughing. (Trawick-Smith 2010, p.549)

Playing and resilience

Lester and Russell (2008a), guided by concepts developed by Sutton-Smith (2002, 2003), suggest that playing is a potent form of emotion regulation, a key feature of resilience, and is marked by the capability to co-create vibrant mo(ve)ments where what might normally be described as excessive or over-the-top emotions can be safely expressed. The children's sense of anticipation and exuberant release as the train passes overhead, the girl's expression of disgust ('yuck') at the boy's exploration of the possibilities presented by a *world made of poo*, and the enchantment of *strawberry mermaids* are examples of the ways in which children co-create opportunities to express primary emotions (anger, fear, disgust, shock, sadness and joy) while keeping them in check by recognising that what happens is a parody (Sutton-Smith 2003). Playing makes fun of them while simultaneously experiencing and experimenting with their 'real' emotional qualities. In other words, the feelings generated in these playful encounters are 'not real' but arise from a different actualisation of the virtual field in which it is okay to express them because the consequences are different. The 'what if...' of playing instigates an 'as if...' emotional repertoire.

Sutton-Smith (2002) introduces a metaphor of the circus to highlight the ways in which the interplay of emotional repertoires maintains a playful disposition and associated range of responses. The animals in the circus represent the possibility of danger, the clowns symbolise the disruption of conventions and the acrobats turn cartwheels as they disrupt physical safety. Yet all of this is framed in a circus tent where hopefully nothing dangerous occurs – it is the simulation of danger that generates the thrills and joy. From this, it is possible to present disposition as an environmental-relational property, in-between, rather than an individual capacity. Playing emerges from an affective-atmosphere (the conditions in the *bedroom scenario* during the children's sleep-over) rather than an individual act of choice and deliberation.

To summarise at this stage, the relationship between playing and resilience capabilities can be found in the expression of desire as a force that flows between bodies, materials and their affects. It is actualised in mo(ve)ments of connections that defy rational explanations and common sense by subverting the normal course of events. It is not a matter of personal choice and freedom but an intra-active process that unsettles the identity of individuals. The co-creation of playful moments is both evidence of and productive of organisms being well: the significant term is 'co-creation', produced in-between the movements of bodies and materials and not given from outside. As such, playing is a form of 'self-health' by preserving the capacity of bodies to be open to the possibilities that exist at any moment to form mutually beneficial relationships.

The connection between playing, well-being and the development of adaptive systems that enhance a capacity to bounce back from adversity and cope with stress has attracted increasing interest in multi-disciplinary research and policy (see Lester and Russell 2008a for a detailed examination of diverse research studies in support of the relationship between playing and resilience). Lester and Russell's (2008a) study contains the significant qualification that the complexity of this relationship across entangled mind–body–environment systems and processes resists specific cause–effect claims about the efficacy of play. However, while policy-makers acknowledge the importance of supporting children's capacities to be resilient, the traditional understanding and application of this concept remains rooted in the wider context of neoliberalism, the individualisation of life and the value attributed to childhood as a period of deficiency and neediness. This perspective starts from the assumption that through the application of expert knowledge and a series of supposedly objective biomedical and psychological measurements, it is possible to determine the resilient profile of children and make judgements about what they might need to enhance their capacity to withstand stress. The identification of 'resilient factors' adopts a binary approach: either you possess or lack what is necessary. It is a form of governance concerned with individual responsibility and self-regulation, with practices designed to enclose the body and keep it under control. As noted in Chapter 1, these are exercises in bio-power designed to create compliant subjects who are not only controlled within the plane of organisation but wittingly and unwittingly collude in the maintenance of these systems.

The increasing proliferation of 'resilience' training programmes (happiness, emotion regulation, mindfulness) in the education system is indicative of the hope invested in instilling personal qualities in children that will enable them to be flexible and adaptable in the face of increasing uncertainty. To be autonomous and self-regulating is *what is the opposite?*

the hallmark of the neoliberal subject; to be otherwise is the mark of deviancy. Resilience, within the dominant logic of capitalism and developmentalism, negates the importance of movements in-between bodies and materials. The potential relationship between play and resilience, as developed in this account, is reduced in policy to highly causal and instrumental connections (play builds resilience by teaching children skills of risk assessment, or encouraging children to empathise and regulate their emotions and so on) that perpetuate a deficit model of 'well-being' and continue to give licence to adults to organise and structure play activities designed to promote resilient qualities. When children display vivid emotions and lively movements, they are, for the most part, met with adult disapproval that questions the possible benefits of such playful antics. Jostling on a wall, creating *worlds made of poo*, snapping elastic on pants, with their emotional tenor and expressions of disgust, excitement and novel movement patterns, would run counter to mainstream accounts of emotion regulation that encourage children to 'keep a lid on' and suppress these exuberant outbursts as a measure of 'self-control'. Indeed, in some cases where these examples have been used in workshop sessions with adults, children's behaviour provokes concerns over safeguarding, bullying and anti-social behaviour.

Resilience is a buzzword that has assumed central importance across all aspects of government policy, from mental health to climate change. As with the concept of well-being, there are contested meanings and little clarity. The primary focus in policy terms remains largely on the individual 'resilient child', whereas the evidence would suggest that resilience arises from the health-enabling capability and resources of the environment (Ungar 2011). While this may appear to be increasingly recognised in policy in the discourse on 'resilient communities', the environment is secondary to the changes that occur at individual level: 'It is theorised as important only to the extent that it provides a forum in which resilience-promoting processes that contribute to individual growth take place' (Ungar 2011, p.4). One central critique that has particular relevance to this discussion can be found in MacKinnon and Derickson's (2012) consideration of the contemporary material-discursive effects of resilience through state agencies and policy. They offer an alternative viewpoint that highlights the ecological, contingent and dynamic nature of resilience that brings a socio-political dimension to the discussion:

Put another way, if alternative social relations are to be realized democratically and sustainably, and in ways that are wide-reaching and inclusive (as opposed to uneven or vanguard driven), then uneven access to material resources and the levers of social change must be redressed. To that end, we offer resourcefulness as an alternative concept to animate politics and activism that seek to transform social relations in more progressive, anti-capitalist and socially just ways. In contrast to resilience, resourcefulness as an animating concept specifically seeks to both problematize and redress issues of recognition and redistribution. (MacKinnon and Derickson 2012, p.255)

There are some pertinent issues from the above extract which are introduced briefly before going on to look at the implications of this for thinking differently about play. It recognises that resilience is not simply an individual capacity but is formed through relationships with the social and material world. This reinforces the general trend in ecological studies that highlights the importance of interactions in-between an individual and a facilitative environment. However, it adds a critical political dimension to thinking about what it is to be resilient. The focus switches from what a person needs to be able to survive in an uncertain world to challenging the ways in which stress and uncertainty operate against citizens; this is a significant movement that switches focus from individual strengths and weaknesses to systems and processes (political, economic, cultural, social and material) which act to the advantage of a minority and inflict hardship on the majority. The notion of resourcefulness is an attempt to draw attention to the ways in which communities may resist and challenge forms of oppression and redistribute resources to their advantage.

The political dimension of children's play is explored in more detail in the next chapter, but for now MacKinnon and Derickson's account of resourcefulness is put to work with Ungar's (2008, p.225) attempt to produce a mobile definition of resilience:

In the context of exposure to significant adversity, whether psychological, environmental, or both, resilience is both the capacity of individuals to navigate their way to health-sustaining resources, including opportunities to experience feelings of well-being, and a condition of the individual's family, community and culture to provide these health resources and experiences in culturally meaningful ways.

Given the main argument developed in this chapter, the claim is that playing is a primary form of children's navigation to health-enabling resources. While navigation may imply a movement towards something that already exists, the application here is different in that playing marks a collective redistribution of everyday environmental resources to children's momentary advantage. This also acknowledges that for the most part the prevailing environmental conditions of childhood are produced by adults as a plane of organisation that regulates children's movements and desires through a panoply of material-discursive arrangements. Thus, for example, the school classroom is over-coded with materials, symbols, practices, routines and habits, technologies and so on that clearly position children as pupil-subjects, expected to follow the rules established by the school. Of course, these are necessary to make things work and for children to be educated, but they also have exclusionary effects – certain behaviours are rewarded, others frowned on. Yet despite this apparent regimentation and regulation, there are always opportunities for breaking out of order. Children can navigate around these conditions to produce mo(ve) ments, or Deleuzian 'lines of flight', that reconfigure time and space to their desires (see Figure 3.1).

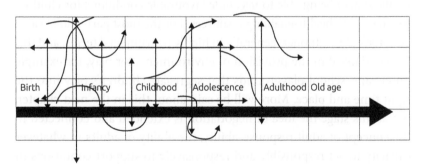

Figure 3.1: Lines of flight on a plane of organisation

These are subtle navigations through what is happening at any given moment rather than pre-planned, although they may become embedded in a repertoire of performances designed to enliven the practicalities of children's everyday existence. These disruptions are evident in the very early stages of children's participation in education systems, as Gallacher's (2005, p.17) example of nursery children illustrates:

On warm, sunny days nursery staff liked to take their breaks outside in the toddler room garden, which is next to the staff room, extending the out of bounds staff room classification into the garden. The children would routinely climb on the benches in the music corner to watch them through the window until they were told to 'leave the ladies alone'. Other routines attempted to alter the staff-designated function of spaces. A popular one involved running across the room and jumping on the sleep mats piled up in storybook corner. The children would do this in groups and often extended the play to 'squashing' and pushing each other on the mats.

Children may subvert and directly counter adult authority and rules. For example, when the class teacher's attention and gaze is not directed at children (writing on a board, back turned to the class) or the teacher leaves the room, children may 'doodle, pass notes, whisper, make faces, giggle, mock and satirise adults' (Sutton-Smith 1997, p.111). However, the teacher, 'while "absent", is still present as an invisible reminder of the ways in which normal boundaries are maintained, adding to the precarious nature and excitement of playing' (Lester 2014a, p.202).

The second part of Ungar's (2008) definition refers to the importance of communities (family networks and friendships, institutional and public space) being able to *negotiate* favourable conditions for children to navigate to health-enabling resources. For the most part, adults value children's play, although generally in highly instrumental terms, and this is materialised in the provision of environments for play, for example public and school playgrounds that segregate children's play into the right time and place. More will be said about this in the next chapter, but at this stage the idea of negotiation is extended and connected to the concept of adult response-ability, the ability of adults in whatever capacity to act responsibly and responsively to support conditions in which moments of play might emerge. This recognises that adults have significant influence in shaping the conditions of children's lives, thereby contributing to the production of environments (and all that this term implies) that may be more or less conducive to play. Negotiation, as a process of resourcefulness, moves attention from the needy and deficient child to the forces that underlie the inequitable distribution of resources and subject these to critical scrutiny; it is a political-ethical manoeuvre that will be addressed in more detail in the following section.

Children's right to play: a right to life

Having developed a broader relationship between play and being well, we now turn our attention briefly to the issue of children's rights. This is a theme which has been explored in a series of publications (Lester 2013b, 2017; Lester and Russell 2010a, 2014a) and a summary of these emerging positions is developed in this section. In undertaking this task, it is important to highlight at the outset that this is not an anti-rights gesture. Undoubtedly, the Convention on the Rights of the Child (CRC) has made a significant contribution to improving the lives of children across the world, although of course much remains to be done. Working with the principle and/and, the discussion extends the conceptualisation and enactment of children's rights, with specific reference to Article 31 (commonly referred to as 'the right to play'), as a political-ethical movement that repositions children's play from the margins to the middle of thinking about the constituents of a 'good childhood' (Lester 2017).

As a starting position and pursuing concepts developed in Chapter 2, the current construction of rights, as expressed in the CRC, presents a universal, decontextualised and abstract account of what it is to be a child. There are numerous critiques of the Convention at conceptual, implementation and practical levels. The idea of a universal child, constructed from a minority world viewpoint, perpetuates a highly selective and idealised image that becomes a colonising yardstick to make normalising judgements about childhoods across the globe (Lester 2017).

The 54 Articles that constitute the Convention should be viewed as indivisible but are often presented under three broad themes: protection from adverse conditions, provision to support healthy development and participation rights which support children's self-determination. Collectively, and as a considerably simplistic generalisation, the formulation of rights is underpinned by concepts from biology and developmental psychology (protection and provision) and the relatively modern social studies of childhood (participation). And within this, rights of protection and provision position children as needy and dependent, while participation rights perceive children as competent and active agents in the construction of their worlds. The first two themes are relatively uncontentious; who would deny the importance of ensuring that children are safe from harm and able to thrive? Claims made on behalf of children from some of the poorest regions of the majority world highlight the multiple and profound threats to children's survival. As such, each individual body is entitled to be protected and provided for to maintain survival. It is an approach that lends itself to technical application by identifying what children need to maintain health and well-being and ensure there is provision to meet these. Having produced a categorical list, the issue becomes one of elaborations to these inalienable rights to ensure they are being protected and enacted, including the publication of general comments which offer detailed guidance about states' responsibilities and ways of implementing children's rights.

The enactment of children's protection and provision rights assumes common sense, a framework which appears natural and, after all, who would dare to criticise the value of these articles? Against this, the seemingly trivial concerns over whether children are consulted or not would pale into insignificance; participation rights can only be considered when basic welfare rights are secured. However, as Lester (2013b) comments, there is a danger in promoting the primacy of protection and provision rights as it detracts from considering childhood as a relational and participatory space and perpetuates a deficit and needy construction of childhood.

The intention is not to dwell on these important and well-rehearsed positions and oppositions but to pursue the line developed to date in this account by suggesting that, contrary to the current reading of rights as individual entitlements, the enactment of rights must be viewed, as with life itself, as a relational achievement. It recognises that there are multiple ideas and practices in circulation about the processes of 'life' and the ways in which human, non-human and material worlds co-exist. However, the individualisation of rights and childhood and their material-discursive effects reduce the dynamic and emergent process of life into fixed identities and definitive subject–object relationships. As previously noted, play is caught up in this process as an instrument that can be used to support learning and development. It is noteworthy that Article 31 has traditionally been linked with Article 28 (a right to education without discrimination) and Article 29 (a right to education that develops personality and respect for others) in state-reporting procedures. This narrow understanding of play has inherent limitations that prevent a broader appreciation of the ways in which children co-create moments of playfulness from the conditions of their daily lives. Another example is introduced here to refresh ideas about playing and to extend into a different way of thinking about children's right to play. It is drawn from an opportunistic encounter and observation of an adult and two children sitting in a cafe in a leisure centre (Lester 2018, p.83):

> The adult was looking at/playing with his mobile phone, sitting opposite the 2 children, both of whom had glasses of soft drinks with straws on the table. One child nudged the other's elbow as he was about to take a drink; the child who was nudged managed not to spill the drink and laughed, put his drink down and jostled the other child. The attendant adult looked up from his phone and the children became still, the adult returned attention to the phone and after a very short period the first child lightly flicked the ear of the other which brought a muffled cry of pain and laughter, and a move away from the other child by sliding to the edge of the seat and half turning away while at the same time sucking some of the drink into a straw, turning around quickly and spraying the other child. At this point the adult told them both to 'stop messing about'. The children paused, one child saying 'he started it' while the other child denied this and said he had 'sprayed him'; both were smiling as they aired their grievances. The adult again told them to stop messing about after which they sat quietly until the adult's attention returned to the phone, before a highly furtive process of nudging and jostling started again, with extremely quick and light touches passing backwards and forwards between the children above and below the table and further muffled cries and laughter. The pace increased and movements became more vigorous until the adult said 'come on, drink up, we're going'; the children quickly finished their drinks and left with the adult – as they moved off there were further jostling movements between the children as they became entangled together, almost as if in a dance routine with haphazard steps.

The discussion to date has presented playing as an entanglement of bodies and materials that are always in motion (moving and sensing) and continuously and inextricably responsive to local conditions. It arises from an ever-present and impersonal virtual field to produce (individuate) moments of metastability, a state that assumes a precarious 'identity' we might recognise as 'play' while appreciating that a body and play are resistant to general classifications and only temporarily stable. Such playful arrangements (assemblages that are in-between and intra-actively composed) are transient and even though at times they may appear to be repetitive, they always contain the potential for becoming different. It is an estimation, projection and coordination of moving bodies and materials into the almost future; pleasurable dephasings or falling-out-of-step replete with relational potential (Manning 2013). Playful assemblages are always composed and produced rather than given:

> Matter's dynamism is generative not merely in bringing new things into the world but in the sense of bringing forth new worlds, of engaging in an ongoing reconfiguring of the world. Bodies do not simply take their places in the world. They are not simply situated in, or located in, particular environments. Rather environments and bodies are intra-actively co-constituted. Bodies…are integral parts of, or dynamic reconfigurings of what is. (Barad 2007, p.170)

These moments are marked by a degree of uncertainty. In the cafe scenario, this may be seen through the subtle movements by the children to jostle and disturb each other while avoiding drawing the attention of the adult – they cannot go over the top for fear of censure. When they are admonished for 'messing about' it adds to what is happening rather than closing it down; the children need to be more discreet in what they are doing with the materials and each other. This augments the vibrant emotional content as the children make minor adjustments and re-adjustments to maintain this state of being well, movements that are a collection of messy, provisional and embodied ways of getting on in everyday life.

Of more general interest is the dynamic and asymmetrical relationship between adults' and children's expectation of behaviour in public space and the multiple layers of implicit and explicit disciplinary actions, surveillance and modes of control that delimit adult–child interactions. Adult actions are shaped by wider societal expectations of managing children's behaviour in line with what is 'acceptable', namely that children's presence in public space should demonstrate the maturing attributes of being adult (Ryan 2010). Failure to do so is likely to bring about subtle and less subtle gestures of censure from disapproving bystanders. Moments of playing in a cafe, dancing at a bus stop and so on are not 'anti-social' or criminal movements, but the general conventions associated with behaviour in public space impose a 'soft criminality' lens on this apparent disorderliness (Cloke and Jones 2005). However, it would be somewhat absurd to suggest to the adult as he tells children to 'stop messing about' that he is infringing their right to play. Equally, returning to the observation of children *becoming dogs* in the supermarket in Chapter 2, it is possible that the mother might ask the children to stop being silly, or that supermarket staff tell the children off while at the same time giving the mother a stern look as if to say, 'Why are you not controlling your children?' These responses may stifle the potential for *becoming dogs* to emerge but, as with the cafe scenario, there is every likelihood that other playful moments will emerge. The habits, routines and ongoing negotiations that enable children and adults to get on together are stepping stones to sustainable ways of becoming (Braidotti 2006).

The notion of abstract and universal rights simply does not work with this relational messiness. The ongoing negotiations, tactics, manoeuvres and movements in-between children, straws, adult, mobile phone and so on cannot be reduced to general themes and classifications which would presuppose an already known abstract subject that is irreducible to any single entity. Neither can this, and all the other examples included to date, be subject to universal rules of law that define what is right and wrong and associated schemes of moral obligations, choices, freedom, rights and responsibilities. Deleuze's pragmatic philosophy proposes another way of conceiving rights as continuously enacted in a relational field in which bodies and materials are always enmeshed. It should be highlighted that this attempt to overcome the abstraction of rights from everyday contexts does not lead to a vague and empty relativism (the idea that everything is contingent, local and specific and there can be no guiding principles for ethical judgements). While renouncing universal accounts of what is right or wrong and moral codes of orthodox dogma, it provides a robust alternative of ethical account-ability and response-ability that can evaluate singular events by how far they enhance or decrease the power to act. It is a creative and responsive approach 'that respects the complexity of our times' (Braidotti 2012, p.170).

From this perspective, ethics is not merely an exercise in thinking about justice, but is caught up in everyday practice, working with the power relationships that are always present to establish and sustain empowering relationships as far as possible within the assemblage and to counter negative and constraining forces that may inhibit the expression of desire. Ethical practice will be considered in more detail in Chapter 5, but the following story, recounted by a primary school lunchtime supervisor while participating in a series of professional development workshops looking at adult practice to support children's play, is included here as an example:

> There was one particular child, aged 7, who recently spent a large part of playtime pretending to be Batman, with his coat spread over his shoulders as a cape and making accompanying noises. He would 'fly' around the playground bumping into groups of children, sometimes to their annoyance, while at other times children would play along for a while before he drifted off again.
>
> On this particular occasion a teacher was also on duty with the playground supervisor, and seeing the child's behaviour and the disturbance he caused at times to other children, called the boy over to reprimand him for disrupting other children's play and 'why couldn't he play properly'. As the playground supervisor commented, she felt powerless to say anything at this time and stood alongside the teacher with a sense of unease. Having carried out his role, the teacher started to walk away issuing a final comment to the child 'and anyway, you are not Batman'. At this point, the playground supervisor, who was still facing the child but preparing to walk off with the teacher turned to the child with a smile and said 'Na na na na na na na na, na na na na na na na na',[1] winked at the child and walked away. (Lester 2011b, pp.19-20)

This is a minor example of ethical practice, of the ways in which children's difference can be both suppressed and supported. In discussion, the playground supervisor spoke of her discomfort with the actions of the teacher and her own sense of relative powerlessness, but because of her participation in the workshops, she asked herself the question 'What would Stuart do?', not with an expectation of getting an answer but as a way to plug into another assemblage, another way of imagining the world differently and acting accordingly. It is, following Deleuze and Guattari (1988), an act of becoming-minoritarian, in

---

1   My representation of the theme tune from the Batman TV series.

which the supervisor encounters the child's world, not to colonise or over-code it, but simply to make a friendlier world with them by countering oppressive forces that seek to diminish the power to act and create playful/joyful moments. At the same time, the supervisor makes decisions about the limits of her own power; to explicitly challenge and undermine the actions of the teacher would, in this context, be very dangerous and may have little benefit for herself or the child playing at Batman. In this context practice is less about overthrow or revolt and more focused on refashioning and loosening adult power to keep alive the possibility of a child becoming Batman. It also suggests that participation is not neutral or apolitical; as previously noted, the moment of confirmation of becoming Batman marks a collective ethical desire to affect and be affected to enable life to go on in a livelier manner.

True to the concepts emerging in this account, this ethical instance is not located within a subject with individual moral agency but is caught up in the lines of movement in-between, a set of intra-actions with the desire or intent to maintain ethical sustainability for life to go on. Each of the examples contains 'remarkable points', composed from concerted actions to keep the play alive (often despite adult interference). 'What if…', 'what happens…', 'na na na na' – all are ways' of keeping the movement moving while at the same time giving it a temporary form. This is never a matter of individuality but a relation of response-ability to all the components (the 'others' that are not other but part of) that constitute the environment in a 'world that is always already an ethical matter' (Barad 2012, p.69). Rights are concerned with cultivating relational conditions for children to be well, and a right to play is much more than simply making provision for children in dedicated time/spaces to support learning and development.

Summary

Working in concert with concepts developed in Chapter 2, the relationship between play, well-being, resilience/resourcefulness and rights is thoroughly entangled to offer a perspective of playing as life going on in an affirmative manner. This is not the individual life of a self-enclosed subject interacting with passive materials. In this account, life is a process of continuous variation that occurs through dynamic transformations in the myriad encounters in-between bodies and things. Bodies have a desire to compose themselves into assemblages that increase the power to act and to affect and be affected to produce beneficial states of being. For children, this collective capacity, or following Deleuze and Guattari (1984), this 'desiring-machine', is often expressed in the co-creation of moments of play. Such desire is a force that flows in-between and is 'experienced in those moments of connection with life that defy common sense, resist dominant cultural interests and power relations and in an untimely manner unsettle the identity of individuals' (Jenkins 2011, p.40).

While what Deleuze and Guattari (1988) term 'molar' assemblages seek to order and control by constraining the possibility for what bodies can do and become, these are not self-determining; 'molecular lines' and 'lines of flight' can escape from the rigid lines of segmentation to produce novel compositions, taking bodies in unexpected directions and 'in the process adding to the richness and diversity of daily life' (Fox 2012, p.126). These are self-organising processes, a collective form of self-protection that has intensive affects by making life a little more vibrant and forming extensive creative connections with other bodies and materials.

Policy discourse of play and resilience, with play seen as an instrument to increase the capacities of individuals to cope with uncertainty and stress, is another form of progress rhetoric which fixes bodies to the plane of organisation. The zeal of play campaigners, while certainly well intentioned, perhaps overstates the claims of the usefulness of play in terms of instrumental outcomes. A more modest approach seeks to overcome ideas of certainty and cause–effect relationships; in this sense modesty is not a weaker position but one that, as with playing, constantly poses the question 'what if...' as a challenge to orthodox and common-sense ways of accounting for life. In this account, playing actualises a world that is always pulsing with life and reveals that the apparent ordinariness and mundanity of everyday life is anything but (Highmore 2011). Concepts of play are set free from the dogma of progression and associated claims of individual freedom and agency to become minor ethico-political movements that, as with play itself, challenge the forces of neoliberalism and the individualisation of life.

This account also offers a different conceptualisation of rights that is both particular and universal as it is concerned with the production of affirmative relations in-between bodies, things, histories and futures. Of necessity, it implies a larger sense of what it is to be 'human' to take account of the environmental conditions that enable all of life to flourish. This becomes the founding principle for an approach to public health that does not offer normalising accounts of what it is to be healthy nor target individuals for their failings but instead focuses on the capability of environments to offer heath-enabling resources. In the context of this chapter, this involves a right for children to navigate to/co-create time and space for playing and the response-ability of local communities to negotiate, both directly and through everyday practices, favourable conditions for children's mo(ve)ments. There is no blueprint for this, 'ethical practices are relational, emergent and specific, but without these practices well-meaning policy/promotional prescriptions become blunt instruments' (Lester and Russell 2014c, p.255). In the absence of any direct cause–effect relationships to establish advantageous circumstances for navigating playful moments, it remains possible to gain greater wisdom in understanding how local conditions may act to support or constrain play through cartographic practices that are attuned to processes, movements, sensations, things and their affects.

Issues of environments for play, ethical account-ability and response-ability will be discussed in more detail in the remaining chapters. But at this point, a brief mention is made of UNCRC (2013) General Comment 17 and the promise this holds for moving away from individual rights to spatial rights and justice. The claim made here is that rather than being simply a reminder to states about their obligations to support children's right to play, General Comment 17 can reconfigure understandings of rights as thoroughly relational, spatial and contingent; indeed, it can readily be subsumed into Article 6 and the right to life – to play is to live. This requires a rethink of 'public health' as an ethical account of the conditions of children's lives and a response-ability to foster conditions in which play and life can go on. A right to play does not make sense in isolation or aligned merely with the provision and progression Articles of education. There is no difference between a right to play and a right to life. Children have a right to navigate to health-enabling resources; adults have an ethical response-ability to support this.

To conclude this section, it is worth repeating that mo(ve)ments of playing are expressions of children being well as they co-create and contribute to the production of a sufficient stock of good things in everyday life. Whether this trickles down into future states is not knowable, but the intensive and extensive affects of playing are likely to maintain an anticipatory readiness and desire to seek out opportunities in the almost-future to cultivate further playful movements. One of the distinguishing features of playing which sets it apart from other health promotions is that it simply doesn't need promoting! It is children's way of co-creating their own health resources, not something given to them from outside their *milieux.*

CHAPTER 4

Play and Space

Introduction

Following the movements of previous chapters, this chapter begins to consider the implications for thinking about a 'play space' and how this might translate into ethical practice in terms of developing account-ability and response-ability to maintain favourable conditions for playing. But first, there is a brief recap of the central and entangled lines of enquiry pursued to date:

- Playing is an ongoing, indeterminate and emergent flow of imaginations, movements, materials (and/and/and…) in-between bodies that produce distinctive co-created moments of time and space that always contain within them the possibility for going elsewhere.

- While eschewing categorical distinctions and definitions, it is possible to discern that such time and space creations are marked by a tenor of pleasure; they bring more to life through the style, rhythm and affects of their movements contributing to the smooth running of life systems and processes (what might be termed 'being well').

- The use of the term 'life' in this context is not an individualised account but refers to an impersonal life that courses through the unique formations composed from discourses, things, bodies and so on, intertwined in encounters.

- Entanglements always have a spatial element; they take place somewhere. Space is a relational achievement and, as with the intransitive use of playing in this account, one might also refer to this process as 'spacing' as a way of injecting movement into this term.

Tag on a tango swing as choreography

In a move to extend concepts developed to date another example is introduced that works with the above state(ment) of play and life and at the same time offers an opening to conceptualising a 'play space'. It is an edited account from observations recorded at an adventure playground:

Two boys (aged about 10/11) were playing a game of tag, using the circular platforms that surrounded a rope swing. It was evident that these two were part of a larger group of players, the rest safely ensconced in the hut at the top of a tower. It was also apparent that the game had a rule of not going on the ground, which constrained the two adversaries to the platform and other structures. There was also another implicit rule which meant that these two could engage in reciprocal bouts of tagging. This led to the two children standing facing each other, in very close proximity, but not touching. The person who was 'it' would tag, and immediately receive a tag back from the other, often increasing the force of the contact in an attempt to push each other away and create a moment to flee; and then there were brief moments when both stood poised ready to tag without actually doing anything. There was a restless dance between the two, and as one looked to retreat, the other followed; it was almost balletic in the choreography of action, bodies and affects, tensions and laughter. But this was also situated; the platforms were an integral part of this dance, and there was only one way out from the circular platform – the walkway that led to the tower – and so the space had strategic meaning within the context of this play. Both children sought to manoeuvre the game to the part of the circular platform closest to the 'escape' route and then one child decided he was going to make a break, tagged the other child and turned to run away but was pushed/tagged in return, diverting the child beyond the escape, and the other child seized the moment to run along the platform and up into the next level.

This singular example with the improvised movements in-between serves to work with the concepts and examples developed to date.

There is a *milieu* composed from the perceptions, sensations, imaginations and memories of moving bodies and the physical arrangement of the environment; the playground platform is central to what happens as it provokes possibilities and constraints for action. The positioning of bodies in relation to the platform generates prospects for movement that at times are quite frantic while on other occasions are subtler and more pensive. From this sense, the platform performs in relation with everything else, like the lines in-between tiles in the museum, or the pink mermaid sweets, or gooey-like stuff. Thus, any *milieu* is both composed and composing, which makes distinctions between subjects and objects redundant. The form that a body takes is composed from the ecological processes at play in the *milieu* at any given moment: the sudden dash to escape the other child changes everything. What is of interest here is how does this singular moment happen given the 'complex collusions of speed and slowness' (Manning 2013, p.17) available at any given moment? This turns attention away from or at least defers products, fixed identities and end points, or what Massumi (2013) refers to as the 'resting places' of process.

As noted in the previous chapter and to reinforce a central point, bodies emerge as an assemblage. But the arrangements of bodies, platform and everything else is a temporary affair and this formation will fall apart as children drift off elsewhere and the platform becomes entangled with other bodies, movements and so on. These formations are important resources for developing relational capabilities and repertoires of response-ability that can augment the power to act. Chasing each other across a platform is nothing and everything out of the ordinary; life taking place in a minor key (Manning 2016).

Continuing the use of examples, this chapter presents a viewpoint of a 'play space' as a process rather than a fixed environment. It establishes the foundations for thinking about conditions that may support the emergence of such play spaces and continues the movement away from seeking to determine the 'what' and 'why' of play to paying attention to 'how' playful moments might occur. Given the unpredictable and opportunistic nature of playful performance, there is no simple cause–effect relationship between adult actions and children's play and this inevitably has implications and considerable challenges for professional practice.

Co-creating play spaces

Following on from the introductory attempt to take stock of some of the key ideas introduced, this section considers the term 'play space', a phrase that is often used to describe an adult-designed and designated place for playing but in the context of this account is an altogether different proposition.

Becoming trees in the art gallery

Another example is presented here to develop the argument. It is a playful mo(ve)ment that has gained increasing prominence in working out ideas and comes from an observation during a visit to see an exhibition of landscape paintings by David Hockney and later reproduced in Lester and Russell (2014a, p.298):

> The gallery was very busy, and movement was restricted as we followed the flow of people through the various rooms. My attention was caught by two young girls (probably aged around 5/6 years old) with attendant adults who appeared very immersed in the paintings, certainly more so than the children who spent time chatting, moving through the crowd holding hands and occasionally breaking out into skipping movements around bodies, at one point sitting on the floor together and doing a small hand-clapping routine. My gaze became more focused as one child stood in front of one of the large landscape paintings stepping over the marked line on the floor which tacitly placed a restriction on adult encroachment to the immediate space around the canvas. Placing her back towards one large tree in the left of the picture, the young child positioned her arms to align with the main branches, effectively mimicking the shape of the tree. The other child stood facing her friend and helped to manoeuvre her arms into a closer copy before standing alongside and adopting a position to represent another tree. This child then proceeded to 'blow' as if it was windy and her friend began bending and shaking in the breeze, and reciprocating with blowing on to the 'other' tree and provoking a similar shaking response. Shortly afterwards they appeared to become conscious of being watched and moved away, giggling before disappearing into the crowd.

As with other examples to date (notably *walking the lines in the museum* and *tag on a tango swing as choreography*), there is very little, if any, verbal communication but somehow through the coordination or collusion of moving bodies and things the temporary form of 'becoming trees' is individuated. To add to the linguistic representation above, one can take Ingold's (2011a) simple and single 'life line' (Figure 2.1) to produce a meshwork of lines of movement (Figure 4.1) as they resonate and become entangled to produce recognisable features of playing or 'messing about'. This form of making diagrams is an experimental attempt to focus on movement, a state of more-than representation, and more will be said about this process later in the discussion.

Figure 4.1: Becoming trees

Following lines of enquiry established to date, it is possible to discern the ways in which the children's moving bodies become entangled with other bodies, paintings, lines on the floor and the general atmosphere of the gallery to produce a 'play timespace' of becoming trees (and sitting on the floor and weaving through legs and…). In this situation, Hockney's paintings affect and move the children in the encounter; indeed, the production of this singular timespace would not occur without their presence. The points of interest are the movement and affects that are produced as the children wander through the gallery. Manning and Massumi (2014) eloquently express this process by imagining a situation in which you are late for work and need to negotiate a crowded pavement with bodies all around moving at different speeds and in different directions, and the material properties of the environment (such as waste bins, kerbstones, puddles, cracked and uneven paving stones). A body (movements/sensations) is attentive to the 'gaps' that appear in the coming and going of things, although this 'gap' is not empty but formed from the configuration of moving bodies: it is a field of relationality. The children in the art gallery are attuned to these openings as a way of 'getting on', of moving from a constrained to more open space. They are both present to the openings as they happen – not pausing to deliberate and plan – but attuned to the 'in-between' and the possibilities this contains:

> The experience then is all movement-texture, complexly patterned, full of change and transition, teemingly differentiated. You're surfing the crowd even as the crowd is surfing you. Despite the rush, this is not without joy. You revel in the fluidity of your trajectory, without focusing on it as a feeling tone separate from the movement. You have performed an integral dance of attention, seemingly without thinking. (Manning and Massumi 2014, p.10)

This would suggest the moment of becoming trees is a thoughtless act, but it could be that it is 'thinking in movement': every movement of the children is a performed, embodied and embedded analysis of the composition of the field and the promise it holds for *becoming trees*, or animals, or children, or anything – but becoming different.

Clearly, the gallery is not designed for playing per se and is certainly not designated as a 'play space' in the common sense of this term. The space of *becoming trees* does not exist before the children's mo(ve)ments and once the children have moved off back into the crowd, it is no longer a play space, although there may be some residue of this for the children and observers. It is not possible within the context of ideas introduced to date to isolate these movements and determine when and where the children are playing. The desire to classify places a border that demarcates and fixes play (as indicated in Figure 4.2). This 'cut' across movement has inclusionary and exclusionary effects: if the moment of becoming trees is 'play', do all the other movements indicate a state of 'not playing'? Who could say where play starts and ends in this picture? The very act of trying to classify into these arrangements encloses and confines play to a specific location and in doing so cuts life into segments.

Figure 4.2: Cutting play from movement

The identification of clearly defined and enclosed activity (the transitive use of play: 'playing trees') has troubling material-discursive effects, particularly in terms of adult approaches and support for children's play. Its foundations lie in a particular abstract understanding of 'space' that has attracted increasing critical attention, as the next section briefly elaborates.

What is 'space'?

As with everything else discussed to date, concepts of 'space' are complex; there are numerous and contrasting readings that contain multiple meanings (Harvey 2009). The word has acquired a dominant common-sense application in everyday conversation and more professional contexts without us being fully aware of what is meant by this apparently simple and straightforward term. A taken-for-granted sense of space may be troublesome as it conceals the possibilities that a more nuanced appreciation offers. Following Harvey (2009), the art gallery in the *becoming trees* story above may be portrayed as a Euclidian 'abstract space', the space of planners, architects and other technical practices that lead to the design of a purposeful physical environment that acts as a background for activity (mainly viewing portraits and other artistic products). As such, space is formal and quantitative; it can be fixed, measured, mapped and classified.

This dominates understandings of space in the modern world and produces an emotionless reduction to the basic 'raw material', lying inert and waiting for humans to shape it for their desires. It is from this perspective and associated practices that space is defined and bound into exclusionary spaces or segments (public, private, states, regions, grids, urban, natural and so on), each with their own power relationships. This is the Deleuzian 'plane of organisation' where segmented spaces, while performing different functions, are closely connected to establish a normative account of the 'individual', situated in relation to other individuals, things, movements, measurements (early years settings, playgrounds, classrooms and so on). This is the basis for the process of *differenciation*, the possibility of drawing distinctions and classifications between separate beings. Returning to Figure 1.2, the act of enclosure that cuts a body from the environment masks the movement of holding a pen, 'taking a turn around the paper before continuing on its way to wherever it would go and whatever it would do next' (Ingold 2011a, p.148). A plane of organisation insinuates itself into all sorts of everyday habits and routines that assume common sense and as such appear beyond question.

In contrast, and drawing on the examples of playful movement introduced to date, space may also be presented as a relational achievement brought about by encounters between heterogeneous bodies and materials (Massey 2005). Life is not lived in fixed space but on the move in-between, propelled by a 'vast array of past experiences, memories, and dreams accumulated directly and indirectly from their engagements with the world, as well as a wide array of anticipations and hopes about the future' (Harvey 2009, p.137). From this view, disparate influences flow from everywhere to everywhere else. Rather than the classification of things into separate parts, subject/object relations and fixed identity, relational space is open, messy, fluid, multiple and indeterminate. These flows and forces can assemble to form an event, or metastable moments (as witnessed in the lines of movement of children becoming trees). Massey (2005) presents a compelling argument for revitalising imaginations of space with three key propositions:

- Space is recognised as the product of interrelations, as constituted through interactions (but following Barad, we might use the term 'intra-actions') that occur at all levels of analysis 'from the global to the intimately tiny', which in this reading would suggest at molecular level of bodies and atomic – or sub-atomic – level of matter. This accent on relatedness challenges essentialist accounts of identity as something fixed and pre-constituted, proposing instead that it is constantly being formed through encounters with other bodies and objects to produce 'space'.

- Given this, space is always a sphere of possibility and multiplicity; there are many ways of forming relationships and equally multiple ways of perceiving the world. The story of the world cannot be explained simply by minority world accounts. Massey (2005, p.11) contends that any 'serious recognition of multiplicity and heterogeneity itself depends on a recognition of spatiality', opening the world up to greater imagination of what is possible.

- Space is always under construction: given the first proposition that spaces are the product of relationships that are ongoing and embedded in material practices, the future (spacetime) is always open; there are always connections yet to be made.

Massey's three propositions draw on Deleuze and Guattari's development of ideas from Bergson suggesting time is not a continuous and homogeneous reality; this is merely an illusion since, following the concept of relational space, there cannot be a true succession and progression of things that can be measured by time since one space-state disappears when another is produced. *Worlds made of poo* no longer exist as spacetime once the child ends with 'I dunno' and they are replaced by another production. Time may be presented as the continuity of a multiplicity of 'temporal becomings' and as such cannot be broken down into discrete units but must be merged with space to produce a 'spatio-temporal' event, or a 'timespace' (after Harvey 2009) that is always open to multiple experiences and modalities and therefore always in the process of being created. These territories are not necessarily demarcated or delineated; however, they can be affective complexes, 'hazy, atmospheric', but sensed nevertheless, as intensities of feeling in and through the movement of bodies (McCormack 2013, p.7). Within the examples included to date, it is possible to imagine that the desires of children in the art gallery are actualised through an extensive relational capacity to move between adult bodies, create a gap on the floor and cross the line to stand in front of the painting. This is accompanied with increasing intensity of affect that augments the power to act (Spinoza's *potentia*); there appears to be little obstruction to the flow of movement.

But while spaces are always open to new possibilities, this is not an unlimited process; not everything can happen and there are constraints on what might be achieved at any given moment. Children's playful formations are fragile and fleeting, lines of movement may be suppressed and blocked by more powerful others (Spinoza's *potestas*, which also includes the power of 'things' to repel as well as attract). As noted in the previous chapter, dominant implicit and explicit expectations of children's movements in public space collude to limit possibilities for action. A warning from the gallery attendant about not over-stepping the mark, a casual comment from a parent fearful of disapproving looks from other adults, warning signs about not over-stepping the mark and so on, might rein in children's movements. Such spatio-temporal relations are not predicates or essences of a thing but 'dimensions of multiplicities' (Bonta and Protevi 2004, p.94). A play timespace is composed from multiple sensations and movements that are sensitive and susceptible to environmental conditions which in themselves are always a reflection of arrangements of power.

Spaces are not neutral but cut through by relationships that might increase or decrease opportunity for playing. There are many formations that inhibit possibilities for playful and affirmative compositions; multiple practices, habits and routines consciously and pre-consciously organise and operate on moving bodies in very active ways by producing dominant affective registers that shape and constrain possibilities for becoming different (McCormack 2013). Though not fixed and static, they tend to attune movements to a specific end – what Lefebvre (2004) refers to as a form of dressage or entrainment through repetitive patterns that inculcate habitual ways of being. Thus, for example, it is possible to discern how habits, practices, routines, material arrangements (material-discursive effects) and so on produce a patterning or rhythm in a school classroom to establish a purposeful atmosphere which choreographs movements of both adults and children alike. However, this is not totalising: there are multiple arrhythmic movements that temporarily break apart order and stability and potentially generate creative expressions. No matter what dominant productions of space intend, there is always something which escapes and gets out of order. The next section will examine one of the major adult spatial productions for children's play – namely the playground – to critically examine the underpinning and entangled conceptualisations of space, play and childhood, and the ways these become played out in practice.

The production of children's 'play spaces'

When asked to describe a 'play space' most adults would cite examples of public and school playgrounds; places where they may have played as children and now take their own children. It immediately situates children's play in a certain spacetime, performing a significant cut in spatial arrangements to create environments where children 'belong'. As the National Trust for Historic Preservation somewhat wistfully comments:

> On warm spring evenings, blustery fall afternoons, and sticky summer days, when nostalgia and memories brush past you, where does your mind go? Where did you spend many hours as a school-age child? For most of us it was a playground, whether climbing the playground equipment or running circles on the athletic field, letting our imaginations take us anywhere and everywhere. (O'Shea 2013)

The traditional approach to supporting children's play in the public realm is through designing segregated locations to a predictable pattern and making a causal connection between what is offered in these sites in terms of equipment and materials and what children are expected to do with this environment. The existence of playgrounds has become a dominant trope in public imagination and this is evident in the last serious policy formulation which addressed children's play in England (Department for Children, Schools and Families, DCSF 2008), with considerable investment in the development of new and upgrading of existing local authority playgrounds. The rhetoric of New Labour's English *Play Strategy* highlights the ambiguous policy relationship between play and space, noting, for example, that there should be a variety of supervised and unsupervised places to play in local neighbourhoods and there should be safe and accessible routes to children's play spaces. The implication here is that a 'play space' pre-exists children's play in an identifiable site. Thus, it becomes possible to suggest that 'play spaces are attractive, welcoming, engaging and accessible for all local children and young people, including disabled children, and children from minority groups in the community' (DCSF 2008, p.5). In contrast to this, *The Play Strategy* also recognises that children have a playful stake in public space and this should be acknowledged by their neighbours, while at the same time qualifying this by stating that children should 'play in a way that respects other people and property' (DCSF 2008, p.5).

This ten-year strategy for supporting children's play very much rests on the assumption that a play space is an adult-designed and sometimes supervised facility for play and this was the primary focus for the first stage of implementation of the plan. Undoubtedly, this led to significant investment in upgrading play facilities. The pros and cons of this innovative strategy would warrant a volume in itself, and the intention here is not to dwell too much on these, especially given the early demise of the strategy with the formation of a Coalition Government in 2010, but rather to critically consider the idea of a playground as another 'inaugural gesture' (Massumi 2002), that is, an unquestioned assumption that this is the way to plan for children's play. In doing so, this section extends into (and revisits) the dominant construction of childhood and how this permeates thinking about the relationship between play and space before presenting a different approach to policy formulation that brings together UNCRC (2013) General Comment 17, the innovative approach adopted by the Welsh Government's (2010) Children and Families (Wales) Measure and the concept of 'play sufficiency'.

It should be made clear at this stage that what follows is not an anti-playground position: it maintains the and/and principle developed in Chapter 1. Playgrounds, and indeed the wider provision of public parks, are important community assets and attractive locations which children will navigate towards for playing (and the associated benefits of 'being well'). However, the continuing central focus on the provision of playgrounds at the expense of a wider consideration of spatial policy and the constituents of a 'good childhood' is a very limited negotiated response in support of children's right to navigate to health-giving resources (Ungar 2008) in the practices and routines of their everyday lives. This becomes even more pressing as austerity measures have significantly reduced the capability of local authorities to maintain children's playgrounds and it is timely to consider alternative approaches to the issue of planning for play. But there may also be something more fundamental about the continuation of the common-sense relationship between childhood, play and space that warrants a more critical analysis.

A brief genealogy of children's playgrounds

The intention at this stage is to apply Foucault's (1991) genealogical investigative method to develop a critique of the current production of children's playgrounds, with specific focus on contemporary themes in the UK. This attempts to reveal the power relationships between understandings of childhood, play and space and their historical foundations; as such it is a 'history of the present' to bring about a 'revaluing of values'. Genealogy seeks to work away at the edges of the inaugural gestures that shape and limit what is imaginable by opening up new possibilities and associated practices that can change the world. As an opening to this, a brief account of the history of the playground movement and underlying values is developed, recognising that this glosses over the complexity and variability in approaches.

The modern playground can be traced back to the mid-19th century and appears in a variety of different guises and locations. For example, sand gardens originated in Berlin, Germany in 1850 and later the idea was imported to the United States (Frost 1992). Here, the idea of a playground soon gained public support in the late 1880s and early 1890s in northern industrial cities, usually attached to settlement houses (Howell 2008) and as the idea caught on a national organisation – the Playground Association of America – was formed to spread provision across the US (Gagen 2000). In the UK, the 1859 Recreation Grounds Act recognised the need for children's playgrounds in 'populous areas' and made provision for land to be made available. Since this period, initially through the actions of voluntary/charitable groups, the number of playgrounds grew in urban residential areas. The Physical Training and Recreation Act (1937) provided further support, along with the early efforts of the National Playing Fields Association (Woolley 2008).

At the outset, the move to create segregated environments for children had little to do with valuing play but instead playgrounds were an instrument to control and shape children's spatial behaviours and placements (Gyure 2006). Theodore Roosevelt (1907), addressing the Washington Playground Association, stated:

> City streets are unsatisfactory playgrounds for children because of the danger, because most good games are against the law, because they are too hot in summer, and because in crowded sections of the city they are apt to be schools of crime.

Equally, Hart's (2002) study of New York reveals that the history of planning children's play environments represents an expressed need to contain children, to keep them off the streets, safe from traffic and unsavoury influences. The desire to physically enclose children to specific locations was driven by social and moral reformers as part of a wider movement, including staffed playcentres and free kindergartens, to develop institutions to address concerns about children's welfare. Alongside public playgrounds, schools also embraced the importance of and provision for playtime.

A research review of historic examples of this specific form of provision highlights how the accompanying rhetoric of exercise, control and promotion of school ethos remains in contemporary discourse and practice (Ramstetter, Murray and Garner 2010). The review concludes that playtime makes a valuable contribution to children's social, emotional, creative and physical development. However, these general assertions are tempered with some ambiguity arising from competing demands and perceptions about the relative merits of playtime within an increasingly demanding curriculum (for example, the binaries of play and work, freedom and control, risk and safety, nonsense and rationality). Playgrounds and playtime are imbued with adult understandings of the nature and value of childhood, the role of schools as educational institutions, understandings of adult responsibilities for children, moral panics and so on.

The connection between philanthropy, education, moral welfare and developmental psychology produces a playground as a block of spacetime that aligns with other segments on the plane of organisation to examine, discipline and normalise children's behaviours. As more progressive ideas about child development and education emerged during the 20th century, the value attributed to this form of provision became more complex due to the presumed relationship between play and healthy development increasing in popularity (Gyure 2006).

While the early playgrounds contained functional equipment (swings, slides, seesaws and climbing frames, with, for example, 'monkey bars') designed to instil an element of control into children's movements, contemporary versions evidence a variety of motifs including adventurous, creative, imaginative and natural themes.

Playgrounds have acquired multiple value, often espoused in remedial terms in response to contemporary concerns about childhood, children's deficiencies and their futures. Yet for the most part there is a causal conflation between the considerable, and often contested, research into the benefits of play and the importance of playgrounds as sites for providing these benefits. This is reflected and strengthened in the design and promotion of playground sites, for example the contemporary association of playgrounds and their role in promoting active lifestyles for children and adults alike. This movement harks back to the original 'jungle gym' playground designed to exercise children's bodies to use up surplus energy that otherwise might find more deviant outlets but is rebranded as a response to fears over the growing 'obesity epidemic'.

Another significant modern theme is the playground as a site for promoting creativity and innovation in behaviour – skills deemed to be valuable for the successful progression of children to become responsible citizens in a changing world. Design becomes more open-ended, with consideration given to a range of materials, landscapes and equipment to support novelty and so on.

But this can only go so far: accompanying this apparently benign trend is general anxiety and risk aversion around children's play and play provision and the potential for injury while playing at designated adult-designed locations. This has led to a reduction in the range of environmental features and an increase in control over children's behaviours. This is clearly a reflection of wider societal trends in which increased concern with risk and an associated 'blame culture', fed by media stories, gives rise to a protective discourse in which adults perceive children as vulnerable and in need of protection from the dangers of the world, including the ways in which they may present a danger to themselves and other children (Bundy et al. 2009). This is nothing new: from their inception, playgrounds have always been understood as spaces where adults control, order and discipline children's bodies, emotions and thoughts following the prevailing ideology of the period

(*The Lancet* 1913, 1924; Thomson 2005). Nowhere is this more evident than in the contemporary construction of the 'natural playground', as is critically explored in the next section.

The natural playground

The rhetoric that surrounds the design of and justification for public playgrounds is fully evident in one of the major contemporary themes in provision, namely the natural playground movement. Again, it should be stressed that what is offered here is not merely an oppositional stance but an opportunity to connect the inaugural gesture of 'planning for play' and its dominant articulation through the playground movement with the wider discourse of childhood and adulthood and the increasing separateness of children from adults in the modern post-industrial world. This is not simply a divide that acknowledges a degree of biological immaturity but is a representation of a different value between adult and child. Childhood and adulthood are held by common sense to be the opposite of each other; adults are burdened with responsibilities while children are carefree and as such this period of innocence needs to be nurtured and protected (Cunningham 1995). It marks the construction of minority world childhoods in time and space as a 'privileged domain of innocence, spontaneity, play, freedom and emotion in opposition to a public culture of culpability, discipline, work, constraint and rationality' (Aitken 2001, p.7). Developing the historical background to this discourse, Aitken (2001) considers the 'classical' works of, among others, Rousseau, Thoreau, and Emerson, who saw children and childhood as pre-social, a state that contains a natural moral goodness. The state of childhood is an age of beauty and purity in which children are thought to possess wisdom that is no longer accessible to adults. This relationship is the result of centuries of scientific and popular discourse that privileges and values children as products and wonders of nature, prized for their natural beauty and state of innocence and purity. The image of the natural child acts as another powerful representation of an individual enclosed organism (see Figure 1.2), cut off from the external world, where nature lies in wait to maintain childhood naivety and protect children from the worst excesses of modern life. In this account, nature stands as an inert, passive, ever-present, unitary background against which humans construct their lives.

The depiction of (generally working-class) children playing in their immediate squalid and dangerous environments collides with the image of Rousseau's natural child (Read 2011), which in turn gives rise to the importance of playgrounds as sites of protection, not merely for children's safety from danger but also for the preservation of children's innocence. Following Rousseau, the period of childhood is the closest to nature as the source of all good things, in sharp contrast to the polluting influence of adult society; nature assumes a naturally advantageous position as an antidote to the evils of society and at the same time holds the promise of society's ultimate salvation (Taylor 2013). This comes at a time when the period of childhood in the minority world is of increasing adult concern, fuelled by media reports and bio-politics (with central themes that feature various anxieties based on permutations of variables related to children's health, well-being, loss of contact with nature, technological 'threats', risk, increasing educational pressures and so on). These fears are articulated in a range of campaign materials and reports, typified by the following extract from a National Trust publication:

> Our nation's children are…missing out on the pure joy of connection with the natural world; and as a result, as adults they lack an understanding of the importance of nature to human society. If we do not reverse this trend towards a sedentary, indoor childhood – and soon – we risk storing up social, medical and environmental problems for the future. (Moss 2012, p.2)

Against this somewhat alarmist backdrop, it is unsurprising to see the emergence of the natural playground movement as a remedy to these ills.

While Rousseau distinguishes the state of childhood as a time of innocence and closeness to nature, another line of philosophical thought produces this period as a time of irrationality, when children are ruled by passions and desires that need to be overcome if they are to become rational adults. Stemming from puritanical thoughts encapsulated in the phrase 'spare the rod, spoil the child', it advocates that children's natural desires need to be tamed for fear that they will become devils. The natural will of children needs to be tamed in 'much the same manner that the spirit of feral horses is broken so that they lose their naturalness and become compliant and domesticated' (Aitken 2001, p.32). Only those with the ability to construct and order meanings from senses, that is, humans and more specifically 'man', can have a sense of 'nature' as something apart from mind. Therefore, to be human is to transcend the confines of nature to which the lives of all other creatures are bound (Hinchliffe 2007), no longer deceived by primitive urges, basic perceptions and bodily sensations. As noted in Chapter 3, the idea that there is an external environment apart from being human is a powerful act of inversion founded on and perpetuated by philosophical arguments that promote human mastery or control over nature and natural forces (Harvey 1996). It sets human agency apart from the world, delineating one from the other by highlighting human qualities of self-reliance, autonomy and independence.

While apparently paradoxical, these two strands (romantic and puritanical) combine to produce a powerful effect on the western adult imaginary of childhood, presented as a 'natural' phenomenon (Lester 2015a). In contrast to the autonomous rational adult, children are heteronomous, subject to laws of nature, irrational and emotional (Hinchliffe 2007). The purpose of childhood is to progress from this state to become reasonable, *beyond* the laws of nature. For this to occur, children should retain their natural innocence and sense of wonder by being close to nature and it falls to adults to protect them from the violence and ugliness of contemporary society. Childhood and nature become entangled and invested with hope, 'a powerful utopian vision of adult hopes enacted through multiple practices designed to both protect and propel the child forward to moral maturity' (Lester 2015a, p.57). It has powerful performative effects, notably in the growing demand to restore children's contact with so-called natural environments (see Louv 2005 for a particularly influential account). For Louv and other passionate advocates of the 'natural child' movement, children's and the planet's salvation rests with reuniting children with natural restorative environments and reconferring the role of 'moral teacher' on nature (Louv 2005, p.187). In doing so, Louv insists on the clear demarcation between nature (good) and technology (bad) for children. As Taylor (2011, p.429) comments:

> The parallels between these moral discourses point to the mutually constituting relationship between childhood innocence and pure

nature, but they also shed light on the ways in which highly essentialized discourses of nature authenticate and morally justify essentializing discourses of childhood. In other words, the moral authority of nature lends enormous weight to the truth claims of childhood innocence.

An adult desire for children to be situated in nature marks the search for a utopian other time (lost childhoods) that can be reclaimed through a utopian other place (pure nature), a seductive idea expressed in many therapeutic programmes as searching for the 'inner child', in order to become 'more natural and hence more morally authentic' (Taylor 2011, p.429).

Given that children's play, as previously suggested, is held to be a defining feature of childhood, it is invariably entangled across the above themes as an expression of children's innocence, sense of wonder and their future success. Play as progress merges with other modern play rhetorics of self-expression, identity formation, self-actualisation and creativity (Sutton-Smith 1997) to produce idealised and 'organic' play forms (Brewer 2012). When placed alongside romantic characterisations of play as natural, free, instinctive, non-literal, irrational and so on, playing is presented as a distinct form of behaviour that is a mark of children's heteronomy. This fixing of nature, childhood and play generates a range of contemporary spatial productions and practices, most notably the production of 'natural play environments', increasingly a key tactic in the management of childhood. The following is a typical illustration of the natural playground rhetoric (Stoecklin 2000, no page number):

> Discovery play gardens offer children chances to manipulate the environment and explore, to feel wonder and to pretend, to interact with nature, animals and insects, and other children. They are environments that encourage children's rich and complex play and greatly expand the learning opportunities of old-style playgrounds. Children's discovery play gardens are places where children can reclaim the magic that is their birthright – the ability to learn in a natural environment through exploration, discovery, and the power of their own imaginations.

While the natural playground movement is generally well intentioned, such an uncritical account perpetuates and strengthens the long-standing romantic construction of childhood and aligns with proximate segmented spatial productions to silence and denigrate critical accounts of other ways of life (Alaimo 2010). Despite claims of 'naturalness', natural playgrounds are organised bounded environments that act on the desires of children. The playground is a technology of conduct built from a dual understanding of play that acknowledges this form of behaviour as an expression of freedom and its instrumental value in shaping children as citizens (Ryan 2010). They are spaces to overcome the deficits of being a child by being a certain child (with an innocent and playful nature) in a specific location and time (natural). They govern fields of action of both children and adults by constraining what can be legitimately thought, said and done and configuring certain forms of relationship between adults, children, space and play. The production of knowledge is stabilised and innovation constrained, adding up to what Clegg (1989, p.89) calls an 'obligatory point of passage'. The associated rhetoric of the movement is designed to win adult hearts and minds and produce valid knowledge on the best ways to raise children, and it becomes both the source and the destination of authoritative statements and actions (Ryan 2010). This is generally reinforced by the marketing slogans of the playground industry; the natural playground becomes wholeheartedly another tool of neoliberalism and bio-power. The natural playground is presented in contrast to the 'urban' nature of the greater part of childhood – urban spaces which must somehow be inferior because of their lack of 'naturalness'– fostering negative views of urban childhoods and associated threats to childhood innocence.

The nature/human binary produces a stable and durable picture of both childhood and nature. But this is not a 'truth': it becomes stable, or an inaugural gesture, through the exercise of power. The question is, what does the discourse of the natural child contribute to maintaining dominant power structures? Undoubtedly, there may be conditions (perceptions, affects, materials, landscape features and so on) in which playing is more likely to emerge in an indefinite arrangement. But this is a different form of landscape than currently prevails in the deterministic discourse of much of the natural playground movement. As with the broader playground movement, it is evident that placing children is never a neutral practice (Gullov 2003) and the ways in which the institutional and public spaces of childhood are planned and arranged speaks volumes about adult attitudes to children and their place as citizens in democratic society. This genealogy now moves on to consider another form of provision for children's play that may offer a counter perspective to what has been introduced to date. Given that I have spent much of my professional practice working in these locations, this may appear to be a eulogy for this form of provision, but it is also set within the context of the inaugural gesture of a playground.

The adventure playground: a counter movement?

While the traditional public and institutional playground seeks to exercise spatial control over children's everyday lives, a different movement can be found in the emergence of adventure playgrounds (APs). This can be traced from an original concept (while wary of claims of origins and essences) attributed to Thomas Sørensen, a Danish landscape architect who noticed that children appeared to play anywhere but adult-designed playgrounds and envisaged a 'junk playground' that children could shape to their own desires. The success of the junk playground at Emdrup in Denmark was noted and later imported to England by Lady Allen of Hurtwood, and the first UK adventure playground opened in Camberwell in 1948.

The adventure playground movement sought to overcome the controlling influence of traditional public playgrounds by creating sites in which children's playful freedom of expression could be fully supported. To this aim, play leaders or adult supervisors were appointed to provide resources and offer a degree of 'light' supervision to maintain an open environment in which children could have a greater element of control over what happens. As such, they were promoted as environments which enhance playing rather than attempt to censor and limit it. But, as Kozlovsky (2008) suggests, this did not remove the power of adult intention for children's play but reframed an instrumental approach in a different manner.

The formative years of the adventure playground movement in England coincided with concerns about the rise in delinquency, particularly among boys, and the need to create spaces where children could 'play out' their anxieties and frustrations that arose from living under stress during and immediately after World War II and in impoverished 'slum' conditions. The proposal to develop community-based and organised adventure playgrounds, as a part of post-war reconstruction, was one of the first examples of 'bottom-up' collaborative planning and the introduction of a new form of 'citizenship' by creating sites where children could play in a permissive and supportive environment that may in turn lead to them overcoming their aggression and becoming more responsible citizens. As such, adventure playgrounds were a vital part of a negotiated response in local communities and have established themselves as valuable resources for both children and adults alike, and long-standing APs continue to provide an important timespace (see below). Pivotal in this long-standing value is the role of the playworker and more is said about this in the next chapter. Ward's analysis of the 'junkyard' playground movement portrays the space as 'living anarchy', a microcosm of a free society:

> With the same tensions and ever-changing harmonies, the same diversity and spontaneity, the same unforced growth of co-operation and release of individual qualities and communal sense, which lie dormant in a society whose dominant values are competition and acquisitiveness. (Ward 2008, p.114)

While the AP movement is diverse, and each playground reflects local history, culture, physical landscape and so on, they present and espouse a different image of the child, generally reflecting childhood as a social construction and co-creating sites of freedom of expression and the formation of children's culture.

This counter movement offers a form of provision that (potentially) produces molecular lines and lines of flight to deterritorialise rigid molar formations and expectations (Deleuze and Guattari 1988) and by doing so problematises the normative standards of such arrangements. Playing, as a self-organising and dynamic process that increases children's collective power to act, inevitably disrupts adult order and control. These minor movements can instigate subtle changes within the system, yet for the most part they are somewhat elusive and intangible. It may be argued that a founding principle of APs is that rather than differentiating children with regards to their successful progression to citizenship and associated subjectification (son/daughter, boy/girl, healthy/unhealthy), they are sites where children can actualise different ways of being, a 'becoming-child' in a Deleuzian sense. As APs are settings that seek to maintain a prevailing playful feel, to become is not to attain or reinforce a fixed form or identity but to 'find the zone of proximity, indiscernibility or indifferentiation where one can no longer be distinguished from a woman, an animal, a molecule…unforeseen and non-pre-existent' (Deleuze 1997, p.1), or to put it another way, 'to play'.

The persistence of community-based and often locally managed APs over time speaks volumes about their value to children and adults, as noted in a small-scale research project in the South West of England that explored adult memories of attending APs as children alongside past and current playworkers (Williams *et al.* 2016). The research was carried out by a team with considerable experience in developing and managing adventure playgrounds in the UK and at the outset there was a collective effort to go beyond the peak moments of playground life (those things that stand out when recalling memories) to apprehend the seemingly mundane and everyday practices and routines that contributed to the production of timespace that felt different for both adults and children alike. These are things that generally 'go on and on in the background…stuff that is often unnoticed, often unsaid, often unsayable, often unacknowledged and often underestimated' (Horton and Kraftl 2006b, p.259).

I didn't go anywhere, I was on the coach

For example, the following story, taken from a resource manual for a playwork continuing professional development (CPD) programme (Lester and Russell 2010b, pp.7–8), features an apparently mundane encounter:

> There was one particular child (Raymond) who was a regular on the playground and it would be fair to say that in today's language Raymond would be described in whatever the current jargon is as a 'school non-attendee' with associated diagnosis of 'learning difficulties'. On this occasion, Raymond was sitting with the playworkers and there was a general question 'what have you been doing today?' Raymond contributed that he had 'spent all day on the coach', which immediately sparked interest – 'where did you go?' Raymond's somewhat perplexed response was 'I didn't go anywhere, I was on the coach.' We tried to find out where the coach went, but all Raymond said was that it didn't go anywhere – he stayed on the coach and watched TV! It eventually emerged that Raymond was actually referring to his 'couch', which led to great laughter from all.

This story of nonsense and confusion (and many other similar, apparently minor stories) assumes significance without effacing its singularity as an occasion when things are slightly different, often acquiring the status of 'legend' alongside more serious stories. These often taken-for-granted examples matter: they are constitutive of affective complexes and hazy atmospherics (McCormack 2013) that while often beyond linguistic representation, may be 'sensed'.

To an outsider, the dominant and defining feature of most APs appears to be the large, generally wooden, structures (towers and connecting platforms, slides, zip wires, swings); these are the physical foundations of most contemporary playgrounds and seen as the source for risky and adventurous experiences. But when starting to think about how these sites mattered, such objects become less central (that is not to deny their attraction for children). While many APs may share these iconic structures, the contexts of practice are singular locations. Each playground is a unique configuration and collusion of human/ inhuman/inorganic forces that establish a special dynamic rhythm/ atmosphere over time. This is not fixed but open to reconfiguration and rearrangement as well as solidifying to produce a site that holds what might be referred to as a 'prevailing playful feel'. Adventure playgrounds are produced by multiple people and materials at multiple moments in time; they are processual spaces rather than a fixed product:

> Relational specificity is always a processual arrangement of agencies and actors that never precipitates sites as a stable point of origin or a specific knowable point of destination…the key thing is that site is sensed as a nexus of ongoing relations rather than something concrete existing in advance of these relations. (McCormack 2013, p.35)

The playful feel or atmosphere of any adventure playground is more than the sum of its parts. Bodies, materials, imaginations, histories and so on generate a unique refrain, a collusion of forces that brings together 'an extraordinary juxtaposition of signifying objects, images, and practices' (Bednar 2011, p.18) that may cohere materially, visually and spatially into significant spaces central for 'playing'.

However, there is an inherent tension between the espousal of the freedom and anarchy of APs and often externally imposed instrumental purpose. On the one hand, the low-intervention mode of playworkers who largely display confidence in children's ability to co-create their play from the materials at hand (Allen 1968) produces APs as *terrains vagues* which children can manipulate to their own desires. On the other hand, the pull of powerful molar normalising forces and the plane of organisation that shapes what it is to be a child places expectations of control, order and progression. From the outset, playworkers have struggled to maintain the original ethos of the junk playground movement in the face of external pressures – the very first junk playground leader resigned his post when his committee wanted him to control and organise activities (Cranwell 2003). And with the growing domination of neoliberal economics and associated political regimes, these tensions have increased as 'new public management' accounting systems exert a stranglehold on the provision of public services. Market-orientated thinking pervades aspects of life that traditionally have been valued according to a different set of norms. Contemporary molar tendencies determine the 'value' of things (what counts) and apply pseudo-scientific technical measurements to make judgements in terms of the worth of public services. In relation to children, this is generally reduced to the contribution that provision makes to the making of a future productive and consuming citizen. These forces have not by-passed the adventure playground movement and have had deleterious effects.

Much community-based playwork provision has disappeared and often those settings that remain have surrendered their original values and beliefs to fit in with policy requirements and associated funding streams. And so even though they may have revolutionary possibilities, adventure playgrounds, as part of the wider provision made for children, continue to sharpen the relational and spatial divide between adults and children within a broader neoliberal framework in which childhood is valued as a period of preparation for becoming an adult, and institutional settings are increasingly required to control and organise space to ensure desirable progression. Perhaps the more recent iterations of the adventure playground under the New Labour *Play Strategy* (DCSF 2008) highlight this dilemma – given a universal strategy with limited time for implementation, the new playgrounds largely abandoned the self-organising, bottom-up, community-action grounded nature of these spaces, and were replaced by adult-idealised representations designed to recreate some idealised vision of childhood with adult 'play sculptures'. In doing so, children are used to approve these intentions through a 'consultation' process designed to bring children onto the adult plane of organisation (Deleuze and Guattari 1988). The potential deterritorialising capabilities of the junk playground movement have become over-coded to produce another institutionalised space (Lester 2013a). The adventure playground, now often conflated with the rhetoric of a natural playground, produces an idealised and romantic version of childhood (more 'Swallows and Amazons' than 'Lord of the Flies').

Playgrounds on a plane of organisation

The above brief analysis of the development of public and institutional playgrounds highlights an inherent tension and paradox in terms of understanding and supporting children's play. The design of traditional playgrounds and staffed play provision produces locations that seek to normalise play behaviours, an adult production of space that represents a wider construction of childhood as a period of play, creativity, adventure and a time to be 'in nature'. Underpinning this is a rhetoric of the importance of these sites for successful development, leading to claims of their benefits for physical health, problem-solving skills, creativity and imagination and even neural development. Thus, playgrounds continue to maintain a high profile in policy and resource allocation. They are the right place for children to play: 'Playgrounds are very much about censoring and restricting types of play deemed undesirable and displacing them from places deemed dangerous or corrupting' (Kozlovsky 2008, p.171). The foundation for the development of public playgrounds was a means to engender and engineer a specific version of the child as healthy, vigorous and productive and to counter/overcome the problem child of poor environments and associated problematic personal and social behaviours. Modern-day versions may not explicitly express such stark intentions, but the descriptions of contemporary playgrounds still present a particular image of the child at play and contribute to governing the child; 'they are both a way of structuring the field of possible action and a mechanism through which young citizens are invited/incited to recognise their responsibilities' (Ryan 2010, p.771). Normativity is enacted by a collective state apparatus (itself not a separate, boundaried entity), which is the conduit through which lives are governed and become self-governing. These apparatuses are sites of technical practices, 'seeking the best methods and procedures for delivering predetermined outcomes – a stable, defined and transmittable body of knowledge but also implicitly a particular subject' (Dahlberg and Moss 2005, p.2). As Deleuze and Guattari (1988, p.159) famously assert, 'you will be organized, you will be an organism, you will articulate your body, otherwise you are just depraved...you will be a subject nailed down as one'.

Playground design often substitutes a narrow range of physical activity for the spontaneous play in diverse environments that children seek out. The examples of playing introduced to date occur, after Ward (1979), anywhere and everywhere, produced through the movements and encounters in-between bodies and things. Not only do playgrounds fail to satisfy the complexity of children's desires (while bearing in mind that children can and do use these sites for generating playful expressions as the example below clearly illustrates), they also tend to separate children from the daily life of their communities, exposure to which is claimed to be fundamental to the development of civil society (Ward 1979; Hart 2002). In this sense, civil society refers to the equitable distribution of valuable health-giving resources for all citizens, most notably in the context of the discussion to date the ability for children to navigate timespace for playing. What is needed, argues Hart (2002), is not more segregated playgrounds, but a greater attempt to negotiate neighbourhoods that are safe and welcoming for children, responding to their own preferences for play close to home, with their friends and in locations that children can temporarily occupy and where they can deterritorialise adult inscriptions.

Looking beyond the playground, an adult plane of organisation operates across multiple scales to structure children's everyday routines and spatial practices, generally based on the twin pillars of protection and provision (Lester 2013b). Continuing the exploration of spatial concepts (and again emphasising that this is not an attempt to synthesise different theoretical positions), the plane of organisation is 'conceived' space (Lefebvre 1991), that is, representations of space produce an idealised and pre-defined image of space commensurate with Harvey's (2009) abstract space. Conceived space is shaped by the dominant order of society, which in the context of this account refers primarily to neoliberal economics, developmental psychology, political regimes and their inaugural gestures which permeate policies, codes, legal systems and knowledge about space. This conception of space is enacted by planners, engineers, developers, architects and policy-makers and is mediated through a range of verbal/non-verbal codes and signs that emerge in a dominant discourse of space in any society. Thus, space becomes segmented, ordered into specific institutions and locations that while performing to their own internal logic act in concert with the dominant conception of space. Rigid segmentation produces sites and hierarchies of entrenched power that predetermine the hopes and expectations of what one can do and become. Molar lines of organisation (Deleuze and Guattari 1988) maintain borders between these segments, enclosing children in childhood institutions, each with their set of spatial practices, or what Lefebvre (1991) refers to as perceived space, designed to reinforce dominant accounts and establish common-sense, taken-for-granted habits and routines by which people manage to go on with life.

Such practices help to ensure continuity and some degree of cohesion in social relations; they maintain order and purpose. Lefebvre's concept of spatial practices is updated by Thrift (2008) and Amin's (2006) consideration of spatial maintenance and repair systems, a complex series of processes to keep space working, largely running in the background with powerful material-discursive effects. They seek to stabilise and order within a normalising plane of organisation, ensuring desire does not get out of hand and shaping them into 'normal' patterns of behaviour. Thus, for the most part, maintenance systems are designed by adults to suit adult purposes and reinforce children's position in everyday life as subordinate.

Yet, as Deleuze and Guattari (1988) remind us, while a plane of organisation seeks to establish order, it always contains the potential for becoming otherwise. Molecular forces are interspersed into molar structures and are potentially disruptive as they arise from bottom-up, experimental processes (Saldanha 2010). As suggested earlier, a plane of organisation cannot close off all desire, and children's playful urges will seek to find improper expression between the cracks and crevices of ordered space, producing 'lines of flight' (Deleuze and Guattari 1988) that delimit the constraints seeking to enclose creativity and different ways of becoming a child (Lefebvre's 'lived space'). And while there may be a mismatch between adult design intention for children's play and what children value, this is far from straightforward.

The dangerous river

The following child's story, 'the Dangerous River', written rather reluctantly as a piece of homework about what the child did during the weekend, highlights the creative ways in which children may create their play narratives and movements:

Once upon a time there was a dangerous river next to a volcano. The river was surrounded by a jungle.

Suddenly the volcano erupted – a fire demon came out.

Me, Alan, Danny, Michael and John all ran.

He threw a fire ball at us – it landed in the water with a SPLASH.

We jumped into a boat and the current took us down.

A crocodile came – we jabbed it but its scales were too hard. It smashed the boat. We heard a loud BANG – and again – but this time it was a louder BANG!

We just managed to get on the bank. The fire demon threw another fire ball at us.

We ran into the jungle and a snake bit Alan. It was a cobra.

We quickly reacted – we shouted help.

Nobody heard us, but all of a sudden he was healed.

We ran to get away from the fire demon. He threw some molten lava at us – the jungle was on fire. We were trapped!

The fire was getting closer and it was too close. It suddenly disappeared – we were thinking where it went and wondering what was that bang.

We looked back at the jungle that wasn't there.

We saw a hut on the horizon – we ran to it. We all knocked on the door – nobody answered. We looked through the window – we ran back to the river and made a hut out of wood. I caught a big trout and we cooked it.

The next day we made a raft and sailed on it on a calmer day.

But when we got further down, there was a whirlpool. We tried to get away from it but we didn't succeed.

Me, Danny and Alan were the only ones that survived. We swam to the bank – we made another raft. We all fell off and when we were under water we saw a big squid. It tried to attack us – but we grabbed the bank. Arrows were coming out of nowhere. We ran and ran until we were all out of breath. We jumped onto the raft and got away. We remembered the big squid. I just saw it lurking under us. I shouted look and pointed at the big squid.

We went rushing down the river.

By then the fire demon was very angry because all his fire balls missed.

When we were further down the river there was another jungle…

This tale draws on specific landscape features in the playground and the wider park. As an adult observer, I was a remote witness to the movements of the group of children but could not appreciate the narrative that accompanied this. The story is a replay of some of the moments that occurred and are explained by the child; for example, the 'volcano' was a large mound with steep sides, grassed over in places while in others worn away by children sliding down the hill; the burnt-out hut was the old bowling pavilion, long disused and derelict; the crocodiles were the above ground roots of the best climbing tree in the park; and the jungle was the tangle of bushes that grew around the edges of the park. When the parent and now grown-up child went back recently to retrace the story (after a period of about 12 years), most of the locations had disappeared, largely on grounds of health and safety (the roots had been covered over as they were a trip hazard), visibility (all vegetation at the boundary of the park had been cleared for security reasons) and (adult) aesthetics (the bowling green hut had been restored and fenced-off from public use and a wild flower area established, with accompanying signage requesting people not to walk in this area).

This representation contains within it 'abstracted musings' (Philo 2003, p.18) and visualisations that connect with real places and people and that 'happily fuse the real and the imagined, often displaying deliciously chaotic geographical imaginations' (ibid.). Such narratives are also essentially 'poetic': imagined symbols and real experiences combining to create meaningful expression of states of being. It endures as a reminder, not an accurate picture but a reverie that is imbued with significance; while seemingly minor, these things matter. It once again reinforces the capability of children to be resourceful – able to navigate timespace for playing when conditions allow. In line with the previous discussion, such acts may be everyday micro-political manoeuvres simply to create more favourable states of being.

Summary

This chapter has added to the discussion to date by assembling the apparently straightforward terms 'play' and 'space' into a complex formation that generates different ways of thinking about a play space beyond the traditional ways of accounting for this relationship. By doing so, it connects key threads or lines of enquiry to date, with reference to Deleuze's ontology of the virtual, individuation and the production of the actual to suggest that life, as a process of 'spacing' always contains within it the possibility for becoming something different.

Current dominant economic, political, social, intellectual and technological forces find expression through institutional policies, organisational structures, practices and feelings. These form a plane of organisation or a complex network of heterogeneous materials which are over-coded with dominant meanings to produce a space that seeks to fix the identity of the child-subject as economic investment and preparation for economic productivity, measured by targets and assessment. Molar assemblages may express patterns that seek to establish equilibrium through a molar structure or 'state apparatus' that erects a dominant way of accounting for space and spatial practices and imposes a set of pre-established standards that demands conformity by subjects.

The remaining sections of this book broaden the discussion beyond playgrounds to build on understandings and practices of play/space and rights to consider the ethical-political implications for democratic processes and spatial justice.

■ CHAPTER 5 ■

The Micro-Politics of Playing

Introduction

Several decades ago Colin Ward (1979) presented a picture of children's play as an expression of protest over the conditions of their lives. Children co-create timespace when they can momentarily reclaim the materials and detritus of their environments and shape them to their advantage. Thus, for example, children can chalk the streets (Ward 1979, p.81), occupy waste spaces (p.98), make go carts (pp.134–135) and find multiple ways of using found objects (pp.82–83). This chapter revisits Ward's significant observations and commentary to extend ideas about playing, space, rights, life and everything else discussed to date as a prelude to exploring the implications for professional practice.

Ward's evocative description and accompanying black and white photographs of children messing about in the city reflect his wider engagement with anarchist philosophy, notably Kropotkin's (1972) exposition of 'mutual aid' and morality rooted in a superabundance of life that demands to be exercised to increase the power to act. Anarchy, as a political philosophy, is much maligned in contemporary academic and popular discourse, and has generally fallen into disrepute and been largely abandoned. Anything labelled anarchic (including aspects of children's play) is readily dismissed as disorderly and lawless. However, there is no single 'anarchy' but many disparate historical and contemporary accounts. Certainly, an anti-authoritarian stance is present in most of anarchism's earliest proponents, but it was largely a stance that was highly libertarian in nature and form.

A more recent perspective, meanwhile, offered by May (2007), seeks to combine traditional accounts of anarchy with aspects of post-structural philosophy (in particular Jacques Rancière) to propose that power, per se, is not a negative force but becomes oppressive when it dominates: power operates deleteriously. Anarchy is a movement that resists the harmful effects of all forms of domination that can occur anywhere and everywhere, for example in the classroom, the privilege afforded to cars over pedestrians, or, in May's (2007) examples, a company's deduction of payment to contracted workers because of sickness, the public domination by mainstream media that veils the interest of the elite that funds it and so on. As such, it is a political philosophy concerned with everyday life. This notion is revisited later in this chapter, but at this stage, and in relation to the ideas presented about play and life, power is presented as a force that is situated in-between people (and things) and generative power overflows from mutual relations in an intensive and extensive manner. As with posthumanism, anarchism recognises that there is no primary central organising system for life, only forms of relationships that might enhance or reduce the capacity of life to flourish. As discussed to date, conditions that enable mo(ve)ments of playing to emerge are practices designed to enhance states of being, to release forces of desire to see what more bodies can do.

Playing as political action

While I am cautious of presenting play as anything other than itself, the processes by which bodies and materials collude to produce beneficial states has significant implications for rethinking the nature of ethics. As noted in Chapter 3, posthuman ethics is not concerned with the application of a universal moral code (how one ought to live), but is enmeshed in everyday practices and encounters, working with ever-present power relationships to co-create empowering relationships and to counter constraining forces that limit the capability to thrive (how one might live). This inevitably situates the enactment of ethics as a 'political' movement, concerned with cultivating favourable conditions for life to flourish. The intention at this stage is to further explore the 'political' nature of playing before setting this in a wider context of democratic processes. It is not an attempt at synthesis but rather a nomadic and rhizomatic exploration to see how things become entangled and to cut the world differently by shamelessly poaching concepts to see what more might be said and done. It seems timely given how the apparent spread of anti-democratic forces of repression have gained the upper hand in national and international politics.

No going on the field

Another example is introduced at this point, an extract from an observation of children at playtime in a primary school:

> It had been raining during the morning and the rule for lunchtime play was 'no going on to the field', reinforced by the playground supervisors as children come out to play. Previous observations had highlighted the attraction of the field for children, notably a group of older boys who regularly played football in this area. As this group entered the playground they started to play football with a stone on the tarmac playground which brought a swift intervention from a playground supervisor who reminded the children that they cannot play football when the field is not in use for fear of hurting the smaller children. The boys moved to the edge of the playground where it bordered onto the field and began jostling in an attempt to push each other onto the grass, while at the same time keeping a watchful eye on the position of the playground supervisors. The movements became more frantic until one of the boys grabbed the hat of another child and threw it onto the forbidden area. The child went to retrieve it, and as he neared the hat the remaining children shouted to the nearest playground supervisor: 'Miss, [name of child] is on the grass'. The supervisor approached the group, by which time the boy had retrieved his hat and returned to the others. The supervisor said that he knew the rule and had to 'go and stand on the wall'.[1] The child protested his innocence, trying to explain what had happened but this was ignored by the supervisor who led him to the designated punishment spot. The remainder of the group followed a short way behind and when the supervisor had moved away began to jeer and tease the child on the wall, who became increasingly

---

1 A form of punishment in which children had to go and stand against a specific part of the school with one hand on the wall until told that they could move away by a supervisor.

'angry' (with a 'play-face') until one child got too close and he left the wall to chase and grab him. This immediately brought more shouts from the rest of the boys: 'Miss, [name of child] is off the wall', which gained the attention of the same supervisor, who came over and asked the boy to return to the wall or he would be sent to the headteacher, while ordering the group of teasing boys to stay away: 'Can't you find something to play?' They moved off, smiling at each other.

Ward (1979, p.97) comments that 'one of the things that play is about, intermingled with all the others, is conflict with the adult world'. However, following Ward's reading of Landauer (1910), the notion of play as protest does not imply some grand revolutionary act in which structures are completely overturned but rather a more minor and modest way of revolutionising ideas, materials, bodies and symbols through these everyday mo(ve)ments. As Landauer (1910, p.3) critically notes:

> The state is a social relationship; a certain way of people relating to one another. It can be destroyed by creating new social relationships; i.e. by people relating to one another differently.

Thus, the collective efforts of the group of boys to play with the dominant 'no going on the grass rule' begins as a minor experiment to transgress without getting caught but escalates into a more flagrant breach of the rule. In doing so, it makes a mockery of the rule itself as the adult is tied into enforcing order. The subsequent punishment, while seeming to be harsh and isolating, is simply another opportunity to enliven the practicalities of the playground on a day when their desires are frustrated. As such, the disturbance of adult regulation and control is not simply rebellion or destruction, but an act of creation – the chance to see what more can be done with the environment than the 'reality' that others seek to impose on their lives. The adults supervising the playground are not passive in this process and may, to a certain extent, collude with what is taking place by enforcing the rule that allows for the possibility of becoming different.

Sutton-Smith (1997) also explores the political nature of children's playful expressions in the rhetoric of child power and identity, a theme, he suggests, which has attracted little attention in the study of play, particularly the view that the content and style of children's play acts as a compensation for their general life conditions. Sutton-Smith (1997, p.115) suggests that any subordinate group will have a hidden transcript, a 'behind the backs' critique of the power structures that seek to position them as inferior, citing Scott (1990, p.xi):

> I suggest, along these lines, how we might interpret the rumour, gossip, folktales, songs, gestures, jokes, and theatre of the powerless as vehicles by which, among other things, they insinuate a critique of power while hiding behind anonymity or behind innocuous understandings of their conduct... Together these forms of insubordination might suitably be called the infrapolitics of the powerless.

Through their subversive playful acts, children can appropriate and reconfigure aspects of a largely adult-determined world; the challenge is to test how far they can go without bringing adult approbation. And even when adults do 'catch' children, the consequences are generally minor; thus, a casual adult command to 'stop messing about' to the two children in the cafe may temporarily restore order, but the playful desire remains and leads to more subtle movement to continue with what is generally seen as misbehaviour in this context. Similarly, the children on the school playground push the adult boundaries and even collude with adult authority ('Miss, he's on the grass') to extend possibilities. But where conditions are favourable, that is, they have time and space to themselves, much of the play will remain covert and hidden away from the gaze of adults; children understand that any attempt at disturbance, of expressing intense desire, will be largely viewed as misplaced, unexpected and generally unwelcome, and such disorder needs to be subjugated and annihilated (Mozère 2007). Returning to the bedroom scenario introduced in Chapter 1, the first sign of an adult coming upstairs may lead to children immediately stopping what they are doing to return to their original 'lights out' position, with accompanying emotions that may place children at the edge of hysteria as they try to control their laughter and feign stillness. While the adult may exhort children to settle down and go to sleep, the affective atmosphere of the bedroom remains highly charged and is likely to erupt as soon as the coast is clear.

The examples given to date are embodied ways in which children play with identity, enacting and transmogrifying as 'becoming-children' in novel and fluid formations (Katz 2004). Such behaviours may be presented as 'political' in that they produce moments that reconfigure the existing order of the world to satisfy their own urges; moments in which children 'resist, conform and negotiate on their own terms, even if these struggles and negotiations do not and cannot be carried out in official political arenas or follow conventional political modes' (Kallio 2009, p.6). This is not programmed Politics (upper case 'P') in the traditional sense of party/adult politics and formal democratic processes. Rather, children's playful mo(ve)ments and imaginings continually question and problematise the given order of things by asking 'what if...' and find expression through 'as if...' actions that acknowledge a different world is always possible. It is a form of contingent political (lower case 'p') action that is always contextual and relational, concerned with making the best of the situation here and now, 'not with some fantasized future, with small concerns, petty details, the everyday and not the transcendental' (Rose 1999, p.279).

By playing, children expose the power structures and associated routines of their everyday lives to scrutiny, often drawing on their presumed innocence to push at boundaries and transgress existing power relationships that might, under other circumstances, meet with adult disapproval; after all, it is 'just playing'. Recent work with gallery staff from a children's museum nicely illustrates this process. There is a taken-for-granted (tacit, unwritten) rule of 'no running' in the museum; however, detailed observation of children's movements reveals highly novel and creative ways of circumventing this expectation as children skip, dance sideways, walk quickly with long strides and so on. This may raise a question about the value of the rule of not running, but its constraining existence invites children to invent a whole series of movements that play at the edges of adult expectations. There may be times when gallery staff intervene to remind children who break into a run, and this public reminder acts as a further invitation to move in more creative and subtle ways.

Equally, children may entice adults to collude in their subversion of norms and decency, as Opie (1993, p.31) recalls a conversation with children:

> Two of the boys jumped up on a shoe locker... 'try putting your fingers in your mouth and pulling it sideways, and then say "I was born on a pilot ship." It comes out "I was born on a pile of shit".'

More is said about this process later in this chapter but at this stage it is worth repeating and reinforcing the application of 'affect' in considering play as a political movement. Affects are forces that arise in-between; children's playful encounters dispose a body to engage with the world by establishing affirming connections with other bodies, space and materials that increases a collective power to act (Deleuze and Guattari 1988). The 'body' in question is not individual and enclosed but emergent, leaky and without organisation; bodies come to be through the assemblages or *milieux* they co-compose (the process of individuation, after Simondon 1992). Given that bodies are 'always more than one' (Manning 2013), affective forces are dynamic and in a state of constant flux; as well as affects that increase a body's capacity to act, there are also forces that limit and constrain movement.

Musical worms

These are the interrelated processes of de- and reterritorialisation, as illustrated by the following observation of children's play in an after-school club in the UK (Lester 2011a, 2013b). The opening period to the observation reveals adult control over children's movements through the design and implementation of a series of party games, part of a programme concerned with the theme of 'music'. Children are organised into playing 'musical chairs', with one of the playworkers controlling the music and as the game develops, children are eliminated and have to sit with the playworker on a bench until the game is over. At one point, two boys who have been eliminated start to play fight and the worker separates them, making each child sit either side of her. At the conclusion to the game, the playworker announces that they will be playing 'musical statues' next. And it continues, children eliminated, getting bored and adults getting more exasperated at trying to control what they deem to be disruptive behaviour. After a while, a playworker announces that it is snack time and they leave the area with a sense of growing exasperation with children's apparent ingratitude for the efforts they have made to 'provide play'. Following this...

> A small group of children aged between 5 and 8 years old congregated around a CD player that had been used for adult-structured activities (musical chairs, statues, etc.) and then abandoned as the adults

prepared snacks. A child asked one of the adults, 'what can we do now?' and the adult responded, saying 'I don't know,' and walked away. At this point, one of the children tentatively suggested to the others they play 'musical worms'; it was fairly apparent that the child was responding spontaneously and creatively, and when other children looked interested and asked 'how do you play it?', the notion developed into a concrete idea as the child responded 'you wriggle around on the floor like worms, and when the music stops you have to flip over on to your back and the last one over is out'. Following this explanation, another child asked if he could provide the music rather than use the CD player and the other children all agreed to this. And so the game began – the child humming a tune, while the worms wriggled on the floor (with much laughter). As the child stopped humming, the worms flipped over, and a decision was made about who was the slowest. Under conventional game rules, the last person is generally 'out', but in this game the children negotiated that the person who was last should provide the music for the next round and so all continued to participate in the game. After a short period, it became apparent that the real attraction for the children was in providing the music and the worms became increasingly reluctant to turn over when the music stopped; everyone wanted to be last and there was a period of worms gracefully turning in slow-motion. In unspoken recognition that the game was changing, one child suggested that the first worm to flip over should provide the music for the next round and so the whole process started again with the worms energetically throwing themselves over as they attempted to 'win'. (Lester 2013b, pp.30–31)

The game of musical worms is constituted and emerges from the immediate materials at hand which in turn are shaped by forces near and far: the maintenance routines of everyday life and spatial practice interpenetrate molar forces (Deleuze and Guattari's plane of organisation and Lefebvre's conceived space) to impose order and control over children's desires. The adult programme of activities, while well intentioned, serves to reinforce how the space works but also contains within it the ever-present possibility for becoming different: musical worms may not have occurred without musical chairs. These are not random events, acts of escapism or negations of everyday routines but are 'organically connected to [them] and intensify the vital productivity of daily life' (Gardiner 2004, p.242). The adult-designed locations of childhood, while striving to limit and direct children's desires, can never fully contain these; they are fluid spaces co-created from heterogeneous materials and forces (Prout 2005). 'Musical worms' is an assemblage formed by the intra-action of never fully fixed materials that collude in a dynamic manner to affect and be affected by the flow and movements in-between. The apparent 'order' or identity of musical worms is emergent, continually reworked and reshaped. There is no central organising system, but biological and social forces weave novel, unpredictable and complex networks of relationships that cannot be accounted for in traditional ways.

Playful mo(ve)ments transform bordered space into participatory spaces; children are still caught up in adult-constructed spatial demands, but they can recruit them into their own playful desires and subvert or resist them. They are illustrations of ways in which subjects, while seemingly produced and constrained, can also act with purposeful desire in the diverse spaces in which they are positioned and 'engage in a performative politics of re-inscription' (Youdell and Armstrong 2011, p.145). No matter how far institutions seek to construct borders and limits to children's desires, they are always porous and open to children's playful inversions and subversions; 'people cross these borders bringing with them conflicting ideas, experiences, ideals, values and visions (all the things that make up discourses) and different material resources' (Prout 2005, p.82). The collective power that children hold over bodies and materials during play constitutes the ways in which they simply go about their daily lives. It denotes a pre-conscious political sensitivity and sophistication that is largely unrecognised and unnoticed in debates about children's participation. Yet such moments are important; not only can things be different during play, there is also the possibility of more of these moments to come. As previously noted, such moments are acts of resourcefulness, that is, they are reclaiming and repurposing resources that are generally limited and controlled by more powerful others. Through playful participation, children are making their own provision by appropriating the materials at hand and by doing so are engaged in self-protection through co-creating moments of being well. This offers a different cut on the three themes of the UNCRC of provision, protection and participation (Lester and Russell 2010a).

To reinforce a critical point that permeates this account, playing produces moments which are pleasurable, and for the time of playing children get a sense that life is better and can maintain a sense of optimism that things can simply go on (Kraftl 2008). *Worlds made of poo* (Chapter 2) is not a complete overthrow of existing order but a form of 'soft subversion' (Guattari 1996) or micro-political lines of flight initiated by a collective desire to break away from the plane of organisation by generating emotional resonances that are life affirming.

Playing and 'becoming democratic'

The above rendition of playing/spacing places it as a fundamental democratic process, a political movement that abstracts children from the sovereignty of adults. Children's play is improvised, opportunistic and unpredictable – not planned, site-specific or pre-figured. Aitken and Plows (2010, p.332), citing the work of Benjamin (1978), note that play, rather than being mere imitation, marks the capacity to affect and be affected by the world; as such, 'young people's capacity to play is also a capacity to re-conceive history and geography, which in turn creates a moment of revolutionary possibility' or a form of bio-power from below (Hardt and Negri 2009). But there is a much broader issue at stake here, one that returns playing to a central position in terms of the process of life itself.

The discussion to date has introduced a range of concepts attuned to the force and flow of an impersonal life that goes on through differentiation, largely based on Deleuze and Guattari's (1994) 'transcendental empiricism'. The next section continues with this analysis, working with what may be Deleuze and Guattari's (1994) most explicit political writing in *What is Philosophy?* and the concept of 'becoming democratic'. In line with their contemporary continental philosophers (notably Foucault), Deleuze and Guattari have been accused of failing to establish a *political* philosophy, with little regard or consideration for democracy and the accompanying production of human rights. In terms of traditional approaches to political philosophy, these claims may be justified: they appear to give little attention to a universal ethics of how one ought to live and how these 'oughts' can be used to make judgements about current systems of governance. Neither do they link ethics with political action to explicitly establish rules for what might constitute sound and just government. Rather than deal with the relative merits, promises or faults of existing systems, whether free-market liberalism or Marxism, Deleuze and Guattari sketch a framework for an alternative and altogether different political philosophy, a movement that varies not only in the vision it provides but also in the level and style of intervention it advocates (May 1994). This is fully in keeping with their overall approach that suggests the purpose of philosophy is to create new concepts rather than verify or falsify existing ideas. Deleuze and Guattari are not anti-democracy, just as they are not anti-rights. However, they do present a challenge to universal and idealised accounts of both democracy and rights. What follows is a summary of this critique, sufficient to extend the idea of playing as an important micro-political process and the promise this presents for a different form of democracy.

In developing this account, I am indebted to Paul Patton's (2000) exploration of Deleuze's political philosophy and Todd May's (1994, 2007) presentation of 'post-structural anarchy', with a signpost to the work of Jacques Rancière (2004), which has been influential in shaping thoughts at this stage. The endeavour is not to present an authoritative reading of Deleuze and Guattari's politics or seek synthesis with the multiple publications by Rancière but to draw on, or shamelessly poach, some of their ideas and set them to work in the study of play. It will also reinvigorate Colin Ward's portrayal of 'play as protest' with a contemporary, renewed interest in a philosophy of 'anarchism' (see, for example, the poet Lawrence Ferlinghetti, anarchist geographer Simon Springer, as well as political philosopher Todd May). As always, the intention is not to arrive at any definitive conclusions or truths but to maintain a questioning stance to explore 'what if…' and 'what more…' can be done and said to make more just and equitable worlds.

As a starting position, and to reinforce a main line of argument to date, the desire of life is to continue, to co-create and sustain favourable conditions for flourishing. This is an impersonal life, a force that is not contained within individual organisms but flows in-between (Ingold 2015). Life emerges and proceeds through diffractive processes, that is, continuous and indeterminate disturbances and adjustments in response to affective forces moving at different speeds and across different registers at any given moment. Affect, or Barad's (2007) concept of agency from the middle, is a 'transpersonal capacity [desire] which a body has to be affected (through an affection) and to affect (as the result of modifications)' (Anderson 2006, p.735). This implies that bodies are always in relation with and open to other bodies and things, a transpersonal, agentic quality of Deleuzian 'bodies without organs', in-between bodies (Pile 2010). An organism's state of health fluctuates according to the intensity of relations that impinge on the body. Desire operates by forming relations, configuring new and extensive assemblages with the widest possible materials at hand to increase the body's force of existence or power (*potentia*[2]) of acting and experimenting with what it might become and so resisting capture by territorialising forces. In political terms, this emergent self-organising capacity of bodies in motion can extend anarchism from a negative position of individual nihilism and opposition to 'power' in all forms to one that is concerned with establishing affirmative relations that compose innovative and singular events. Power is not oppressive; it only becomes oppressive when used to limit the possibility for life to flourish.

While recognising the dangers of making simplistic generalisations, the neoliberal project, and its manifestation in increasingly globalised economic systems, seeks to control the forces of life and usurp them to its own desire, namely the axiomatic of capital. It engenders a certain, yet intangible, affective atmosphere constituted from a juridical, political and technocratic apparatus operating as a form of bio-politics that shapes and conditions bodies as individual. All too often, these systems of domination are upheld as being 'democratic', yet, as Rancière (2010) suggests, these schemes of oppressive power relations are ways of 'policing' citizens through an organisational system of coordinates that divides the community into groups, social positions and functions. Far from being democratic, this process favours those who have a part and excludes those who do not and are thus set apart. It falls to the political and economic powers (as both become mutually entangled) to distribute forms of espoused 'democratic' power; citizens are passive recipients of state distributions. There are those who distribute equality and those who receive it, establishing a hierarchy that can never be equal (Rancière 2010).

---

2   *Potentia* is used here to distinguish an enabling power from the oppressive power that subjugates and hinders affirmative encounters (*potestas*) and this will be revisited later in the discussion.

Given the all-pervasive spread of global and state capitalism, states have become anti-democratic – what Rancière calls 'police' states. They thrive on the willing but unwitting transfer of power from people to a body that is separate from them, with an authority to make laws that must be obeyed – it is an oligarchy in which power resides in a few, abstracted from the many. The framing of what constitutes 'democracy' (the inaugural gesture) is predetermined and citizens are presented with electoral choices that are pre-packaged and generally serve the interests of capital. Popular opinion is fabricated by powerful interests and becomes another instrument of domination by the market rather than genuine democracy. And while there may be different degrees of democratic state government, each remains complicit in increasing exploitation and 'the production of human misery alongside great wealth' (Patton 2010, p.153). This is Deleuze and Guattari's 'plane of organisation' created by molar or majoritarian forces. The term 'majoritarian' does not signify the largest number but marks the ability of those who dominate to form the standards by which the rights and duties of all citizens are measured. Failure to conform to these standards identifies someone as without a part.

In contrast to Rancière's notion of 'police state', a democratic state should be founded on egalitarian principles of the equal value of all citizens; no person's life is of lesser regard or has a greater part than another's:

> Such a political society is an association of equals in which there is no justification for the exclusion of individuals or groups from the widest possible system of basic civil and political liberties, nor any justification for the arbitrary exclusion of particular individuals or groups from the benefits of social and political cooperation. (Patton 2010, p.164)

For Rancière (1999), 'real democracy', or what he refers to as 'politics', is the undoing of police order through a presupposition of all 'speaking beings' having a part. This is not the democracy envisioned by elites but a challenge to ways in which neoliberal democracy operates. It is about democracy as it concerns people who are not in power, rather than as a buttress for people who are. From this perspective, democracy is a counter-movement, a politics that interrupts. It is a mode of life in which people struggle to reclaim power, a form of resourcefulness as alluded to in the previous chapter, suggesting that politics is the will to develop social justice and an equitable distribution of resources. As such, it is the disturbance of the plane of organisation brought about by those who have no part in the formation of the coordinates of this plane. Politics is always relational and intervenes in 'police' states by creative and innovative tactics that uproot bodies from their placements, and liberates free speech and movement from their reduction and location to a plane of organisation. Imagining a *world made of poo* or *becoming trees* has little or nothing to do with 'learning' as determined by majoritarian state systems but these playful mo(ve) ments have power in modifying the field of possibility by actualising a different reality.

As the opening section of this chapter suggests, playing is the exemplification of life's differentiation that invites the question 'What are the possibilities it presents for also thinking and enacting "democracy" as minor political movements that can actualise new ways of being beyond what already exists?' It attunes to individuations, phasings and dephasings, emergent relationships, and the remarkable points between the virtual and actual that always contain 'more than'. Playing opens a line that intervenes and disorders dominant power arrangements. It produces a different spacetime, with its own rhythms and movements, revealing other ways of arranging:

> This call for the coursing of minor gestures within frames of everyday life involves crafting techniques that create the conditions not for slowness exactly but for the opening of the everyday to degrees and shades of experience that resist formation long enough to allow us to see the potential of worlds in the making. (Manning 2016, p.15)

The proliferation of minor gestures is a process of 'becoming-minoritarian' (Deleuze and Guattari 1988) or the creative process of becoming different from the majority; it involves deterritorialising standards and conventions to see what else is possible. The term minor (and associated interpenetration with molar), therefore, is not an expression of scale or a binary opposition but recognises that 'becoming-minor' can actualise different versions of reality that resist standard classification and ordering. Children's play, rather than being an exercise in progress towards autonomy and rationality (the adult common sense of play), becomes momentary spacetime in which life cannot be reduced to what has already been produced and marks the potential to create and work with difference. It may also suggest that the process of playing, far from being an infantile act, is a sophisticated democratic manoeuvre. The recognition that children are political actors and can activate powerful assemblages is a vital component in developing forms of resistance to molar forces.

Negotiating playing at the park

From this perspective, micro-politics is a form of democratic process concerned with everyday practices that enables participation in collective decision-making, while also facilitating the contestation of segmentary forces, as the following example illustrates:

> A child (aged 7) is picked up by his parent from school and on the way home, which is a short distance away, asks if he can go to the local park. The father is familiar with this routine and says he will drop the school bags off on the way home and then they can go off together. But on this occasion the child says he wants to go to the park with his friends (twins of the same age who live immediately opposite). The father says that he is sure they will not be allowed to go to the park on their own and the child replies that the boys' mother says they can go if he goes with them. The father is now in a difficult position and reluctantly agrees but issues a strict warning about coming home in time for tea (even though the children do not have a watch between them). The child calls for the others and they go off to the park. He returns later, and when asked what he has been doing replies 'nothing'. A couple of days later, the father of the child meets the mother of the twins and comments that she was brave letting her children go the park unaccompanied by an adult. She is momentarily confused and replies that she let her children go to the park because [name of child] had called round and said that his dad said they could go to the park if she let her twins go with him.

This relatively simple (and probably familiar) tactic, hatched in advance, was sufficient to counter adult-driven habits of accompanying children to the park; it is a minor subterfuge that opens up a 'crack' in routines, rupturing the taken-for-granted state of affairs and renegotiating differential movements and conditions that are more favourable to the desires of children (and once the pattern is established, also beneficial for adults!). This is a minor example of the everyday acts of deterritorialisation that pervade adult–child relationships. They are actions that become reterritorialised into routines and practices: it is alright to go to the park so long as you are accompanied by 'known' local children. In line with Ward's (1979) account of play as protest, children confront the logic of 'police' systems to highlight the porosity of the plane of organisation. Children are cautious in their experimentation; they are reworking rather than overthrowing. It is, after Foucault, a mode of curiosity not to assimilate what is proper and ordered but questioning bodies, materials and so on to see how they might get free of themselves – exploring what and how things might be changed.

Becoming democratic requires a tactical response attuned to localised police systems. As such, it is bottom-up, emergent, indeterminate; the tactical manipulations of 'keep off the grass' in the playground, a playground supervisor reaffirming a child becoming Batman and the numerous traditional games, pranks and jokes enacted by children are experimental transgressions, molecular lines of movements and lines of flight. They may seem trivial, but they offer a clue to democratic processes that insinuate into dominant power relationships. Deleuze and Guattari (1988, p.178) offer the following guide to such tactics:

> This is how it should be done: lodge yourself on a stratum, experiment with the opportunities it offers, find an advantageous place on it, find potential movements of deterritorialisation, possible lines of flight, experience them, produce flow conjunctions here and there, try out continuums of intensities segment by segment, have a small plot of new land at all times.

Micro-political acts form alliances that can make new connections and animate generous ethical response-abilities, the ability to respond to our part in entanglements with the 'other' that is never apart from and always more than human. They offer an opportunity to reconfigure the ways we think about the relationship between play, childhood and adulthood by inviting questions of what might constitute a 'just' environment. This is not a grand statement of universal justice and rights but everyday relational practices that may leave room for children to take advantage of their immediate conditions and resources, notably through co-creating timespace for playing.

Play, spatial justice and a right to the city

Deleuze and Guattari's (1988) significant tactic of forming a 'new land' is important as it eschews the idea of total revolution, the overthrow of existing systems and their replacement by a utopian state of equality. Capitalist 'democracy' is majoritarian: all accounts of being 'free' are framed by the interests of the market. In line with Rancière (2010), an egalitarian capitalist or Marxist society is impossible. But becoming democratic is 'by its nature that which eludes the majority' (Deleuze and Guattari 1994, p.108). Deleuzo-Guattarian micro-politics presents a fundamentally different order of political activity, concerned with a pragmatic creation of new forms of life and different ways of living. Having a 'small plot of new land at hand' is a more modest tactic but one that contains within it revolutionary possibilities as lines of flight can connect, in a rhizomatic fashion, to build impetus and contain sufficient force for further movements of deterritorialisation. But it is not oppositional; Deleuze and Guattari do not refute the concept of 'democracy' but recognise the potential that molecular movements and lines of flight contain to reconfigure molar segments, hence processes of 'becoming democratic' to form a land yet to come. It also contains an inherently spatial element consistent with ideas developed in Chapter 4. This new land is not a physical surface or backdrop to human activity but, in line with their radical democracy, is relational and processual. This section folds this into further discussion about rights and issues of spatial justice.

In the context of this account, a 'new land' may be one in which a sense of playfulness permeates aspects of everyday relationships and wards off capture by police systems. In this sense, playing is much more than an instrument to be used to steer children towards becoming self-regulating adults who can take their place as capitalist consumers and producers. The political nature of playing is increasingly evident in local and global social movements concerned with challenging the worst excesses and injustices associated with neoliberal economics (see, for example, Crossa 2013; Katz 2004; Pinder 2005; Routledge 2012). Playfulness and humour are valuable ways of forming collective solidarity – participatory, open-ended and playful improvisations, or what Routledge (2012, p.431) refers to as 'ethical spectacles' which can produce absurd reconfigurations of a presumed reality to provocatively question the given order of things. Play, laughter and fun are important qualities in a politics of resistance that confronts the array of injustices and exploitation associated with neoliberal economics (Crossa 2013). These playful political acts are self-organised, contingent and always in motion to create spacetimes of political and ethical possibility.

A new land will always be emergent, giving rise to minor experiments and novel connections. Elements of this will be reterritorialised but desire will always escape:

> [new land] topography is traced by the movement of escaping desire. The fleeing elements can never come to rest because the apparatuses are never eradicated once and for all. Capture will continually reassert itself in forms like state agencies, private property, party organizations, corporations, planning departments, and the like. Fleeing elements of desire must always continue the active process of warding off these apparatuses, preventing the formation of institutions that will try to organize desiring-production, form it up into organs, codify it into machines that are limited to performing a narrow function. (Purcell 2013, p.29)

To briefly reiterate: children's everyday movements and encounters with each other, imaginations, lines on the floor, gooey stuff, works of art, bus stops, all collude to create a momentary distinctive 'space' or indeed 'new land'. Such mo(ve)ments may be presented as expressions of children's desire to affect and be affected to produce a better state of being, a state of being well. As noted in Chapter 3, the composition of playful new lands marks the enactment of 'rights' from the middle of a relational field (the *milieu*), a collective act of resourcefulness grounded in everyday life.

But these movements, at best, go largely unnoticed, or more likely, they are minor acts of deterritorialisation that are reterritorialised through a wide range of material-discursive manoeuvres which combine to delimit children's actions and desires ('play nicely' and 'play properly'). A pragmatic ethical response, therefore, is concerned with issues of 'spatial justice' or, adapting Rancière's terminology, 'spatial politics', in which the part that has no part acts to claim a sufficient stock of good things that enable life to flourish, in this instance by co-creating timespace for playing. The principle of spatial justice presents a radical application of the material and discursive connection between relational space, legal and governance systems and the ways in which they become entangled with political and social norms and everyday habits and routines (Soja 2010). While children are generally good at negotiating time and space for play in their daily routines, this is against a backdrop of inequitable distribution of timespace. Neoliberal government policies have intensified income inequalities and increased social polarisation across multiple scales of organisation (Soja 2010). Uneven development has geographic consequences by limiting access to the 'common wealth' of the material and social world (Hardt and Negri 2009) by shaping daily physical, social and material arrangements. These arrangements are always imbued with power relationships, both oppressive (*potestas*) and benign (*potentia*). It is only in abstract or absolute space that the ideal of equality for all exists. The effort to create a greater sense of democracy and participation of all citizens is continuous, an ongoing struggle between organic and inorganic materials to occupy spacetime that is productive of being well. When we consider children's play, these injustices are, in general, located in children's reduced ability to claim space (to live and play in their immediate environments), to participate in spatial production (to transform the local environment to their desires) and to develop spatial connections (to navigate the environment and form links in-between).

As noted in Chapter 4, space is more than an inert background for human activity but an active force that shapes all aspects of human and non-human life; the spatial, physical and social are thoroughly entangled and mutually implicated across layers of organisation in a messy, non-hierarchical manner. Thus, for example, the layout of roads may privilege drivers' needs over walkers' and so can oppress, exploit and dominate understandings and everyday practice of space, limiting possibilities for other forms of movement through 'common-sense' routines of social control and discipline. For the most part, children's daily lives are structured around adult productions which in turn are generally favoured in terms of adult desires that, through the processes of self-governance and bio-power, are in service to the demands of neoliberal economic production and consumption processes.

From this relative position, it is easy to plan and order children's movements; the allocation of space and time for playing fits in with other provision to form the plane of organisation that fixes short- and long-term trajectories: children should be in the right place and on the right line of development. So already it is possible to discern that the geographies of these productions will have spatial injustices and distributional inequalities; the layout of roads, signage, laws and so on privilege the needs of adult movement over children's. But as children *becoming trees* exemplifies, playing can temporarily reconfigure adult design intentions – a gallery with its 'atmosphere' of cultural reverence can momentarily become a space for play. Rancière (2001, Thesis 8) comments:

> The police say that there is nothing to see on a road, that there is nothing to do but move along. It asserts that the space of circulating is nothing other than the space of circulation. Politics, in contrast, consists in transforming this space of 'moving-along' into a space for the appearance of a subject: i.e., the people, the workers, the citizens. It consists in refiguring the space, of what there is to do there, what is to be seen or named therein. It is the established litigation of the perceptible.

The border designed to segregate road users from pedestrians can become an attractive 'transitional space' as children attempt to carefully balance along the kerbstones or utilise it for a game of 'kerby' and so on. Ward's (1979) descriptions and photographs of children using the 'street', applied in this context as a metaphor for public outdoor settings, including roads, pavements, alleyways, shopping centres, carparks (Matthews *et al.* 2000), highlights the multiple creative ways in which they may temporarily reconfigure space. By using whatever is at hand, children occupy spaces where they generally do not exist and do not count, moving from a position of passive subject to political subject, 'becoming democratic' through having a collective part to play in the production of space. These fleeting and fleeing moments are opportunistic as the following two examples illustrate.

Playing on the benches in the plaza

The first is a chance observation in a large shopping area and illustrates the ways in which children can make use of street furniture:

Walking behind a male adult with a child (a boy about 8 years old) – let's presume it is the child's father. They are walking along the pedestrianised row of shops, the child skipping ahead and occasionally looking around and pausing in their forward movement to see if the adult is behind. They reach a more open space, designed 'plaza style' with a number of benches for sitting (presumably for adults to recover from the trials of shopping with children?). The child jumps onto one of the vacant benches and runs across – at the end is another bench set at an angle a small distance away from the first bench. The child jumps across, lands on the bench, runs across it and jumps off at the end. As he turns around he sees that another boy of similar age has followed his movements. It is not clear at this stage where or if there is an attendant adult. When the second child reaches the end of the bench, the first child climbs upon to the narrow back of the bench and starts to balance across – it is about 4 inches wide and demands a degree of care and caution – arms outstretched and carefully placing his feet and taking small steps forward. The second child follows. As the first child nears the end, he speeds up and leaps from the bench to the floor as though performing a gymnastic display. Without a glance at the child behind, he moves towards the adult and skips off along the path. The second child has also jumped down to the floor in less ostentatious fashion and sidles in a different direction with a broad smile on his face over to the waiting adult.

The frozen food cabinet

The second example, an observation by an after-school club manager, takes place in a supermarket where two women, with three children between them, meet in a supermarket and stop to chat. The children stand around getting increasingly restless. A short while later the following occurs:

The three children, a boy and two girls, start to sidle away from the adults and make their way down an aisle containing frozen food cabinets. One of the girls looks inside the first cabinet and the other two stand alongside, whispering and giggling. The girl slowly opens the door as the other two keep an eye on the adults, and then they all reach in and take out packets of frozen food. They walk slowly along the aisle, continuing to whisper and giggle, until they reach another cabinet

– the girls pass their packets to the boy who places them in the second cabinet and they then take out more packets of food. They return to the first cabinet and furtively place the packets onto the shelves, again with more muffled giggling. By this time, the adults have finished chatting and move off, followed by their respective children.

For these moments, life is temporarily enlivened, sites of adult production and consumption are transformed by children's desire to unsettle and stake a claim, as children, through a playful redistribution (literally in the second example) of resources that works to their advantage. These, along with the other examples presented to date, are minor ways in which children have a part, creating a small plot of land by deterritorialising molar lines to counter some of the dominant trends in spatial production and so-called democracy.

Given that spaces are relational productions, they can be sites of greater justice produced by coalitions of forces that work to overcome inequalities. The quest for greater spatial justice and the challenge to the multiple and often apparently minor and mundane injustices that may limit children's ability to co-create playful mo(ve)ment become a policy linchpin, 'an integrative umbrella for coalition building, a kind of connective tissue or glue that can help to unite diverse and particularised struggles into larger and more powerful movements' (Soja 2010, p.109). Thus, rather than treating play as a discrete, self-contained, time-bound and situated activity, the concept of spatial justice provokes broader questions about democracy and a right to the 'commons' (Hardt and Negri 2009) at a time when contemporary forces of capital accumulation are dispossessing the poorest and most vulnerable of the resources necessary for a 'good life'. Since the global financial crash in 2007/08, the imposition of austerity measures in many minority world countries has exacerbated the gulf between rich elites and those who struggle to have a part. Playing, as a becoming-democratic process, reminds us that no matter what the police seek to control and order, there are always gaps for politics to emerge, that people can learn to use and exercise power to transform the present into more favourable conditions. This issue is revisited in more detail in Chapter 7.

Summary

As with playing itself, this chapter is fundamentally concerned with change rather than maintaining existing conditions. There is a pragmatic ethic at stake when one considers the movement of playing; it is more than simple child's play but contains guidance for avoiding the fascism that is 'in our heads' (Foucault 1984) by playful 'proliferation, juxtaposition and disjunction rather than by hierarchisation and subdivision; prefer[ring] positivity over negativity, difference over uniformity, nomadic or mobile assemblages over sedentary systems' (Patton 2010, p.146). This is not an act of violent revolution and upheaval; the impetus for social change is provided by movements of deterritorialisation and lines of flight, the multitude of ways in which individuals and groups collude to produce moments that deviate from the plane of organisation and molar segments. Colin Ward (1979) argued that it is through the processes of play and imagination that children can counter adult-based intentions and interpretations – a form of politics that challenges state domination.

Applying the concept of spatial justice alongside Deleuzian concepts gives rise to a series of central questions about space: who uses the space, who doesn't and why, how do people contribute to the everyday productions of space, what is the prevailing feel of space and what are the barriers to full participation (used in the sense of playing)? There is no normative judgement to account for these questions; the redistribution of timespace is found in micro-political and subtle shifts in connections, sensibilities, movements, beliefs and practices on the part of individuals and groups. Where they become extensive, when a spirit of playfulness permeates life, micro-political movements can bring about changes in the majoritarian standards themselves. Indeed, without this potential, such movements amount to nothing. The formation of plots of new land, however fleeting, is the effort to expand and strengthen the part that children have as citizens, a form of resistance to dominant forces. And as Springer (2014, p.82) comments, 'hierarchy is a system of organisation that only lives because we allow it to and we eradicate it every time we summon the nerve to laugh in its face', a 'sense of play and pleasure among the ruins of hierarchical social relations' (Ferrell 2001, p.235).

Seeking spatial justice, as an ethical endeavour, reveals and challenges the ways in which the production of space includes and excludes. It questions policies and practices and holds them to account for the contribution they make to cultivating conditions in which children can play. By doing so, dominant assumptions and practices that produce inequitable social and spatial productions are challenged, allowing for the possibility of imagining and actualising other virtualities. Movements of account-ability and response-ability form a state of enchantment with life that counters the majoritarian atmosphere of disenchantment and dislocation and associated state of fear and uncertainty. As with playing, there is a minor utopian impulse, not for a far-off and impossible new order but a new land 'in which the formation of new orders is continually warded off by a generalised condition of collective escape, one that works tirelessly to remain free – perhaps an anarchist utopia' (May1994). As May (2010, p.158) comments:

> Democratic politics is not dead, simply because it is never dead. It is neither dead nor alive. Rather, it comes to life, here and there, when the circumstances are right and people are decided. The project then, for those for whom democracy matters, is not to pronounce upon its fate nor to seek its Archimedean point. It is instead what it has always been: to be ready to engage it, to create it, alongside others with whom one stands and with whom one may share nothing else but equality.

To be ready to engage and create conditions with others for moments of play to emerge anywhere and everywhere, as a democratic process concerned with spatial justice, forms the material for the remaining chapters of this book.

■ CHAPTER 6 ■

Start here for notes

Cartography and Account-Ability

Introduction

Consider these words from Colin Ward (1979, p.88) and bear them in mind as we move from thinking differently about children's play to adult account-ability and response-ability:

> If you find yourself in an inconspicuous place, forget about time and all your pressing tasks, and simply watch and listen, you will develop a kind of reverence for the games of children, for their inexhaustible ingenuity, for the ways in which the rules they devise are more subtle, less attuned to competition and more geared to enabling everyone to have a chance, than the team games devised for them by adults [but you won't always like what you see!].

The previous chapters have mapped out a different reading of the relationship between children, play and space by drawing on Deleuzian philosophy and what might be loosely termed 'posthuman' accounts of life. Having set the scene, the attention turns in the following chapters to how adults might work with these concepts and processes to act ethically and responsibly in co-creating favourable conditions in which playfulness may thrive. It reintroduces the guiding principles established in the opening to the discussion, namely the interconnected processes of account-ability and response-ability: the ways in which adults can take note of children's play and act responsibly/ethically with these mo(ve)ments. For ease of presentation, these principles have been teased apart: this chapter considers the processes of account-ability through using a Deleuzian approach to mapping as a basis for a critical cartography of children's play; it introduces a range of practice-based 'research' methods that includes walking and wayfaring interviews, soundscapes, 'radio commentary' observations, audio-visual materials, mapping movements, diagrams, observation, storytelling, and other creative more-than-representation approaches.

Chapter 7 looks in more detail at some of the ways in which adults may respond to children's desire to play across scales that range from global declarations of 'a right to play', state legislation (with specific reference to the Welsh Government's Play Sufficiency Duty), local policy formulation and a range of professional practices. It is important to remember that the scalar distinctions between near/afar, micro/macro and so on mask the multiple ways in which these interpenetrate and become entangled in the production of spatial practices.

These two chapters also draw on a collection of research projects that have provided the opportunity to experiment with developing a pragmatic, practical and ethical response to the adult's role in promoting and realising children's right to play. These have covered a range of contexts, including the Welsh Government's Play Sufficiency Duty (Lester and Russell 2013a, 2014b) and professional development programmes with Welsh local authorities on an approach to assessing and securing sufficiency of play opportunities; the cultural sector on making spaces more playful, with Manchester Museum (Lester, Strachan and Derry 2014), Chester Zoo, Eureka Museum and English Heritage; a participative action research project with an adventure playground in East London (Lester, Fitzpatrick and Russell 2014); two play settings in Manchester on the value of playwork (Lester 2016b); and a project sharing adults' memories of adventure playgrounds in Gloucester and Bristol (Williams *et al.* 2016).

In line with the process of playing, account-ability and response-ability are manifestations of a pragmatic ethics and a desire to affect and be affected to produce more favourable conditions for playfulness to emerge. However, there is an immediate dilemma here: the dominant 'common-sense' value attributed to play is for its role in supporting adult agendas such as children's education, physical activity, and social and emotional skills development, thus preserving the status of

/ which are?

the majority, and so the formation and enactment of policy and its associated practices promotes play activities deemed to contribute to these agendas. In this molar formation, playing is merely a mechanism for achieving something other than playing, providing a justification for interventions that encourage the kinds of playing that are deemed to develop the right kinds of skills and behaviours. This rationalisation of play is reflected in social policy relating to children and young people (Lester and Russell 2008a; Powell and Wellard 2008) and becomes a totalising material-discursive practice (Lester and Russell 2013b); it sits comfortably within the dominant economic discourse of social policy that 'privileges instrumental rationality and technical practice…[and] in doing so sets up a binary opposition between process and outcome' (Moss 2007, pp.229–230). In this construction, playing is presented as a distinct activity that takes place at specific times and in designated spaces, and which has desired outcomes.

This book has offered a different way of thinking about playing as an expression of children's desires to affect and be affected by the world in ways that produce moments of pleasure and the sense of life being better. This is an affirmative position rather than one of lack. It presents playing as a collective disposition interwoven in the mo(ve)ments of children's everyday lives, as something that emerges from the entanglements of bodies, affects, material objects, atmospheres and whatever is to hand, whenever the conditions allow.

Such a perspective presents a challenge in terms of adult planning for play. Planning becomes less a matter of offering specific activities, places and services (important though these are) and more one of paying attention to those conditions. However, it is not simply about the role that adults can have in supporting or constraining play but is also concerned with democratic processes in which all citizens have a part to play. Adults and children are not separate entities; their lives are inextricably connected even when adults may be temporarily absent. Furthermore, not only are they entwined with each other, they are entangled with the material flows and forces of life itself. Given this, focus is drawn towards the intra-active micro-movements that constitute life going on and the possibilities that these present for becoming different, to make the world anew.

Taking account of the everyday

The composition of affective encounters cannot be reduced to universal accounts (Harrison 2007). Rather than fix and explain this relational messiness by drawing on pre-established concepts that prise entanglements apart, the question becomes one of how to *account* for the ways in which bodies, materials and space co-produce each other. The specificity of playful mo(ve)ments demands approaches that are 'tuned to the particularities of the entanglements at hand' (Barad 2007, p.74) and the differences they bring about. It suggests attention is given to the affective qualities of space combined with a commitment to experimenting with different ways of becoming attuned to these qualities (McCormack 2013). As noted in the introduction, the line pursued presents a pragmatic ethical stance to co-create a playful atmosphere where adults and children can get on and go on together. This is not the preserve of playworkers or others working specifically to support children's play but has wider implications and application for all adults who have a professional role with children, and arguably for all adults everywhere.

Drawing a line at the zoo

We start again with another example:

A new play area is being developed at the zoo, and a fence erected around the site. The zoo has painted the boards with blackboard paint and left a supply of chalk – freely available for passers-by. A young girl with piece of chalk is walking, holding the hand of an adult; as she walks, the child traces a line on the board and lets go of the adult's hand but still walks alongside and continues to trace a meandering line. She then breaks out into a skipping action and the line jumps up and down in response to the change in movement. She jumps up and down – the line peaks and falls before she carries on, now walking quickly to catch up with the adult but still tracing a line. She finally leaves the board, has a quick glance at where she has come from and skips off to hold the adult's hand.

As this example shows, mo(ve)ments of playing are constituted through and with the 'live surface': the sensations, textures, rhythms and intensities of everyday life (Stewart 2007). The familiar ways of children's precarious balancing along a wall, running on to the grass at school playtime, running fingers through gooey stuff, following lines at a bus stop and waving arms in response to an imaginary wind, are among the most ordinary yet meaningful elements of life. They are also mo(ve)ments that go largely unnoticed (Laurier 2013). The unremarkable nature of everyday life, in itself, is not a failing but an expression of the ways in which we are 'at home in the world' (Stewart 2007). Habits are so often taken as mundane routines of little value or something to be cultivated (good habits) or overcome by interventions from others or self-regulation (bad habits). However, they are also vital constituents of the pre-representational real, 'made up of forces that stimulate and transform living beings through their ability to accommodate routines, activities, projects that the emergence of life amidst the real requires' (Grosz 2013, p.218). Grosz proposes that habits not only establish sites of regularity in a world that is constantly changing, but also generate changes in the apparently unchanging world by initiating ease of action to form links with a world that is always open to innovative behaviour. Habits are performative by establishing rhythms and refrains that are a vital component of an affective atmosphere:

> Ordinary affects are the varied, surging capacities to affect and to be affected that give everyday life the quality of a continual motion of relations, scenes, contingencies and emergences. They're things that happen. They happen in impulses, sensations, expectations, daydreams, encounters, and habits of relating, in strategies and their failures, in forms of persuasion, contagion, and compulsion, in modes of attention, attachment, and agency, and in public and social worlds of all kinds that catch people up in something that feels like something. (Stewart 2007, pp.4–5)

We will return to the question of habits in Chapter 7.

Playing, as a very ordinary magic (after Masten 2001), is an expression of desires that matter not only because of the ways in which they produce an intensive difference, but also because they hold the promise of keeping whole clusters of affects attracted to them (Stewart 2007); they are extensive in scope, maintaining an appetite, or anticipatory alertness and readiness (Bennett 2004) to the possibility of further moments of playing. This is play's immense affective and life-enhancing significance.

Given this, in considering adults' role in supporting children's right to play, attention switches from what playing might mean, and is instead turned towards how moments of playing come about and where they might go. It should be evident that this cannot be a matter of templates or blueprints, but rather what is suggested is a Deleuzian processual-materialist approach that, rather than pulling everything apart and fixing it into categories, attempts to get at the messiness of the world, at the formation of assemblages of animate and inanimate matter and the ways they become entangled to affect and be affected in complex relationships.

What is suggested is that accounting for how conditions might support or constrain the emergence of playing (accepting that both may co-exist, as in the examples of the children 'playing with rules' on the grass in the playground) requires a *cartographic* approach. This is mapping that takes into account all that has been explored so far in terms of the power relations in the production of space, children's right to play as a matter of spatial justice, entanglements, affects, mo(ve)ments and life as emerging in-between these assemblages rather than as an individual affair. Rather than seeking to represent meaning as universal claims and proofs, this approach puts to work a range of practice methods that generates a collection of artefacts, or play documentation, that can begin to work with the messiness of practice. While each element on its own may be limited, they collectively combine to give a sense of the rhythms, patterns of movements and relationships, and a series of particular events which is then subject to critical scrutiny to see how they might enhance or limit opportunities for moments of play to emerge. These materials (what might be termed a 'cartography of play') also provide material for experimental, 'what if…' responses designed to see what more the environment can offer for playing.

Mapping as process

Chapter 2 considered in some detail the distinction Deleuze and Guattari draw between mapping and tracing. 'Tracing', for them, refers to the expectation that scientific methods can discover and represent the world in the straight-line teleological thinking of cause and effect, with attendant ideas of predictability and a sense of control over an externally existing, stable 'natural' world. With mapping, however, concepts can roam and mingle freely, connect and disconnect, opening up the possibility for nomadic movement away from order. It draws on a different set of trans-disciplinary navigational tools, each of which can be bent towards 'opening the event to more, more; more action, more imagination, more light, more fun, even' (Thrift 2008, p.20). Mapping brings focus to ways in which organisms and things intensively co-exist and co-create; everything does something and nothing can be delineated as separate and apart from everything else (Barad 2007). It inevitably challenges an anthropocentric account of life; everything (matter and meaning, object and subject, nature and culture) is mutually entangled. As Deleuze and Guattari (1988, pp.13–14) say:

> What distinguishes the map from the tracing is that it is entirely ori-ented toward an experimentation in contact with the real… The map can be torn, reversed, adapted to any kind of mounting, reworked by an individual, group or social formation. It can be drawn on a wall, conceived of as a work of art, constructed as a political action or as a meditation.

Yet tracings and mappings are not binary opposites; as with ideas of deterritorialisation and reterritorialisation, one can become the other (O'Sullivan 2006), maps can be traceable: 'even lines of flight, due to their eventual divergence, reproduce the very formation their function it was to dismantle or outflank' (Deleuze and Guattari 1988, p.14). Rather than making a product, mapping is a matter of ongoing process, of method; once it becomes fixed, it is a representation, an imitation, a tracing.

By way of an illustration, an example is offered here from the partici-patory action research project with the London adventure playground (Lester, Fitzpatrick and Russell 2014) that shows how tracings and mappings can interpenetrate. At the first session with the playworkers, they were asked to draw a representational map of the playground. This in itself was an embodied process, as they worked on a large sheet of paper, moving around it to add boundaries, features and so on, all the while talking about what was where, giving rise to a range of stories and also emotions as the playworkers spoke about how they felt about particular areas of the playground. The process was much more than the production of a map that could then be populated with other forms of documentation; it was itself a mapping, a sensing of the collective and multiple ways of relating to and producing the space. The map came to act as both a plane of organisation and a plane of immanence for other forms of documentation, which included stories, diagrams, mappings of flows and forces of the playground and so on.

Another example is offered from research into the Welsh Government's Play Sufficiency Duty. This duty, introduced as a part of the Children and Families (Wales) Measure 2010, places a statutory duty on local authorities to assess, and as far as is reasonably practicable, secure sufficient play opportunities for children in their area. The statutory guidance (Welsh Government 2014) lists nine 'Matters' that local authorities should take into account when preparing their triennial assessments. Some of these approach 'account-ability' for children's play through 'counting' and through tracing: numbers of children in specific categories (such as age, ethnicity, gender, disability), numbers of playgrounds and parks, specific targeted services and so on. These tracings provide representations of habitual and fixed categorisations of children, space, services and concepts. They 'fix' play into a time- and space-bound activity to be provided. This is important. It is information that is needed, and play provision matters to children as a part of the mosaic of their lives. What is equally important, and often overlooked, is what this approach might exclude. Mapping offers a different approach to account-ability: paying attention to the ways in which children take timespace for their own play productions interwoven into everyday life is an ethical matter of spatial justice. It contributes to (it affects and is affected by) the ongoing development of collective wisdom, and critical considerations of how space might be configured differently (or indeed, how current supportive configurations might be maintained) forms the focus of Chapter 7.

Leopard skin wellies

Lester and Russell (2013a, p.2) open their report on the first play sufficiency assessments carried out in 2012–13 with an account relayed by an adventure playground worker (indeed, the report takes its name from this story):

> When the playground closes in the evening, the play and playworkers sometimes spill out into the local community. The playworker tells the

story of being with a group of children where one boy was decked out in leopard skin wellies and a top hat and was carrying an old vacuum cleaner hose, all items brought from the playground. This spill-over makes playworkers and children highly visible in playful ways and the playworker said that since they started working, first in the community prior to the opening of the playground and then on the playground with this spill-over, local adults have become aware of children's play, and attitudes towards it have changed. This example highlights the ways in which everyday actions and relationships, over a period of time, have a powerful influence in shaping community attitudes and engagement. Of course, it will raise issues; not all adults 'get it' and certainly many of the things that happen on this particular estate 'would be weird somewhere else'.

It is possible to bring mapping-as-process to the detail in this example, following digressions and developing further questions, not as a way of drawing general conclusions but to see what more might be said about the processes of this event. This process revealed connections:

> with innumerable environmental/relational features: the presence of the playworkers, the development of the adventure playground and its responsiveness to local conditions; the relationships between children, playworkers and adults on the estate; an emerging culture in which a resident can put an old trampoline onto an empty space for the children to play with, the provision of play priority signs by the community and so on produce the conditions that contribute to the child playing in that place at that particular time. (Lester and Russell 2013a, p.72)

Of course, as acknowledged, not everyone in this community welcomes children's playful presence on the estate. However, their visibility brings these tensions to the surface and people find ways of getting on together. Undoubtedly the Welsh Government's (2010) attempt to legislate for children's play through a play sufficiency duty is a challenging task; the conditions that might support children's play are complex, contextual and contingent; not just one thing (for example, a planned intervention with an expectation of a causal outcome), but a whole assemblage of small things over a period of time that work together to shape a culture of acceptance that can make this a play-friendly environment.

The process of mapping also employs Deleuze's concepts of refrains and diagrams, which offer an insight into the more-than-representational constitution of rhythms of space; 'a refrain composed of differentiating patterns of affects, percepts, and concepts that exceed any effort to explain' (McCormack 2013, pp.67–68) composed from sounds, light, bodies and materials intra-actively mingling with different forces and flows, a style 'drawn out as series of lines of continuous variation' (ibid.).

Drawing lines at the nursery

Another exemplary account is briefly presented here, based on a personal recollection of the emergence of a *milieu* between an anxious parent and child when it came time to separate at nursery school:

> After several weeks of becoming distraught at leaving time (both adult and child), a rhythm or refrain emerged that involved drawing lines on the reverse side of a photocopied colouring-in picture, readily available at the start of the nursery day; the movement of large wax crayons flowed across the paper, gradually covering all the white space and marking the time to separate. These micro-movements assumed considerable significance, far greater than the nursery teacher's exhortations to the adult to encourage the child to draw properly and stay within the lines of the prepared picture. The lines of two wax crayons over a sheet of white paper established a *milieu*, working from the middle to the outer edges, with different speeds, the child's movements slowing as the paper became increasingly filled with colour. It had its own rhythm, a minor mo(ve)ment in everyday practice that lessened the pain of separation for all concerned.

This rhythmic pattern is an example of the multiple routines and habits that emerge to cope with life and provide the foundations for playful improvisations (Edensor 2010; Grosz 2013). It is a refrain or repetition that holds off falling into chaos and despair while at the same time is always creative and offers moments for becoming different. In this instance, there are multiple diagrammatic representations of this process – the paper covered with coloured crayons – but the meanings of this only exist within each singular moment of intra-activity; each picture is a representation of moving bodies and their affects. There are multiple possibilities for producing refrains: for example, the adult and child could have developed a song, the ending of which could have served the same purpose. Equally it could be a set of gestures, a compilation of materials and so on. But as McCormack (2013) asserts, experimental diagrammatic practice can overcome the distortions of linguistic representations by taking lines for a walk (Paul Klee's description of drawing, 1960) and to apprehend the continuities, discontinuities and rhythmic effects of encounters and movements.

Towards a cartography of play

So, how to produce a map and not a tracing when attempting to account for how the ongoing co-production of spaces might support or constrain mo(ve)ments of playfulness? It is possible to suggest methods, and indeed, some are explored below, but what is equally important is to place such methods in the overall approach proposed, namely that the methods are not attempts to represent reality, nor are they 'data' to be themed and interpreted. They are processual efforts to develop an ongoing sense of and for movements and the co-production of space and of/for children's lines of flight, their democratic practices of deterritorialisation and reterritorialisation. In order to pay attention to playful assemblages that continually emerge and die away, mapping must be wary of becoming tracing, of fixing a static reality. The concept of 'diagram', as a process of mapping and not tracing, 'does not function to represent, even something real, but rather constructs a real that is yet to come, a new type of reality' (Deleuze and Guattari 1988, p.157).

One of the unique features of the approach is that the process is fluid, responsive and grounded in creative action rather than being a series of well-defined steps that are rigorously adhered to irrespective of what happens. It also recognises that while practices may be bound by habits, routines and customs, there is no intrinsic requirement for them to be performed in this way – it is simply the way things have turned out and they could (and still can) work out differently. While a range of performative methods are presented separately in what follows, they work intra-actively and diffractively to compile what Lester and Russell (2013a, 2014b) refer to as 'collective wisdom' in recognition of the multiple ways of 'knowing in being' and that sustainable and ethical ways of knowledge production and action might 'come after and not before awkward mixtures of knowledge and material' (Fitzgerald and Callard 2015, p.19). The application of these methods is always singular and contextual, the melange of disparate, multi-sensual approaches collectively compiles the 'matter' of documentation (Childers 2014). The materiality of bodies, movements, policies, theories, practices and other animate and inanimate objects is mutually constitutive and all these carry equal weight. Many of the methods are now generally accepted as standard approaches – observations, mapping, video and sound recordings, interviews – but they are utilised with a different focus to create new conditions of possibilities. They have value for both discovering a little more about how children move and act in their everyday environments and digging beneath the surface of adult response-abilities.

A nomadic approach: mobile methods

Adopting a nomadic approach invites researchers and practitioners to wander the environment and pay attention to events and encounters between disparate materials, more-than-human encounters between people and things (Banerjee and Blaise 2013). Such events are moments of instruction and reveal the implicit conventions and tacit compulsions that orient child and adult movements. They are also an invitation to sometimes 'stay still', to observe closely the patterns and modes of movements and mutually shaping entanglements of specific situations (Banerjee and Blaise 2013). The encouragement to be attentive produces stories of movement and relationships that would previously have been unremarkable. For example, the story of the girls *walking the lines at the museum* was recounted by a visitor services assistant who had 'slowed down' and begun to pay attention to how these mo(ve)ments emerge. In addition:

> Slowing down to pay closer attention also initiated a conversation with the parent who commented that of all the things in the museum this seemed to be the most attractive at this time. This recollection, rather than objective classification, reveals the ways in which child, adult, floor tiles and so on assemble to produce a singular moment of movement and playfulness. It also marks an enhanced ability to look at the opportunistic formations that occur anywhere and everywhere and to reveal these relationships by telling their stories. (Lester, Strachan and Derry 2014, p.31)

Crouch (2010) refers to this process as 'flirting' with landscape, coming across familiar sites but sensing strange juxtapositions and movements; as these discoveries are made, bodies become more attuned to the possibilities of their existence everywhere and anywhere, as Crouch (2010, pp.5–6) acknowledges, 'even in familiarity and habitual rhythmic engagement, the meaning, our relationship with things, can change in register; slight adjustments of feeling over time becoming more significant'. It also highlights the significance of the patterned floor in the entrance to the museum.

Observation of a teddy bear

Such attention need not always be on human movements. In a study on the value of play provision in Manchester (Lester 2016a), when faced with the challenge of observing frantic activity between children in a playwork setting, my attention turned towards a giant teddy bear (TB) lying in a corner of the room and the ways in which this moved through the environment. This edited extract from observation notes presents the liveliness of TB (Lester 2016a, p.30):

> TB sitting in a corner of an area with settees and large floor cushions. A boy and girl enter the area, pick up TB and start playing tug-of-war with it before the girl lies on TB while the boy drags her along the floor before being discarded. TB is then picked up by three boys who start chasing around the room…one child hit another with it, child fell over and child just checked to see if he was ok – not a big deal – child gets up and carries on chasing other boy with TB. The three boys abandon TB mid-room – a girl picks it up and carries it into the corner with cushions – a boy runs by and casually kicks it (like football) – another boy then takes it into the corner and sits on it, gets up and runs away – at this point TB is in corner between wall and settee. A small girl picks it up and puts it on her back, runs over to a playworker and bumps into him with TB, leaves TB lying on the floor where it stays for a while before a boy dives on TB and pretends to fight it, picks it up and play fights with one of the playworkers who then holds TB and gives voice to it while wrestling boy with it and then makes playful threatening gesture with TB to a girl before talking to her via TB and gesturing with arms.

The process of walking through the museum, adventure playground, local neighbourhoods and school playgrounds at different times also builds a picture of the flows and rhythms of the respective environment, revealing some of the embodied practice-based insights of children and adults in relation to movement and space. 'Flirting' and its accompanying stories make valuable contributions to perceiving and appreciating the important material-discursive lines in-between people, environment, things and structures and their possible exclusionary effects (Jung 2014). This form of 'mood walking' also leads to chance encounters with adults and children. Like participant observation, 'walk alongs' can enable researchers and practitioners to observe and facilitate discussion around situated spatial practices and can often merge with audio-visual methods (Degen and Rose 2012).

Audio and visual methods

These walking methodologies can be complemented with a range of creative and audio-visual methods. In a study on the co-creation of an adventure playground (Lester, Fitzpatrick and Russell 2014), distilling two hours of filming from a static recorder positioned on a roof into five minutes of speeded-up movement presented a different perspective on the range of children's movements and encounters. Equally, recordings of children's movements through the museum gallery space reveal the richness of the fabric and atmosphere of the environment and the playful ways in which children appropriate time and space, engaging with a range of materials strategically placed by museum staff.

Audio recordings or 'soundscapes' can provide insights into the distinctive audible features of spaces and hold the potential to complement more traditional forms of data by adding a sensory dimension and the ambience of an environment (Gallagher and Prior 2014). This can be illustrated by an example from the adventure playground participatory research (Lester, Fitzpatrick and Russell 2014) in which a playworker wandered the playground with an audio recorder to pick up the ambient sounds and then invited other members of the staff team to situate the sounds against specific locations. Through attentive listening, it was possible to discern and become attuned to different qualities of sound, for example the swing area, the sandpit and aerial runway each had a distinctive soundscape. It also brought into realisation familiar sounds that had gone unnoticed as part of the background refrains of the playground, for example the church bell and how this punctuated the rhythms of the playground.

A similar experiment was carried out with playworkers in the Manchester playwork study (Lester 2016a), with playworkers carrying a digital recorder for a five-minute period before passing it on to a colleague to produce an intriguing soundscape of background noises (the sound of table tennis, a balloon being released with accompanying 'fart-like' sound which brought the setting to a standstill) and fragments of conversations in the foreground ('I had to do four minutes', 'Four minutes of silence, wow', 'I had to do five minutes and at the end I got a cross'). The full recording reveals a complex and multi-layered soundscape that might appear, on first listen, to be just 'noise' but which expresses 'ways in which bodies and things create their own unique spaces alongside, between and interpenetrating the environment and all that it contains to compose the feel of the setting' (Lester 2016a, p.39).

Another approach is to produce a 'radio commentary' of events as they unfold, where a member of staff stands to one side for a five-minute period and commentates on what they see in the style of a sports commentator (or any other style). Again, this produces a different account since the performance affects what is recounted.

The images and recordings produced with these mobile methods are not simply a reflection of a pre-existing reality (a representation, a tracing), but are cut from and effect cuts in the world according to norms, values, contexts and processes. While being well-intentioned, in traditional approaches to asking children in interviews about their experiences of playing, their 'voices' become disembodied and their words assume a stable veracity. Given that playing is of-the-moment, opportunistic and often a way of subverting adult intentions for children's use of timespace, it generally resists articulation and representation. The challenge is to bring these minor political actions to the surface in ways that can remain faithful to them. The descriptions of the children playing tag on the swing platform, becoming trees and dancing at bus stops emerge from a desire to not fix and reduce play by classification but to be more attentive to affective resonance and the ways in which play spacetimes emerge and cohere into a recognisable form.

It is a performative practice concerned with describing the details of each singular event. It is more than assumed objective description as it incorporates a sensing state of enchantment, alert to movement and associated novelty, surprise, twists and tensions or 'the capacity to move and be moved by bodies at a distance' (McCormack 2013, p.140). Rather than using methods to produce data, the multi-sensual/mobile approaches outlined above pay attention to the everyday movements and meshworks (between bodies, materials, symbols and so on) that constitute spaces that are amenable to playing.

Diagrams and mappings

Alongside mobile and audio-visual methods, the use of diagrams or alternative forms of representation can be a 'creative force, inventive and experimental attempts that disrupt the taken-for-granted ways of seeing the world, a creative act of proliferation and rupture' (De Freitas 2012, p.557). They offer up the spatio-temporal movements formed by lines of becoming; 'every animate being, as it threads its way through and among the ways of every other, must perforce improvise a passage, and in so doing it lays another line (Ingold 2013, p.132). In line with the earlier discussion on making diagrams, this is not about accurate representation between points but a more performative, aesthetic and artistic way of paying attention to the non-linear, indeterminate, multi-sensory lived experiences of space (McCormack 2013, 2014; Powell 2010). In the adventure playground participative research, playworkers mapped the movements of particular children or members of staff, showing diagramatically the flows of movement as they ranged across the space. Other examples have been presented in the previous section (the lines on the paper to mark a refrain that leads up to the time for the parent to leave the child at nursery), and also the play lines of movement of the boys at the bus stop in Chapter 2 or the entangled lines of the girls becoming trees at the gallery in Chapter 4.

Observation

Observation is a primary form of accounting for how children's play arises from whatever is to hand. Yet here, also, the suggestion is to approach observation as mapping and not tracing. In much research and professional work with children, observation is used as a form of assessment, where adult professionals use apparatuses such as measurements, templates, scales and so on to assess children's development or skills, to impose meaning on to what they see. Despite the need in research and professional literature for observations to be 'objective', Barad (2007, p.139) highlights the 'inseparability of object and the measuring agencies'. The apparatus – which includes not only scientific tools for measurement, but also systems of thinking, material-discursive practices and so on – is entangled in intra-actions with other phenomena; it is not neutral and it performs particular exclusionary cuts on what is observed. The observer is always part of an assemblage of materials, concepts, bodies and histories that are distributed and powerful with the capacity to affect and be affected. The observation of the girls becoming trees was a chance encounter, and 'I' was caught in a momentary web of relationships as the performance unfolded. The important point here is that an attending presence is not adult–child, observer–observed, but connected and enmeshed. The observer is embroiled in the performance, not outside it, and is 'infected by the effort' (Dewsbury 2009, p.326), no longer participant observation but observant participation in life (Blaise 2013; Dewsbury 2009). In order to grasp the rhythms of everyday life one must first let oneself go, 'give oneself over, abandon oneself to its duration' (Lefebvre 2004, p.27). It necessitates caring about the possible worlds that we all help to bring about and sustain; one cannot stay detached, clean and innocent and impose hygienic methods.

Some of the exemplary accounts included in this book are moments which are opportunistically noticed through what might be termed 'accidental ethnography' (Fujii 2014) to signify the unplanned ways in which they emerge; there is no forewarning and no deliberation other than anticipatory readiness to be open to the possibilities that the world presents. This form of playful apprehension can be developed and refined through practice; bodies can learn to be attentive and form an enchanted attachment to the world. It is a state of receptive and generous ethical sensibility towards other things and bodies (Bennett 2001), productive of moments which glow and glimmer, diffractions which resonate and reverberate to sense nonsense (MacLure 2013). Examples are drawn from witnessing events that glowed, whether through direct presence or a more removed position; but all instigate a sense of enchantment and embodied response to the ways in which play, in particular children's play, appears in the fabric of everyday life. It is a position that is more akin to surfing and riding the waves, a precarious state of balance and focused attention to the unfolding movement (after Borgnon 2007) rather than post-event imposition of knowledge.

To treat the ongoing singular events of the world seriously requires a move from a form of empiricism that seeks to codify and denote to one that is oriented towards the task of descriptions that contain a fidelity to what they describe (Latham 2003). Description is a high and rare achievement (Latour 2005) yet simply describing may, in traditional research terms, suggest there is something missing. This is the legacy of orthodox academic requirements that privilege explanations. But Latour (2005, p.35) counters with the claim that if 'a description needs explanation it means it is a bad description'. Transcendental empiricism supports such moves by paying attention to the instability of life and the ways in which thoughts come to life through movement and encounter, demanding a different set of tools that adopt a practical standpoint, methods that can experiment with such messy everyday actions and add to the liveliness of intra-activity. It brings closer attention to those forms of expression, routines, habits, improvisations, sensations, materials and so on that constitute the practices and events of everyday life that normally escape notice. Bodies can no longer be passive vehicles of objective perception and meaning-making; they are central to the practical accomplishments and movements of becoming, 'of matters spooling out without a predetermined destination' (MacLure 2013, p.662). It is an attempt to animate rather than deaden life, to show children's 'doings', flows of movement at different speeds and tempos and their affects, a process of attuning to the subtle diffractive patterns of complex interferences while holding off the louder noises of academic conventions.

This is a position of being witness to the event, observing, attesting, accounting and being accountable to one's visions and representations (Haraway 1997). It is tentative and doomed to fall short – something always escapes. But in a sense, it thrives on these limitations by recognising that what counts as 'knowledge' is always open to further (re)arrangements (Dewsbury 2009). As Jones (2008, p.209) comments, 'we can hope to do children justice by witnessing their lives and making space for them without trying to occupy those lives and render them in adult discourses'. It is this move from representation to witnessing that may hold greater possibility for beginning to think about ethical relationships and encounters. Witnessing holds off classifications and meanings by attuning embodied attention to the multiple ways in which bodies, materials and so on momentarily assemble with a force and flow that we might represent as play.

Storytelling

The encouragement to be attentive produces stories of movement and relationships that would previously have been unremarkable. Stories and anecdotes are traditionally shunned in the search for representing an objectively existing reality. Yet stories have great value. As with observations, they are always singular examples which stand for themselves and cannot be generalisable. But each story contains within it the potential for looking in more detail at intensive processes that contribute to the formation of the event and at the same time lead off into other possibilities, formations and relationships in extensive meanderings. We live in a storied world – the narratives we tell of our experiences. Stories are valuable not simply for their telling, but also for their retelling; they provide opportunities to share experiences and serve as a point of intra-action in-between people. Through storying, dialogue can emerge, supporting the development of a multiplicity of knowledges (collective wisdom); people can share familiar experiences or appreciate difference. For the storyteller, telling stories is a process of sense-making and for the listener, hearing a story can expand their own sense-making and add new possibilities for their own storytelling. Stories can bring theoretical concepts and policy intentions to life, as they reach beyond the cognitive to the affective and embodied. Stories make and add to history as well as imagine possible futures. The examples offered in this book might be thought of as observations and as stories.

Summary

This book has offered a different line of enquiry into children's play that requires different ways of accounting for it as an ethical matter. Mo(ve)ments of playing can emerge from whatever is to hand, forming assemblages from human and non-human bodies, material and symbolic objects, affects and so on, in non-linear and opportunistic ways to co-create moments that have a vibrancy and make life worth living. Traditional research methods or ways of documenting 'what happens' tend to produce tracings that seek to fix and represent play as activity with attendant benefits beyond playing; the process of mapping offers possibilities for more-than-representational ways to account for children's ability to take timespace for their playful co-productions.

Deleuze and Guattari (1988, p.13) urge us to 'make a map, not a tracing', to develop ongoing processes that work with sensual, mobile and more-than-representational methods. From this perspective, account-ability becomes the 'ability to articulate [take account of] how practice affects conditions for playing, what happens, and how this contributes to policy objectives' (Lester 2016a, p.50). The maps and movements, encounters and relationships, and accompanying stories associated with critical cartography bring life to the environment; they are read diffractively, not reflectively, to consider the ongoing and multi-faceted flows of action that play across and through space. In the adventure playground, museum, playwork setting, school playground and in public spaces, the environment is revealed as constituted through, productive of and permeated with flows and forces that establish ever-changing patterns, rhythms and moods. At a broader level, the accumulation of different multi-sensual points of view can be mapped to produce an open landscape of possibilities; the collective (and always partial) assemblage of artefacts and bodies brings a critical lens to bear on everyday rhythms and the ways in which space is always a process of becoming. Concepts fold into each other, disturb and create something new. Account-ability becomes a creative process through crafting maps that are always open-ended.

Over time and through multiple layerings and iterations with visual, spoken and written materials, maps and diagrams, attention is drawn to the contingent patterns of spatial production. While each example is singular, collectively they begin to reveal the ways in which the environment is cut and shaped through practices and routines that may include and exclude opportunities for playing. From this perspective, cartography is always an integral feature of the ongoing participatory relationships that emerge during everyday practices, contributing to the compilation of collective wisdom, not as an accumulation leading not to comprehension but to apprehension of the ever-changing patterns and rhythms of everyday encounters and their effects.

CHAPTER 7

Critical Cartography and Response-Ability

Introduction

The previous chapter considered the process of mapping, of co-producing a cartography of play, as an approach to adult account-ability. Account-ability refers to the ability of practitioners to account for children's play through a range of more-than-representational methods that pay attention to the emergence of playful moments, and to compile a sense of what might contribute to conditions under which playfulness might emerge. In this sense, accountability leads to response-ability, or an ability to be alert and responsive to children's movements in order to maintain a prevailing playful feel. This is the move from a cartography of play to a *critical* cartography. It is how adults can develop a continual ethical responsiveness that can help create a more just distribution of spatial and temporal resources for children. Account-ability and response-ability are not separate processes but are entangled: the process of mapping, particularly as a collective endeavour, not only produces documentation, but is also performative in the sense that the process itself generates change. This chapter considers aspects of and approaches to response-ability as a critical cartography of play, beginning with a discussion on the interrelationship between theory, research and practice before briefly revisiting Ungar's (2008) notion of navigation and negotiation. It then employs this and Amin's (2006) four registers of the 'good city' as sensitising concepts that can work with documentation to create new concepts and approaches to planning and practice that can leave space open for children's own playful productions. It is used here not to arrive at grand action plans but to offer a diffractive reading of the documentation, one that explores the disturbances and differences rather than echoing the same, in order to extend thoughts, knowledge and practices, and to develop rich, multiple readings (Mazzei 2014).

Towards a critical cartography of play

The singular details presented in cartographic documentation pay attention to the mundane habits of children's spaces, and these can then be held up to critical scrutiny. As seen in Chapter 6, habits are more than mere routines of little value, but provide both a sense of continuity and the possibility for change, and establish the rhythms and refrains that contribute to a prevailing playful feel. Grosz (2013, pp.233–34) argues for an understanding of habit 'beyond automatism' in order to appreciate its potential 'paradoxically, [as] a dynamic force that opens up the universe, both its living and non-living forces, to contraction, to contemplation, and thus, by way of deflection, to free action, to radical change'.

Habits of spatial production in work settings and in public spaces are what keep them going, but they can also be exclusionary. It is through paying attention to mundane everyday details that such habits can come to be sensed, through the examples, the stories, the mappings and so on. Two key questions arise through the process of critical scrutiny: 'What more might be said and done beyond the same ways of thinking and acting?' and 'What if...?' As the refrain for much of children's play, can also be put to work in actions of adult response-ability. It is an experimental process rather than implementing solutions to identified problems. 'What if...' experiments are playful, contingent, often opportunistic, and are performed without any great prediction of what might happen.

The chairs

This extended extract from the participatory action research on an adventure playground (Lester, Fitzpatrick and Russell 2014, pp.20–24) gives an example of how critical cartographic methods brought attention to the habits and routines produced through the positioning of a set of chairs, and a series of responses from the playworkers to this.

This story shows how the approaches used in the research project played out through a set of chairs in ways that became quite significant. It weaves its way throughout the data over a period of time, across numerous artefacts such as photographs, videos, mappings, transcripts of sessions and blogs. The story begins on the very first day, when the playworkers were asked to take three photos of the 'play space' that held particular meaning for them. One of the playworkers took a photo of some chairs on the veranda by the entrance to the building. Introducing the photo to the others in the group, she said:

> I've got seating which is my special place. I find that this is a meet and greet place and I'm always standing there greeting the children as they come in. This is the place where the children catch up, what's happened in school, gossiping, lots of playing going on, rough and tumble, chasing around and also it is the last point where everyone meets and says good-bye to each other.

Others agreed that the spot was special, calling it the 'heart' of the place, and noting also the significance of leaving rituals enacted here at the end of the session. Alongside this sense of specialness sat also an awareness, expressed at a later session, that the older users often dominated the area, congregating there loudly and boisterously filling the space, and this was daunting for people wanting to enter the building (although there was another door, this was the main and most visible one). The space was clearly important to groups of teenagers, as highlighted in a mapping of flows that one of the playworkers did during a 15-minute period when only the teenagers were there.

These conversations and other artefacts highlighted the significance of what might be considered a very ordinary space and very ordinary happenings on adventure playgrounds, and this is why it is of interest in this research. The mapping of the flows and movements is intended as more than an exercise in accurate representations of reality, plotting and fixing things in time and space, rather it is concerned with possible relationships and new ways of looking at disparate materials and phenomena, allowing for thinking differently about individual and collective experiences. The photograph [of the chairs] is seemingly devoid of vitality, understood as a collection of material objects onto which the viewer may impose meanings drawn from their own histories and experiences of such spaces. When the site is in operation and the young people move through and occupy the space, each event might be seen as an assemblage of material and symbolic objects, bodies, desires, affects, histories, relationships and so on – a unique moment where elements combine to produce 'what happens'. Previous and subsequent events may be similar but will never be exactly the same. These repeated yet different events become a part of the habits of the space as a whole, understood as the way things are, and also offering the opportunity to be different (Dewsbury 2011).

The seats themselves contributed to the production of a space that was experienced by the playworkers as both special and problematic. It is unclear how long these seats had been there; it is assumed that they had been there long enough for their positioning to become a key and habitual element of the assemblage that produced that space. Part of its significance lay in its position as threshold; one of the playworkers spoke about often feeling that she had to ask the youths to move away from the door, and another spoke of two younger girls not wanting to use the door where the teenagers hang out. So, the positioning of the chairs is significant: being at the threshold of the building affords both the space as meet and greet and the space of intimidation for others wanting to enter the building.

Following her mapping of the flows of movement that highlighted the significance of this area, one of the playworkers said, 'From that I just thought I wonder what would happen if we just move the chairs'. This 'what if…?' question was raised in the research sessions, introduced 'what if…' not as an experiment in the sense that there is no predetermined outcome to be achieved, but draws on the histories, intuitions and perceptions of the playworkers. This open-ended questioning coincided with others deciding to use the chairs as the setting for a planned family open day event, and the chairs were moved in preparation for this from the veranda to form a circle on the open grass before one of the playground sessions. One of the playworkers describes the reaction of one of the regular teenagers to this moving of the chairs:

So, the gates were opened, the first person who comes in is D., doesn't notice they are on the grass, just sees the chairs are not on the veranda, 'A! Where are the chairs!', started to move chairs back; they are not light chairs and he didn't want any help, sat there waiting for someone to come, lying down and dominating that space, reclaiming his territory...he wants that to be his space... It just shows how important that area is to him and all those social interactions there which includes the door – which is probably the one staff use most to go in and out of the building, the door nearest the office, probably the door where you've had most discussions with him. That's his preferred space.

So, two of the seats were moved back almost immediately, and the others were left where they were. The initial moving took place in June, and a discussion with the playworkers in July, just before the summer holidays, returned to the topic. It seemed that not many of the regular children had used the chairs out in the open grass, although one chair had been moved towards the swing, lost its back and become part of the structure – something to land on as a step up to the platform. The story was told of one boy fairly new to the playground who had put his bag on a chair in the new location, sat there for a bit and left it there, with the playworkers commenting 'so it must have felt like a neutral, unthreatening space with the chairs out there in the open'. However, the chairs had been used a lot by parents with younger children, with some of the older children asking why younger ones had started coming more. There was a feeling that although the teenagers still congregated on the veranda, 'there is not the hubbub there was before', and there was also a feeling that the presence of the younger children and parents modified the behaviour of the older ones to an extent, although there were still displays of aggression that co-existed alongside the adults and younger children.

These changes cannot be attributed solely to the moving of the chairs in any predictable, causal or replicable manner. The moving disturbed some of the taken-for-granted assumptions about the space and how to be in it, both for staff and users, and this happened alongside all the other aspects of the production of the play space such as the open day family event, the playbus visits, and perhaps a shift in the ways the playworkers paid attention to the flows and forces in the space as a result of the research project. Throughout the project, the chairs featured frequently and to an extent came to embody the approaches explored. At the end of the summer, for example, two blogs posted in early October mentioned the chairs again. [The project had used a secure online site for ongoing discussion and sharing documentation.] One is reflective, musing on the significance the chairs had assumed:

> The chairs have taken on a new arrangement with one or two near the building, two under the stage and two still out in the middle (where they've been for most of the summer). Reading the day book and registers and realizing that some of the older young people were back, some of the middle-age group from summer were still coming [after-school club]. Friday visits still had a generally younger primary school-age group, and parents and littlies visiting at weekends seemed to reflect the more dispersed and smaller grouping of the chairs! They have taken on a storytelling role for me... Is it true, I wonder?

The other, two days later, acknowledges the shift of the seasons and the end of the school holidays and the possible return of the older users, leading to a decision to (re)place some of the chairs in the social spaces used by them:

Back to school

Some of the older term time users popped in to see who was around. Myself and A decided to move some of the chairs back into the places they like hanging out, to help them feel welcome after a summer of not being there. We put a seat back on the veranda (not right next to the door though) and several back under the ramp/ arch. We left the rest in the middle.

Another playworker commented on her blog that play spaces change all the time, uploading a video clip of a young boy cycling on the veranda in the space where the chairs had been, commenting:

Why does playspace change? Because why not?

The chairs were raised again as a significant symbol of the journey the playworkers felt they had made at a final meeting to review the process and plan a conference workshop.

These 'what if?' experiments are minor mo(ve)ments designed to bring 'what if...' more to the world by remaining faithful to singular events, generating new practice concepts for ethical account-ability and response-ability. From this perspective, the playful entanglement of bodies and materials that comes about through movement, encounters, affects and so on also constitute the emergence of practice wisdom (Lester 2014b). What is known and the 'knowers' of this knowledge co-emerge and shape each other through 'doing' to continually and collectively co-create practice (Keevers *et al.* 2012). This overcomes the orthodox theory–practice divide, and the privilege afforded to the first element in this binary relationship; theory is not something 'out there' but is always performed and materialised through practice in an indivisible manner, as discussed in the section below.

Plugging in: theory, research and practice

Given what has been presented in this book so far, it should come as no surprise that the proposal here is that theory, research and practice do not exist independently of each other but are thoroughly entangled. Research does not create knowledge in isolation, nor does theory under-pin practice, nor is practice a question of merely applying theory. Grand universal narratives, the truths sought by traditional approaches to research and propositional knowledge creation appear clean, neat and tidy, yet experienced practitioners amass practice knowledge that can 'work with the messiness, uncertainty, contingency and co-emergence of lived experience' (Russell, Lester and Smith 2017, p.4). As such, practice is always 'research' based, not in the traditional academic sense of this term, but rather in terms of developing practice-based methods that maintain curiosity and attentiveness to the rhythms, routines, atmospheres and habits that constitute the play environment and the ways they facilitate or constrain children's movements and the emergence of play: practice as re-searching. Theory, too, is valuable for its 'power to get in the way. Theory is needed to block the reproduction of banality and thereby, hopefully, open new possibilities for thinking and doing' (MacLure 2010, p.277). Theory, research and practice ('praxis') might be brought closer together, suggests MacLure, by employing Massumi's (2002) 'exemplary approach' where theory is generated through the use of examples:

> In this context 'exemplary' refers not to an ideal model to which concepts can be applied, but to working at the level of specificities and

singularities to note connections and generate new concepts. (Russell *et al.* 2017, p.4)

This book has followed this line of enquiry by using many practice examples that on their own are singular and cannot be taken to mean more than themselves, but which bring to the surface the details that matter, details which are occluded in grand headline findings and universal cause-and-effect claims. What is offered here is a generative rather than a reductive account of children's play, one that pays attention to what often passes by unnoticed, but with which practitioners are familiar. The mapping-as-process, more-than-representational cartographic approach introduced in the previous chapter is intended to support practitioners to begin to pay attention to these details and to co-produce more and more documentation that can then be held up to critical scrutiny to see what habitual practices and routines might exclude. The intention of critical cartography, therefore, is not to introduce new ideas per se, but to subject existing practice-concepts to scrutiny, to unpick and rework them and reassemble them into new forms; it is always experimental – what more can be done and how might we do it (Lester 2014b)?

This is where we turn to the second strand of response-ability. To do this, two sensitising concepts are proposed, not as theory to be applied, but as concepts to 'plug into' with practice in ways that can give rise to new practices and concepts. They have been shamelessly poached and reworked, and practitioners are urged to do the same, continually creating anew different assemblages of practice, documentation, concepts and other past, present and future desires and forces. 'Plugging in' is another concept from Deleuze and Guattari (1988) that works with the ongoing becomingness of life as an impersonal affair: theory and practice plug in to each other as a 'continuous process of making and unmaking' (Jackson and Mazzei 2013, p.262) to produce something new. The theory–practice assemblage, itself always in formation, of course has other players, each particular to each event, including practitioners, histories, external forces, material objects (the table you use, the cups of coffee) and so on. It is a way of 'thinking with' rather than 'applying' a separate, clean and sanitised theory to messy practices. From this perspective, practice does not neatly reflect theory (or vice versa); it might be seen more as a diffraction: plugging in leads to diffractive disturbances of patterns, and the interest lies in these differences.

Navigation and negotiation revisited: lessons from resilience scholarship

The first sensitising concept comes from resilience studies and has already been introduced in Chapter 3. It is revisited briefly here as it offers a useful thread for weaving through explorations of what adult response-ability might look like.

Drawing on a cross-cultural study, Ungar (2008) discusses resilience as *a process* that acknowledges difference, situatedness and the entanglements of the lives of children, families, communities and environments. He introduces the twin processual capacities of navigation and negotiation: the capacity of children to navigate towards health-giving resources and the capacity of communities to negotiate for such resources.

In the context of adult support for children's play, 'health-giving resources' can be read as the opportunity to take timespace for playing, interweaving it into everyday life. As we have seen from the many examples in this book, play will emerge whenever the conditions allow, and so 'negotiation', as a form of adult account-ability and response-ability, implies working towards creating conditions that will support the emergence of play. Sometimes negotiation may be explicit through formal forms of advocacy (for example, involvement in policy networks, campaigns or more subtle approaches through building relationships and making the case); often, however, it is through small disturbances of the dominant order, as in the example of *the chairs* above.

Amin's four registers of the good city

The second concept was used in the research into the Welsh Government's (2010) Play Sufficiency Duty (Lester and Russell 2013a, 2014b), and has since proved invaluable in developing a critical cartography of children's play with diverse settings. Reading case study data and policy materials from the first stage of implementation of the Play Sufficiency Duty revealed the complex and mobile assemblage of policy formulation and implementation in creating conditions for children's play. As Lester and Russell (2013a, p.78) comment in their concluding statements to the report:

> Children's play is emergent, unpredictable and opportunistic: it erupts whenever conditions allow. These conditions are, as has been emphasized throughout this report, a complex assemblage of material, symbolic, temporal, social, political and cultural factors... Given the messiness and complexity of the issue we do not assert single or absolute truth or causal explanations from the analysis...the Duty is enacted in contingent ways through the formation of relationships constituted from multiple components, each with a power to affect and be affected in the process.

In considering this challenging process, Lester and Russell (2013a) appropriate and reconfigure Amin's (2006) account of the constituents of the 'good city', a concept to be plugged in, worked on, and worked with, when considering data. It is used not to arrive at definitive statements but to offer a diffractive reading of research materials, to extend thoughts, knowledge and practices, and to develop 'multiple readings that are much richer than an easy sense produced by the reductive process of starting with coding and returning to experience' (Mazzei 2014, p.744).

Amin's (2006) account eschews a distant utopian vision of the good life in favour of pragmatic, everyday actions to unsettle inequitable patterns of spatial production through the formation of fragile alliances which collectively deterritorialise existing practices and conditions and guide them towards 'outcomes that benefit the more rather than the few' (Amin 2006, p.1012). It proposes four interrelated 'registers' that take account of and subject prevailing conditions to critical scrutiny: repair and maintenance, relatedness, rights and re-enchantment. The registers and the general terms of their application are briefly summarised here to illustrate the critical cartographic process and the ways in which concepts work with data and data with concepts in an intensive and extensive manner.

Repair and maintenance

Environments are held together by a complex web of vital maintenance routines and spatial practices that operate at different rates, intensities, speeds and scales simultaneously (Thrift 2008). These are necessary to make life liveable, to enable citizens to go about their everyday lives. They run largely in the background, unnoticed and unquestioned in a reliable, regular and predictable manner. They are systems which perpetuate molar assemblages and carry with them a whole series of injunctions, prohibitions, intimidations and exclusions that are targeted at the 'other', anything that threatens the stability of the system by being different, which in this particular case includes the not-yet-adult child.

Maintenance routines are habits that have material-discursive effects. One example is that of the narrative of risk as applied to children and young people's unsupervised presence in public space: they are either at risk and in need of protection or present a risk and are in need of correction. The traditional playground, and its modern iterations exemplified by the 'natural playground' movement (as discussed in Chapter 4), is an important part of routine spatial productions and is presented and accepted as the right place for children's play. Lester (2015c) uses the example of the skate park as a modern version of a playground targeted at specific users. The performance of skating (boarding and rolling) occupies many attractive public spaces – car parks, pavements, shopping precincts, public buildings – and 'just about any other paved space they could get their wheels on' (Howell 2008, p.476). Skaters use the urban fabric in unique ways and by doing so challenge capitalist norms and reassert use value over dominant exchange value (Borden 2001; Woolley, Hazelwood and Simkins 2011). The normative tendencies in urban governance (local authority officials, police, architects and planners, business people and others who may act collectively to produce and determine public space use) appear to conflict with the ways in which skateboarding is embodied and enacted in practice (Stratford 2002). While local bye-laws may be used to criminalise these forms of behaviour and specific design features can be introduced to prevent the performance of tricks and stunts, there is also recognition from urban managers that some provision should be made for this activity. But this is often not made in the spaces that skaters value (Howell 2008).

At a wider level of analysis, children's play is a heterogeneous form of behaviour that is expressed in diverse spatial contexts. While children will play anywhere, features in the contemporary environment have significant material-discursive effects on many children's ability to create timespace to play. There is no universal pattern and there are significant variations in children's spatial lives. While we must be wary of making reductive and normalising statements that diminish the creative, mundane ways in which children negotiate their way through their everyday environments,[1] it is generally accepted in research studies, policy discourse and popular media accounts that children are losing the freedom to explore and play in their immediate environments (Karsten and van Vliet 2006; Malone and Rudner 2011; Prezza and Pacilli 2007; Veitch *et al.* 2006).

Research, in general, would suggest that contributory factors for the apparent decline include changes in education policy and the de-zoning of school admission policies, perceived safety of the residential environment and 'stranger danger' fears (Carver *et al.* 2012; Gill 2007), and urban design/planning which privileges the movement (and parking) of cars and increases fears about children's safety (Malone and Rudner 2011). A critical cartography subjects the taken-for-granted, local, common-sense habits and routines of space to scrutiny to discern how they might include/exclude and takes action to counter exclusionary forces and practices. The intention of this register, following Amin (2006), is to revitalise and foster a sense of hope and generosity to overcome the sense of disenchantment that currently prevails in relation to children's playful presence in public and institutional space. These are small local experiments, for example rearranging routines at school lunchtimes to enable an equal distribution of timespace for playing, temporary street closures, and protecting local 'waste ground' from economic development (for further examples, see Lester and Russell 2013a, 2014b).

Relatedness

This register is concerned with the ways in which adults (parents, professionals and others) 'take care' of children's position as children and not only as adults-in-waiting within their communities. As such it addresses how understandings of childhood and play shape relationships, attitudes and actions at various interwoven scales of

---

1   See, for example, Morrow and Mayall (2009) and Myers (2012) for a counter perspective on the contemporary production of 'needy' children.

organisation. This is a central feature in terms of an ethico-political approach to supporting conditions for playing and counters the humanist/individual tendencies which position childhood on the progressive line of development, an organism cut off from the environment. It also critiques the ways in which difference is 'cut' along a range of performative axes (age, gender, disability, race, class and so on). These movements are not simply about mapping difference but about diffractively reading how difference is constituted and the ways in which these processes are embedded in power structures (Aitken 2010). It draws on alternative concepts including rhizomes, assemblages, lines, meshworks and intra-action, to present life as an emergent relational achievement that is always going on. It refutes the separateness of children while recognising their separability (Lee 2005) and their desire to sometimes be away from adults to co-create moments of playing.

This is not simply the preserve of children; numerous authors have highlighted the value of playing and creative activities for adults and children in building relational connections and obligations (Anderson 2006; Burkitt 2004; Duff 2009). Children are in(ter)dependent and the ways in which they negotiate their degrees of dependency are complex, contingent, entangled and always provisional. Spaces are not pre-figured and fixed but formed through 'a myriad of practices of negotiations and contestation…and intersecting trajectories' (Massey 2005, p.154). They are always open to becoming different through everyday heterogeneous encounters and movements that complicate notions of identity and difference (Duff 2009; Massey 2005). Attention to the conditions of relatedness highlights fluid everyday 'spacings' that open space to vibrancy, liveliness and disruption, calls attention to the possibilities they afford for more democratic processes through addressing rights of presence, and contests the facts of difference (Amin 2004).

Rights

Intimately connected to issues of relatedness and contrary to the dominant discourse of individual rights and entitlements, the approach taken here moves away from seeing children as individual rights bearers towards holding rights in common. The contemporary approach to children's rights, grounded on the notion of a universal childhood, presumes that separate rights are inherent to any being that falls into this category. Terms such as freedom, rationality, responsibilities and choice are presuppositions of a universal and abstract subject (Deleuze and Guattari 1994). The dominant discourse of human individuality positions bodies as isolated thus negating the movement of life as a process of continuous variation that occurs through dynamic negotiations and transformations in myriad encounters of bodies and things (Deleuze and Guattari 1988). By doing so, it creates a subject that needs to overcome childish desires and transcend their current heteronomous state and it establishes all-embracing conditions to steer children to this end. In this context, rights act as molar lines that seek to appropriate and dominate the desires of children and in the process also fix 'adults' to this plane of organisation; adults are expected to protect children being exploited by disruptive forces (Tarulli and Skott-Myhre 2006).

The argument developed in this book is that playing is a creative expression that reconfigures bodies, materials, relationships and so on to become different, not the same. The focus is on what bodies can do rather than on who they are or should become; rights are not externally administered but constituted through intra-active encounters, 'a positioning of rights as immanent potential...[concerned] with the process of situated, particularized, embodied rights *creation*' (Tarulli and Skott-Myhre 2006, p.193, author's italics).

This is not an anti-rights gesture but a preference for an ongoing relational, open-ended, and creative process of rights formation that is always situated and inventive in response to the prevailing conditions (Lester 2016b). Lines of flight, and their respective expressions and representations as moments of playing, are molecular forces which create a path between adult and child (as can be seen in the many examples offered throughout this book), undoing molar accounts of these identities, notably the power of adult expectations of children's behaviour. It is here that adult and child are becoming-minoritarian, abandoning molar distinctions to co-create conditions that enable the common desire of living beings to flourish.

Common-sense productions of space and spatial practices subjugate the identities of both children and adults through subtle and not so subtle institutional materials and symbols that pattern relationships in an unreflexive manner (Mozère 2006). Disciplinary power (Foucault 1991) produces a 'subject', a position that is always situated in diverse spaces and restrained or liberated by accounts of what it is to be a subject. Playing, as a process of de-subjectification, can transform humanist subject positions. Just as children may temporarily disturb order, adults can also overcome the constraints on their actions by more powerful others, contributing subversive acts to the disturbance of adult–child relationships and engaging in 'a performative politics of re-inscription' (Youdell and Armstrong 2011, p.2). The following interview with a playworker is another example of this process in action, drawn from Lester (2011b, p.11):

> The playworker works in an after-school club situated in a community centre, sharing space alongside a range of other community-based projects. The manager of the space has some very clear ideas about children and play, particularly around the idea of play-fighting and children's aggressive superhero/war play. This leads to the imposition of a zero-tolerance approach to these forms of play, reminiscent of Holland's (2003) analysis of approaches in Early Years Centres that reprimand children, when moving into these play behaviours, 'we don't play with guns here'. The playworkers, who are directly accountable to the manager yet at the same time sympathetic to children's desire to engage in these forms of play, have evolved a response that ignores play-fighting while the manager is away from the setting, but colludes with children in being aware when the manager is around and they adopt a much more secretive approach, which may include such things as using fingers as 'guns' and shooting each other behind the back of the manager, playing dead and even threatening to 'tell' the manager when this form of play emerges (both adults and children).

This minor and cautious engagement is concerned with the here and now to open cracks in molar productions of space and identity. It suggests that rights are enacted with adults who bear witness to and attempt to favour children's movements, becoming attentive to, and enchanted by, the possibilities in molecular events for becoming different and learning how to affect and be affected by them (Duff 2013; Jones 2008).

Re-enchantment

Amin's (2006) final register is adapted to consider the ways in which environments (private, institutional and public) may be made more open to children's playfulness by reawakening a sense of enchantment, a common theme that appears throughout this book. To be enchanted is to 'assent wholeheartedly to life' (Bennett 2001, p.159). That is not to deny the numerous challenges that life presents, but an attachment to wonder enables an ethical, generous response and holds off an overwhelming cynicism that is so prevalent in the clichés of neoliberalism, notably the mantras that 'there are no alternatives' and 'we are all in it together'. The exemplary accounts introduced throughout this discussion are minor affirmative moments of being enchanted with the world, a constant reminder that it is possible to become otherwise, to 'receive and provoke surprises' (Bennett 2001, p.163). The idea of initiating surprises coincides with an approach that seeks to open up space to disturbance, pursuing a line of 'what if...' to imaginatively disorder the world on behalf of others (Cloke and Jones 2005). What emerged from one Welsh local authority's detailed research into children's play movements and patterns as part of a response to the Play Sufficiency Duty (Lester and Russell 2013a) was the value children attributed to indeterminate or banal spaces. These are spaces that result from a temporary lack of planning and suspension of the driving economic and aesthetic forces that seek to eradicate friction and disorder, reduce complexity, and privilege the needs of adults and of the economy in public spaces.

However, it is a considerable challenge for adults with responsibility for everyday 'maintenance' routines (planners, architects and so on) and ethical acts of relatedness to consider the possibility of indeterminate spaces, where things are not fixed once and for all. Playing, as an assemblage of bodies and materials and their affects, produces a different form of reality, actualised from a virtual field that is beyond the aims and linearity of planning and design systems:

> Planners typically start with the actual, move into the pre-actual and then back into the actual. When they do this, the intention is not to explore becomings in their own right, but to explore the becomings that are likely to be actualized. Or, in other words, the focus of existing methods of plan making are always anchored around the actual realm. (Abrahams 2013, p.6)

While planning is inherently a highly speculative task, it is driven by economic and political forces that promote certain forms of desirable (producing and consuming) behaviours while restricting others (performative and disorderly). These forces act to control public and institutional space to serve particular interests and deny the idea of 'democratic publicness' (Paddison and Sharp 2007). When it comes to 'planning for play', designers always work backwards from the actual, most notably, the 'playground', and embellish this with other possibilities that fit this already existing template. As market forces, unleashed from regulation, increasingly dominate the shaping of the urban landscape, there is a need to consider a counter perspective that prioritises those dimensions of urban dynamics that contribute to the enrichment of life, a different form of governance that admits the right to the city for all citizens. For Lefebvre (1991), this includes the right to the co-production of the city, to meet and gather, to use space and objects according to desire rather than a unitary function, and to play (Lester 2014a).

It is here that attention switches from the provision of segregated space to the spatial-relational features in which playfulness may thrive. This resonates with Hillier's (2008, 2011; Hillier and Abrahams 2013) application of Deleuze's plane of immanence to planning theory and the challenge for planners to work with the virtual realm and to consider 'what might be' without becoming caught up in how things might be actualised in practice. The environments that children and adults move through are dynamic and always open to more; as Massey (2005) reminds us, spaces are always relational. The encounters and entangled connections between humans and non-humans generate an affective atmosphere, sometimes vibrant and playful while at other times scary and threatening. These positions are not fixed and immutable. As Lester and Russell (2013a, p.77) assert:

> Re-enchantment is an experimental approach; it eschews end-states and outcomes and works with things in the making, uncertainty, surprise and astonishment – the very qualities that distinguish playing. This, according to Healy (2004 p.89), leads to a consideration of 'the role of governance in relation to the generation of events, objects and situations which encourage people to feel wonder and awe, enjoyment and pleasure'. It is an approach that moves away from old ways of

thinking to focus on the dynamics of spatial interactions (as in leopard print wellies) with matching dynamic sensibility and sensitivity that switches attention from providing play to consider the conditions under which playfulness thrives.

The research studies featured in this book highlight a range of spatial interventions designed to open up space for playing by the provision of a number of experimental 'playful prompts' and 'what if…' experiments, for example marking a hopscotch grid in a main gallery or unrolling a length of kitchen roll along the middle of a room at a museum (Lester, Strachan and Derry 2014), putting a line in the after-school club (Lester 2016a) or moving chairs at the playground (Lester, Fitzpatrick and Russell 2014). These actions were instigated in an experimental fashion, not with any expectations of solving identified problems or providing specific play experiences, but to see what might happen, what more was possible.

As may be evident from this brief overview, Amin's (2006) registers are inextricably connected, mutually influential and cross-cutting. Thus, 'no-ball games signs, road arrangements, work patterns, media influence, institutional timetables, layout and practices, adult attitudes and so on, collectively structure the rhythms and patterns of children's spatial lives' (Lester and Russell 2013a, pp.42–43). And of course, this patterning is dynamic, contingent and contextual. As the *leopard skin wellies* story introduced in Chapter 6 illustrates, children are very good at using favourable conditions from the materials at hand to navigate and negotiate their way through their everyday environments. These movements are not readily accounted for by technical research processes alone (counting the amount of greenspace, measuring children's ranging behaviours, qualitative judgements about playgrounds and so on) and children's rich situated knowledge is rarely captured in common forms of consultation. A critical cartography and associated methodologies attempt to work with the messiness of everyday entanglements to map local ways in which children get on with their daily lives. These form the basis for the ongoing and open formation of 'collective wisdom' (Lester and Russell 2013a) as the foundation for adult response-ability to enact 'affective disruptions' (Aitken 2010) that bring about more equitable forms of spatial justice for children and adults alike.

Planning for play

Given all that we have covered to date, the very idea of planning for play is questionable from a range of different perspectives. Dominant understandings of play tend to fix this phenomenon as a special activity that requires separate time, space and things. But what has been proposed here is that playing cannot be reduced to a 'thing' but is always contingent and eventful, a singular expression that is situated at a particular moment in a certain style and with a force that we might as adults refer to as 'play'.

What may be apparent from the analysis to date is that 'providing play' is something more than designating spaces and times as play spaces. Play is not a subsidiary and separate process set apart from the real world; and given its intimate connection with the full range of everyday activities and spaces, it needs to be considered as an integral feature of all space. As Stevens (2007) highlights, leaving room for play in the midst of everyday spaces can promote a much wider range of playful activity than providing 'free' space in isolation.

Given the everyday, spontaneous nature of the formation of playful moments, accounting for play in causal terms is obviously not possible or desirable. It should also be clear that given the nature of 'playing' as discussed here, there can be no template or blueprint to follow. Stevens (2007, p.197) acknowledges that 'playful acts often pay little heed to the instrumental concerns which urban designers typically aim to serve, such as comfort, safety and legibility'. Playing, as an assemblage of bodies and materials with its own unique force and flow to establish a relational spacetime that is different, inevitably challenges both the aims and linearity of planning and design systems that are historically driven by economic and political acts aimed at promoting certain forms of desirable behaviours while restricting others. Institutions, materials, practices, symbols and policies all combine to present a picture of childhood as a 'regime of truth' (Foucault 1980) which assumes a naturalness, order and common sense. Such a plane does not operate by coercion, but power becomes woven into the very fabric of everyday lives as a *dispositif.*

In the design of unsupervised play spaces, inevitably the focus is on material content, with particular physical design of spaces expected to produce specific forms of playing. Technical artefacts such as planning diagrams, maps, the naming and categorising of equipment or zones in catalogues become 'inscription' devices (Latour and Woolgar 1986). What is essentially a subjective conceptualisation becomes fixed and named and thus given authority through these devices, which Rose (1999, p.37) describes as 'little machine[s] for producing conviction in others'. Playgrounds have assumed the status of common sense; they are spaces that meet children's play needs and are the rightful place for children to be; children and young people playing elsewhere in the public realm may be seen as being 'out of place', as evidenced through the restriction of in(ter)dependent mobility and the use of age-based curfews, 'mosquito' devices and other exclusion techniques (Beunderman, Hannon and Bradwell 2007; Lee and Motzkau 2011).

At a wider level of analysis, the planning profession is bound up in a history of professional expertise, knowledge, practices, edicts and regulations that shape plans as rational and controlled accounts. It is, following Lefebvre (1991), inherently ideological, a conceived production of space that represents specific dominant beliefs and value systems that in turn shape planning objectives, goals and ultimately 'plans' that define how we use space. Gunder (2010) situates planning ideology in a neoliberal context in which market forces are supposed to produce a better version of society than other ideologies, especially a state-directed form. Thus, planning is not neutral. Gunder highlights the rise of collaborative planning (the notion that stakeholders should be engaged in planning and development processes) not as a counter to neoliberal ideology, but as a further capturing of people into an uncritical commitment to planning and development processes; children are brought into adult participation arenas to support predetermined processes and agendas.

Spaces are always sites of negotiated and contested meanings and as such they will often be conflictual (Hillier 2005). Playful use of public space offers a reminder that space cannot be fully fixed and presents a wider, more democratic use of the public realm that connects with the right to the city expressed by Lefebvre (1996). It also conjures up new uses that disrupt existing conventions and form new relationships, which in turn are subject to continuous reformation. Adapting from Amin (2004), play spaces are temporary placements of ever-moving materials. Of course, this is simply not confined to playing, as all spaces are brought about by 'dwelling, affinity, immanence, relationality, multiplicity and performativity' (Amin 2004, p.34). Yet as Hillier (2005, p.273) comments:

> As planning theorists and practitioners we seem to have had a pervasive commitment to an ontology of being which privileges end-states and outcomes, rather than an ontology of becoming which emphasizes movement, process and emergence.

Healy (2004), in a general discussion about the challenges of governance in a time of considerable economic challenge and change, highlights the dominant rhetoric of the importance of creativity and innovation for growth. At one level, this is an argument for releasing market forces from the straightjacket of regulation so that creative industries can flourish (or fail). Market processes are supposedly driven by the creative responses to the behaviour of consumers, as well as seeking to influence change in consumer habits, for the purpose of making profits. But Healy introduces another meaning to consider the dimensions of urban dynamics that counters pure economic accounts of innovation. A broader approach to creativity of cultural life establishes a different emphasis, namely that of enriching human life. It is accompanied by placing value on the aesthetic of urban life as a challenge to the over-emphasis on material wealth. This dimension for Healy (2004, p.89) 'leads to a consideration of the role of governance in relation to the generation of events, objects and situations, which encourage people to feel wonder and awe, enjoyment and pleasure'. The complexity of spatial flows, forces and arrangements that constitute urban life suggests a different form of governance which allows for experiments rather than an emphasis on precise outputs and outcomes.

Hillier (2005, p.274) reinforces this point, stating that there is a need to move away from old ways of thinking to focus on the dynamics of arenas of interaction, and that new approaches demand 'a dynamic sensibility which recognises the complex interrelation between place qualities and multiple space-time relational dynamics rather than relapsing into a focus on traditional analyses of, e.g., territorially contained housing markets, labour markets and land use and transport interactions'. And one might add to this list the traditional sites developed for children's play.

In reconfiguring the theoretical foundations of planning, Hillier (2005, p.276) turns to non-representational theory and associated philosophical underpinnings: 'from Thrift I take the conceptualisation of planning as magic; a creative activity in which multiples of different elements and forces – physical, psychical and verbal – perform together'. Hillier also draws on actor network theory and the geo-philosophical work of Deleuze and Guattari to arrive at an approach to planning that allows for the unexpected to come into play and 'things not to quite work out as expected' (Hillier 2005, p.278). This suggests that planning is an experimental process, where problems are not solved once and for all but are rather constantly recast, reformulated in new perspectives. This leads to a reformation of strategic planning as:

- the investigation of 'virtualities' unseen in the present

- the experimentation with what may yet happen

- the temporary inquiry into what at a given time and place we might yet think or do.

Of course, the idea of planning as 'experimental' does not sit comfortably in the current political and economic climate. However, it does offer up the possibility of making new connections and possibilities for spatial productions, thereby identifying key practices and underpinning social, economic and political structures which constitute the formation of assemblages. This would identify forces that seek to include the neglected, violated and dispossessed while at the same time work to counter exclusionary aspects of spatial practice. At a practice level, it finds expression in Stevens' (2007) conclusions from his analysis of play in the public realm. Stevens suggests that in considering the playfulness of space attention needs to be given to:

- the function of space: the ways in which space does and does not support playful use

- publicness: freedom to access space

- performance: opportunity to act in front of others in personally meaningful ways

- the ways in which the features of urban structures and their organisation as urban space give rise to playful possibility.

Attention switches from providing play to the conditions under which playfulness may thrive. This is an important distinction as it pays attention to more general conditions under which social, affective and material resources may facilitate the expression of children's playful desires, what may be referred to as 'play-enabling spaces' or the 'playful feel of space'.

Cushions and childbirth: tuning in

The following example is based on an observation of children's play in an after-school club. My role was 'independent assessor' as part of a quality assurance scheme for playwork:

> The playworkers from the club were seated in a corner of the main indoor play space, appearing to chat with each other, but totally 'tuned in' to what was happening around them, what Hughes (2001) refers to as being in an 'indifferent' mode. I joined the group, with my back half turned to the room (and children's play). I was aware of a game that emerged with a group of children making their way around the edges of the room without touching the ground. They had balanced precariously across the top of a bookshelf and appeared to reach a point where they could not progress. One of the children caught the eye of a playworker, who appeared to 'instinctively' know what was happening and picked up a cushion and threw it at the child without saying a word. Following this act, the playworker returned their attention to the other playworkers. The child caught the cushion and used it as a stepping-stone to be able to progress with their journey around the perimeter. At the same time, another group of children (girls aged about 8–9 years) were making a den using tables, chairs, blankets and sheets. After completion, the girls entered the den and shortly afterwards a girl screamed at the top of her voice. My attention was immediately drawn to this and I prepared to move to the space of the den. The playworkers remained seated and following the scream the girl shouted out, 'My waters have broken!' This was followed by another girl's screams and commentary 'Mine have too'. The playworkers had noticed that prior to entering the den, the girls had collected dolls and soft toys and placed them up their dresses/sweaters and were playing at maternity wards.

What happened here was children's play – non-linear and emergent behaviours that were adaptive to each other and the affordances of the environment. The playworker responses adopted a position of being with while at the same time being apart from the children. These shared moments can be found in everyday relational processes between children and with adults.

Circle time

Another significant example is introduced at this stage to illustrate this point, taken from Maritta Hannikainen's (2001) research into adult–child playful actions and ways of being and getting on together in a kindergarten in Finland. The observations from this study, and subsequent conversations with Maritta at the International Council for Children's Play conference in Estonia (2012), have been significant in shaping my thinking and doing, and one specific extract is presented here.

Kindergarten (along with schools, healthcare settings, playgrounds and so on) are segmented spaces aligned to a plane of organisation. They are abstract and conceived productions (Lefebvre 1991), planned and designed to reflect the dominant values attributed to education and articulated in policy, curricula, standards and inspection regimes. The value attributed to this timespace correlates with the overall intention of education, the purpose of childhood and, by inference, adulthood (Kraftl 2006). Their physical design reflects the primary function of space for education and learning (terms which in themselves tend to become conflated), and there are constant reminders to children about their place within the institution through teaching practices, design of furniture, seating arrangements, educational symbols and materials, codes, and protocols for behaviour which collectively act on children's mobility and agency (Leander, Phillips and Taylor 2010; Lester 2011a). The school space is produced as a site that privileges adult status and power and this is communicated in everyday spatial practices and routines (Devine 2002). Yet there always remains the possibility of children's and adults' desires reconfiguring dominant accounts, as illustrated by the following observation of circle time (Hannikainen 2001, p.127), a fairly mundane routine that generally reinforces power relations: the teacher sits on a chair with children sitting on the floor around this. On this occasion, the normal pattern was disturbed by an injection of nonsense:

> The kindergarten teacher, Sara, begins the roll call: 'Magnus?'

Magnus replies: 'Yes, [here].'

Sara: 'Peter?'

Peter: 'No, [not here], I am down inside Magnus.'

Peter, Magnus, Tine, Natalia and several other children nearly split their sides laughing. Peter, too, smiles at his success.

Sara asks, with a twinkle: 'Are you down inside Magnus?'

Peter asks: 'Yes, isn't that a rather silly thing to say?'

Sara: 'Frankly, yes.'

When the roll call reaches Katrine, she says that she, too, is down inside Magnus. The children laugh.

Sara points out in a surprised voice: 'Now there are two children down inside Magnus.'

Nadja: 'Then he must give birth.'

Tine: 'Two in his belly, no, two in his ears (the other children laugh)... no, two in his nose (all the children giggle and laugh)...no, two in his little peter (meaning: penis)...'

Peter continues: 'No, two in his bum.'

Peter and Magnus laugh so much that they almost fall off their chairs.

This is an act of co-creation: the teacher and children's shared desire to affect and be affected initiates molecular mo(ve)ments that temporarily hold off the mundane routine of registration. For this brief period, a normalising account of being teacher and pupil is suspended and reworked and by doing so the space (composed from bodies, materials, imaginations and so on) is livelier, 'allowing for an intensity of becoming different while creating the extensive possibility that things can go on becoming different' (Lester 2013b, p.33). 'I am down inside...' is a collusion or individuation productive of a playful haecceity ('thisness'), a non-personal block of spacetime with a different speed or rhythm (longitude) from established patterns and different affects (latitude) as laughter ripples around the circle with increasing intensity. This act of deterritorialisation is almost seamlessly reterritorialised as circle time comes to order, but it is never the same – always repetition with difference – as there is a greater possibility for more of these shared moments to emerge in daily habits and practices, as Hannikainen's study illustrates.

These irruptive events allow for a world in which new relations and assemblages are always possible, what Hardt and Negri (2009) refer to as 'biopower from below'. This acknowledges that freedom – taken here as an expression of Deleuze and Guattari's 'plane of immanence' – is always a precursor to power and forms of resistance to dominant forces are 'simply the effort to further, expand and strengthen that freedom' (Hardt and Negri 2009, p.82). Deleuzian excess proposes that affective life must always exceed attempts to make it into an object-target for bio-power and state practices.

Summary: enchantment and practice account-ability and response-ability

This chapter has built on the concepts introduced throughout the book to consider adult response-abilities in supporting children's right to play. Rather than seeking to plan and predict, practice is concerned with reading and sensing the feel of the environment, its moods and atmosphere. Sensing may be the most expansive aspect of practice, yet it is generally overlooked in the drive for objectivity and meeting predetermined outcomes. In terms of children's play, it requires paying attention to moments of uncertainty, ambiguity and indeterminacy and their affects, 'a sense of the "tone" of any situation, the play of singularity, which *might* (and only might) produce new virtualisations' (Thrift 2004, p.85). It marks a state of enchantment.

Given the indeterminate nature of playing, there is no blueprint for professional practice; each moment of playing is a singular example crafted from the prevailing circumstances of everyday life. Rather than fix and explain this relational messiness by drawing on pre-established concepts that prise things apart, practice is concerned with accounting for the ways in which bodies, materials and so on produce distinctive formations marked by their own rhythms and atmosphere. This implies being attentive to the particularities of movements and sensations of playful moments and to experiment with methods that can discern these qualities rather than over-code them with ideas from outside the example. This form of practice accountability also determines adult response-ability, the ability to develop a repertoire of practices that maintain favourable conditions in which play and life can flourish. One last example is introduced here to illustrate further what paying attention to mundane moments might look like in practice.

Can I put you in the bin?

Practice is concerned with everyday relationships as the following example reveals. In conversation with a playworker in a residential setting, a discussion took place about the apparently trivial and mundane stuff that happened in the previous session. The playworker struggled to respond, falling back on describing play activities that took place and when gently pushed to go beyond this, a smile played over her face and she recalled a moment when she was sitting alongside a child, both silent, when the playworker turned to the child and said, 'Can I put you in the bin?' The child turned and smiled at the playworker and moved closer before silence returned.

The playworker acknowledged that she wasn't fully aware of where this question came from, other than it 'felt right at the time'. Such apparently mundane moments matter; they are singular instances that generate a refrain of difference in the making; the playworker is not a social worker, teacher, parent or other adult, the child is not a 'problem'. It is a shared moment of becoming together and makes a minor contribution to maintaining a play territory. But they largely escape explicit articulation and become lost in externally derived technical accounting systems.

Given that a constellation of such moments constitutes a playful atmosphere, critical attention needs to be paid to these everyday rhythms. It requires a set of practice techniques that hold off forces of individualisation, counter the privilege afforded to representation and defer the imposition of interpretations and meanings for as long as possible. Such techniques may be presented as cartographic approaches that pay attention to mapping the unpredictable, indeterminate and multi-sensory intra-actions, the spaces of in-between, and the refrain of the environment. They do not seek to represent something that already exists but are drawn towards movements and sensations; they are concerned with wayfaring as a process of continual movement rather than destination-focused tracings (Ingold 2011a).

This approach is further elaborated in the mapping and diagram-making experiments developed with playworkers at an adventure playground (Lester, Fitzpatrick and Russell 2014) that foregrounded movement through the environment to reveal hitherto unnoticed patterns, rhythms and habits. The diagrams generated from increasing attentiveness to everyday arrangements of bodies and things are forms of composition which draw expressive lines of movement that are imbued with sensations and entangled with all sorts of matter; they are processual rather than products. When these diagrams are overlaid they begin to reveal complex patterns and affects that continually and intra-actively constitute a playground territory that has a degree of consistency (a predominantly playful feel) but not in any continuous manner; there is no beginning or end to these movements, they form a refrain with habits and routines that always contain the potential for moving otherwise.

Adult practice, professional or otherwise, that seeks to support children's right to play as a question of spatial justice is an ongoing process of developing the ability to pay attention to mundane mo(ve)-ments of playfulness that can emerge from whatever is to hand and working to co-create conditions that leave space open for more of such mo(ve)ments. Largely, children are able to navigate and negotiate through adult control of time and space to find such possibilities; adult account-ability and response-ability lie in recognising this and, where necessary, negotiating (explicitly or through small 'what if...' experiments) for space to be open to virtualities and not only the actual. Amin's (2006) four registers of repair and maintenance, relatedness, rights and re-enchantment offer helpful sensitising concepts to work with in this endeavour.

CHAPTER 8

An Ending that is Not an Ending

Another line of becoming

At this stage of writing a book, the expectation is that everything is brought together into a neat conclusion and recommendations are made for the future. In line with the general tenor of this piece, this will be resisted as far as possible. The focus on processes (*how*) rather than product (the *what* and *why* of playing), and the accompanying concepts and practices developed in this account hold off the idea of reflection and reflexivity which would seek to subject and judge experiences to an ideal image of thought and maintain a boundary between an individual subject and an external object. Life goes on through a process of diffraction – disturbances and agitations that keep life moving. This book is an account that attempts to illuminate differences as they emerge in everyday encounters and to remain faithful to these singular examples as far as possible. It is beset by limitations of representation but does not dwell on these; it continues to experiment with ways of getting out of oneself and to open up an ontological and epistemological and ethical space of encounter.

This is not an end but another line of becoming; there is much more to say and do. I have wrestled with this narrative alongside writing for different audiences over a considerable period of time. Concepts coalesce, rub up against each other and diverge in all kinds of unrestrained ways. They compose a plateau where there is no origin or destination, just intensive movements that generate more concepts and lines of enquiry that demand further attention. However, within the limitations of this form of writing there has to be a product. But it should be reiterated, narrative is a process rather than an end state.

Following Deleuzian lines of enquiry, the question is not what playing means but how does it work and how might it be worked differently. Common-sense valorisation of play and associated material-discursive effects would situate it to certain times and places, and structure and organise progressive activities in which choices come already produced, weigh(t)ed, packaged and promoted to ensure that individuals make the right choices. It is just one way in which life is cut apart to meet the demands of capitalist processes of consumption and production; a closed-circuit where forces of production create things to consume and consumption creates ideas of what needs to be produced (Ingold 2011a). On this plane of organisation, value is ascribed to ways of being that accumulate capital (social, cultural, economic); playing nicely is a prime cliché of this movement, and not to do so is a sign of deviancy.

Children's positioning as largely needy, immature and separate from adult worlds operates to the detriment of children and adults alike. It places notions of children's rights in a dominant protectionist mode, which in turn reinforces children's subordinate status. New public management systems, with accompanying quality standards, outcome measures, tight performance management, pseudo-scientific impact assessments and cost–benefit analyses are just some examples of the technology of government, designed to maintain a steady course to some distant and universal utopian vision and constrain alternative ways of seeing and being in the world. At a time when the discourse of austerity (and all that this implies) permeates social and economic policy, and 'hope' seems to be fading, it is timely to remember the ways in which everyday encounters and clandestine acts can permeate and reinvigorate life. Deleuze's philosophy presents life as both finite and infinite; a single life is temporary and frail (Bennett 2001) and life is always going on. Bodies are not self-contained but only defined by a longitude and latitude. The lines of movement presented in this account reposition a right to play (Article 31) as an intra-active indivisible process productive of particular ways of being; indeed, it may be rewritten as an all embracing ethico-political 'collective right to desire', a statement of play's micro-revolutionary possibilities to bring more to life.

Retracing lines

The main thrust of this account is that life is sustained and sustains itself through play; it is a process of continuous, indeterminate variation to see what more can be done. The main themes that extend from Deleuze into a materialist onto-epistemology overcome the sterile and constraining dualisms of nature/culture, structure/agency, adult/child and so on to present a world that is always being made anew through intra-active assemblages of animate and inanimate material that affect and are affected in the formations they compose. Assemblages are always contingent and emergent; life does not follow a pre-given script or line of development. This alternative presents life as a meshwork of lines, a tangle of relationships and wandering threads that cut through the segmented line of a plane of organisation; they are supple lines 'where the child produces a loop, finds something, claps his hands, hums a ritornello, retraces his steps' (Deleuze and Parnet 2002, p.128).

Playing, following the concepts that I have developed here, is a singular process of individuation, intensive movements and lines of flight that cross thresholds to produce blocks of play spacetime that deterritorialise the given world. Dephasings initiate a temporary coherence or collusion of forces that simply enlivens life. Playing unfolds from the middle, creating a *milieu* of its own that allows for experimentation with affirmative affective experience; it always contains within it the possibility for further transformation – 'What if…', 'What happens if you fall off', 'What counts…'? Children's ordinary minor acts of disturbance actualise a different form of ordering, an unexceptional yet potentially magical form of hope (Lester 2010). They are an expression of belief, not for some out-of-reach utopian ideal, but an everyday form of hopefulness that denotes life can go on. They are reminders that people (adults and children) can change practices, conditions and categorical understandings, however modest the scale (McCormack 2013).

Plugging in again (and again and…)

Writing this account (and the publications cited in it) has been a highly challenging yet productive process. Productive in this sense is not the repetition of a fixed set of pre-existing concepts and practices but a reconfiguration of previously disconnected ideas to generate something new. It started with a desire to think differently about play and has pursued intensive lines that flow from Deleuzian ontology and extend to become entangled with multiple threads drawn from (or shamelessly poached from, after Massumi 2002) diverse disciplinary perspectives. It adds more to current thinking and practices that are largely concerned with the 'is' of playing by cutting play otherwise to see what more might be possible. In doing so, it brings focus to the ontological processes by which moments of play might emerge. As with the process of play itself, it is involved with loosening the rigid segments that would seek to fix adults and children into certain positions to produce other possibilities. But of course, the concepts and practices presented in this account also perform a cut in the world. The intention here is to present an onto-ethico-epistemological manoeuvre (Barad 2007) that has been, and will continue to be, performed in a variety of practice contexts to overcome the forces of disenchantment which prevail in adult anxieties and concerns over children's futures. It is ultimately, after May (2005), a desire to change the world by celebrating the playfulness of life. This is not to set to one side the considerable inequalities and abuses that children face across the globe but to confront and redress these by bringing to the foreground issues of spatial justice and to work towards a more equitable distribution of timespace for playing and all the potentialities this may actualise for creating the world differently.

As noted in Chapter 7, the concepts that have emerged from these writings (recognising that they are not fixed but always intra-actively produced) have been set to work in a variety of contexts. This is not a revolutionary position that seeks to overthrow but a continuous process of plugging in – using whatever formations are at hand to reconfigure arrangements to reform anew. As illustrated throughout the book, new assemblages reshape across multi-scalar locations. For example, the working paper produced for the International Play Association (Lester and Russell 2010a) becomes entangled in UNCRC General Comment 17 on children's right to play, which plugs into the Welsh Government's Play Sufficiency Duty, which plugs into the production of *Leopard Skin Wellies* (Lester and Russell 2013a), which, in turn, plugs into a series of workshops with a Welsh local authority in which new formations are enacted through a series of playful interventions in public space and so on.

Similar movements are evident in the small-scale research projects with 'institutional spaces' (museums, adventure playgrounds, schools, playwork settings) and drawn on in this book as examples of ways in which concepts become entangled with practice to enliven space. Alongside this, the Master's in Professional Studies in Children's Play at the University of Gloucestershire has offered a wonderful testing ground for working with practitioners to consider what more might be done with play and adult response-ability; some of the 'outcomes' from this process are featured in the edition of practice-based research studies (Russell *et al.* 2017).

The process of plugging in establishes extensive connections, and many of the enmeshed strands of practice developed during the production of this piece will continue to be explored in future projects (notably with playwork settings, cultural institutions and continuing support for the implementation of the Play Sufficiency Duty in Wales). As with playing, this is not the pursuit of a deliberative strategic plan but taking advantage of opportunistic encounters to form coalitions that have a collective desire to affect and be affected to produce conditions that enable life to flourish. Writing is not separate from this process but is also a desire to add more to the mix; it is here that the value of the singular example comes to the fore as it draws attention to processes of life on the move to co-create moments of enchantment with the world.

Entanglements of writings, creating concepts, practices, encounters, materials and everything else that is presented here are for the most part micro-political acts to form alliances that can make new connections and animate generous response-abilities, that is, the ability to respond to our part in entanglements with the 'other' that is never apart from and always more than human. At the heart of this is an ethic concerned with the ways in which adults account for and take care of the conditions in which children can play, and by doing so create space for challenging the dominant assumptions and practices of inequitable social and spatial production by imagining and actualising other virtualities.

Moments and movements of hope

Despite the recovery of a more vitalistic outlook in attitudes towards physical and mental well-being, the main underlying perception of our modern, urban-industrial society remains mechanistic and soulless. Over the years, the dominant western worldview has become devitalised and devalued, especially in politics and economics. Let's suppose things had developed in a more balanced, Bergsonian way over the 60 years or more since his death: reason *and* intuition, intellect *and* imagination, matter *and* mind, the physical *and* the spiritual. Perhaps we would have learned from this a greater respect for all expressions of the life force, including our own species.

The story told here is one of enchantment: children's play, with its 'infectious vibrations and energetic morphing' (Bennett 2001, p.168) is evidence of an attachment to life. It is a belief that the 'not-yet' (Bloch 1995) can be actualised and expressed through joyful instants of nonsense and disturbance. They are moments of wondering and wandering that resist the pressure of conformity by producing contemporaneous possibilities or compossibilities (after Deleuze 1993). And for adults, who all were once children, playing also retains and restores a sense of enchantment, a reminder that life continues to surprise, delight and mystify. It marks a state of openness to the fragile and disturbing moments encountered in everyday experience. While disenchantment tales promote a sense of vulnerability, sadness and anger, playing reminds that things can be different by generating 'feelings of being connected in an affirmative way to existence…it is good to be alive' (Bennett 2001, p.156). Enchantment is a sensibility which can be cultivated by pausing and witnessing the apparently mundane movements of children and things. To take advantage of this movement requires rethinking and reconfiguring our position in the world and fostering relationships with other bodies and materials to create new conditions for working with the messiness of singular events.

Deleuze and Guattari's (1994, p.1) opening to their final joint publication asks, 'What is it I have been doing all my life?' My personal response would be quite simply 'playing', which may suggest a somewhat frivolous and trivial use of spacetime. I hope this book has convinced otherwise. A playful refrain persists over time, driven by a desire to explore the possibilities found in the here and now of existence, an 'ongoing practice of being open and alive to each meeting, to each intra-action, so that we might use our ability to respond, our responsibility, to help awaken, to breathe life into every new possibility for living justly' (Barad 2007, p.x).

What if…

References

Abrahams, G. (2013) 'Introduction.' In J. Hillier and G. Abrahams (2013) *Deleuze and Guattari for Planners: Jean Hillier in Conversation with Gareth Abrahams.* Groningen: Aesop Young Academics.

Aitken, S. (2001) *Geographies of Young People.* London: Routledge.

Aitken, S. (2010) 'Throwntogetherness: Encounters with Difference and Diversity.' In D. DeLyser, L. McDowell, S. Herbert, S. Aitken and M. Crang (eds) *The Sage Handbook of Qualitative Geography.* London: Sage.

Aitken, S. and Plows, V. (2010) 'Overturning assumptions about young people, border spaces and revolutions.' *Children's Geographies,* 8, 4, 327–333.

Alaimo, S. (2010) *Bodily Natures.* Bloomington: Indiana University Press.

Alexander, S., Frohlich, K. and Fusco, C. (2014) 'Active play may be lots of fun, but it's certainly not frivolous: The emergence of active play as a health practice in Canadian public health.' *Sociology of Health and Illness,* 36, 8, 1188–1204.

Allen, M. (1968) *Planning for Play.* London: Thames and Hudson.

Amin, A. (2004) 'Regions unbound: Towards a new politics of place.' *Geografiska Annaler,* 86, 1, 33–44.

Amin, A. (2006) 'The good city.' *Urban Studies,* 43, 5/6, 1009–1023.

Amin, A. and Thrift, N. (2013) *Arts of the Political.* Durham, NC: Duke University Press.

Anderson, B. (2006) 'Becoming and being hopeful: Towards a theory of affect.' *Environment and Planning D,* 24, 5, 733–752.

Anderson, B. (2012) 'Affect and biopower: Towards a politics of life.' *Transactions of the Institute of British Geographers,* 37, 28–43.

Ansell, N. (2009) 'Childhood and the politics of scale: Descaling children's geographies.' *Progress in Human Geography,* 33(2), 190–209.

Banerjee, B. and Blaise, M. (2013) 'There's something in the air: Becoming-with research practices.' *Cultural Studies ↔ Critical Methodologies,* 13, 4, 240–245.

Barad, K. (2007) *Meeting the Universe Halfway*. Durham, NC: Duke University Press.

Barad, K. (2011) 'Nature's queer performativity.' *Qui Parle*, 19, 2, 121–158.

Barad, K. (2012) 'Matter Feels, Converses, Suffers, Desires, Yearns and Remembers.' Interview with Karen Barad. In R. Dolphijn and I. van der Tuin (eds) *New Materialism: Interviews and Cartographies*. Ann Arbor, MI: Open Humanities Press.

Bednar, R. (2011) 'Materialising memory: The public lives of roadside crash shrines.' *Memory Connection*, 1, 1, 17–33.

Benjamin, W. (1978) *Reflections: Essays, Aphorisms, Autobiographical Writings*. New York, NY: Harcourt Brace Jovanovich.

Benjamin, W. (1999) *The Arcades Project* (trans. H. Eiland and K. McLaughlin). Cambridge, MA: Belknap Press.

Bennett, J. (2001) *The Enchantment of Modern Life*. Princeton, NJ: Princeton University Press.

Bennett, J. (2004) 'The force of things: Steps toward an ecology of matter.' *Political Theory*, 32, 3, 347–372.

Bennett, J. (2010) *Vibrant Matter: A Political Ecology of Things*. Durham, NC: Duke University Press.

Beunderman, J., Hannon, C. and Bradwell, P. (2007) *Seen and Heard: Reclaiming the Public Realm with Children and Young People*. London: Demos.

Blaise, M. (2013) 'Activating Micropolitical Practices in the Early Years: (Re)assembling Bodies and Participant Observations.' In R. Coleman and J. Ringrose (eds) *Deleuze and Research Methodologies*. Edinburgh: Edinburgh University Press.

Bloch, E. (1995) *The Principle of Hope*. Cambridge, MA: MIT Press.

Bonta, M. and Protevi, J. (2004) *Deleuze and Geophilosophy: A Guide and Glossary*. Edinburgh: Edinburgh University Press.

Borden, I. (2001) *Skateboarding, Space and the City: Architecture and the Body*. Oxford: Berg.

Borges, J.L. (1999) 'Happiness.' In A. Coleman (ed.) *Jorge Luis Borges: Selected Poems*. New York, NY: Penguin.

Borgnon, L. (2007) 'Conceptions of the self in early childhood: Territorialising identities.' *Educational Philosophy and Theory*, 39, 3, 264–274.

Bradshaw, J. (2016) (ed.) *The Well-Being of Children in the UK*. Bristol: Policy Press.

Braidotti, R. (2006) 'The Ethics of Becoming-Imperceptible.' In C. Boundas (ed.) *Deleuze and Philosophy*. Edinburgh: Edinburgh University Press.

Braidotti, R. (2012) 'Nomadic Ethics.' In D. Smith and H. Somers-Hall (eds) *The Cambridge Companion to Deleuze*. Cambridge: Cambridge University Press.

Braidotti, R. (2013) *Posthuman*. Cambridge: Polity Press.

Brenner, N., Peck, J. and Theodore, N. (2010) 'After neoliberalization?' *Globalizations*, 7, 3, 327–345.

Brewer, T. (2012) 'Rousseau plays outside in Norway: A personal reflection on how Norwegian outdoor kindergartens employ Rousseauian pedagogical methods of play.' *International Journal of Play*, 1, 3, 231–241.

Brown, W. (2006) 'American Nightmare: Neoliberalism, neoconservatism, and de-democratization.' *Political Theory*, 34, 6, 690–714.

Bundy, A.C., Luckett, T., Tranter, P.J., Naughton, G.A. *et al.* (2009) 'The Risk is that there is "No Risk": A simple, innovative intervention to increase children's activity levels.' *International Journal of Early Years Education*, 17, 1, 33–45.

Burghardt, G. (2005) *The Genesis of Animal Play: Testing the Limits.* Cambridge, MA: MIT Press.

Burkitt, I. (2004) 'The time and space of everyday life.' *Cultural Studies*, 18, 2/3, 211–227.

Burman, E. (2008) *Deconstructing Developmental Psychology.* Hove: Routledge.

Camfield, L., Streuli, N. and Woodhead, M. (2009) 'What's the use of "well-being" in contexts of child poverty? Approaches to research, monitoring and children's participation.' *The International Journal of Children's Rights*, 17, 1, 65–109.

Carroll, L. (1903) *Alice's Adventures in Wonderland and Through the Looking-Glass and What Alice Found There.* New York, NY: Hurst & Co.

Carver, A., Timperio, A., Hesketh, K. and Crawford, D. (2012) 'How does perceived risk mediate associations between perceived safety and parental restriction of adolescents' physical activity in their neighborhood?' *International Journal of Behavioral Nutrition and Physical Activity*, 9, 1, 57.

Childers, S. (2014) 'Promiscuous analysis in qualitative research.' *Qualitative Inquiry*, 20, 6, 819–826.

Cilliers, P. (2005) 'Complexity, Deconstruction and Relativism.' *Theory, Culture and Society*, 22, 5, 255–267.

Clegg, S. (1989) *Frameworks of Power.* London: Sage.

Cloke, P. and Jones, O. (2005) '"Unclaimed territory": Childhood and disordered space(s).' *Social and Cultural Geography*, 6, 3, 311–333.

Colebrook, C. (2005) 'Introduction.' In A. Parr (ed.) *The Deleuze Dictionary.* Edinburgh: Edinburgh University Press.

Crampton, J. (2009) 'Cartography: Performative, participatory, political.' *Progress in Human Geography*, 33, 6, 840–848.

Cranwell, K. (2003) 'Towards Playwork: An Historical Introduction to Children's Out-of-School Play Organisations in London (1860–1940).' In F. Brown (ed.) *Playwork Theory and Practice.* Buckingham: Open University Press.

Crossa, V. (2013) 'Play for protest, protest for play: Artisan and vendors' resistance to displacement in Mexico City.' *Antipode*, 45, 4, 826–843.

Crouch, D. (2010) 'Flirting with space: Thinking landscape relationally.' *Cultural Geographies*, 17, 1, 5–18.

Cunningham, H. (1995) *Children and Childhood in Western Society Since 1500.* Harlow: Pearson Education.

Curti, G. and Moreno, C. (2010) 'Institutional borders, revolutionary imaginings and the becoming-adult of the child.' *Children's Geographies*, 8, 4, 413–427.

Dahlbeck, J. (2012) 'On childhood and the logic of difference: Some empirical examples.' *Children and Society*, 26, 1, 4–13.

Dahlberg, G. and Moss, P. (2005) *Ethics and Politics in Early Childhood Education.* London: Routledge Falmer.

Dahlberg, G., Moss, P. and Pence, A. (2013) *Beyond Quality in Early Childhood Education and Care.* London: Routledge.

Damasio, A. (1994) *Descartes' Error: Emotion, Reason and the Human Brain.* New York, NY: Grosset/Putnam.

Darwish, M. (2009) *Mural* (trans. R. Hammami and J. Berger). London: Verso.

De Freitas, E. (2012) 'The classroom as rhizome: New strategies for diagramming knotted interactions.' *Qualitative Inquiry*, 18, 7, 557–570.

Degen, M. and Rose, G. (2012) 'The sensory experiencing of urban design: The role of walking and perceptual memory.' *Urban Studies*, 49, 15, 3271–3287.

DeLanda, M. (2002) *Intensive Science and Virtual Philosophy.* London: Continuum.

Deleuze, G. (1988) *Spinoza: Practical Philosophy.* San Francisco, CA: City Lights Books.

Deleuze, G. (1993) *The Fold: Leibniz and the Baroque.* London: Athlone Press.

Deleuze, G. (1997) 'What Children Say.' In D. Smith and M. Greco (eds) *Essays Critical and Clinical.* Minneapolis, MN: University of Minnesota Press.

Deleuze, G. (2004) *The Logic of Sense.* London: Continuum.

Deleuze, G. and Guattari, F. (1984) *Anti-Oedipus: Capitalism and Schizophrenia.* London: Athlone Press.

Deleuze, G. and Guattari, F. (1988) *A Thousand Plateaus.* London: Continuum.

Deleuze, G. and Guattari, F. (1994) *What is Philosophy?* London: Verso.

Deleuze, G. and Parnet, C. (2002) *Dialogues.* New York, NY: Columbia University Press.

Department for Children, Schools and Families (DCSF) (2008) *The Play Strategy.* Nottingham: DCSF Publications.

Derrida, J. (1976) *Of Grammatology.* Baltimore: Johns Hopkins University Press.

Derrida, J. (2007) 'Final Words' (trans. G. Walker). *Critical Inquiry*, 33, 2, 462–462.

Devine, D. (2002) 'Children's citizenship and the structuring of adult-child relations in the primary school.' *Childhood*, 9, 3, 303–320.

Dewsbury, J.-D. (2009) 'Performative, Non-Representational, and Affect-Based Research: Seven Injunctions.' In D. DeLyser, S. Atkin, M. Crang, S. Herbert and L. McDowell (eds) *Handbook of Qualitative Research in Human Geography*. London: Sage.

Dewsbury, J.-D. (2011) 'The Deleuze-Guattarian Assemblage: Plastic habits.' *Area*, 43, 2, 148–153.

Duff, C. (2009) 'The Drifting City: The role of affect and repair in the development of "enabling environments".' *International Journal of Drug Policy*, 20, 202–208.

Duff, C. (2011) 'Networks, resources and agency: On the character and production of enabling places.' *Health and Place*, 17, 1, 149–156.

Duff, C. (2013) 'Learning to be Included.' In D. Masny (ed.) *Cartographies of Becoming in Education: A Deleuze-Guattari Perspective*. Rotterdam: Sense Publishers.

Edensor, T. (ed.) (2010) *Geographies of Rhythm*. Farnham: Ashgate.

Facer, K., Holmes, R. and Lee, N. (2012) 'Childhood futures: Better childhoods.' *Global Studies of Childhood*, 2, 3, 170–175.

Fagen, R. (2011) 'Play and Development.' In A. Pellegrini (ed.) *The Oxford Handbook of the Development of Play*. Oxford: Oxford University Press.

Fenech, M. and Sumsion, J. (2007) 'Promoting high quality early childhood education and care services: Beyond risk management, performative constructions of regulation.' *Journal of Early Childhood Research*, 5, 263–283.

Ferrell, J. (2001) *Tearing Down the Streets: Adventures in Urban Anarchy*. New York, NY: Palgrave.

Fitzgerald, D. and Callard, F. (2015) 'Social science and neuroscience beyond interdisciplinarity: Experimental entanglements.' *Theory, Culture and Society*, 32, 1, 3–32.

Foucault, M. (1980) *Power/Knowledge: Selected Interviews and Other Writings 1972–1977*. New York, NY: Pantheon.

Foucault, M. (1984) 'Preface.' In G. Deleuze and F. Guattari *Anti-Oedipus: Capitalism and Schizophrenia*. London: Athlone Press.

Foucault, M. (1991) *Discipline and Punish*. Harmondsworth: Penguin.

Foucault, M. (2008) *The Birth of Biopolitics: Lectures at the Collège de France, 1978–1979*. Basingstoke: Palgrave Macmillan.

Fox, N. (2012) *The Body*. Cambridge: Polity Press.

France, L. (2010) *You are Her*. Todmorden: Arc Publications.

Frost, J. (1992) *Play and Playscapes*. New York, NY: Delmar.

Fujii, L. (2014) 'Five stories of accidental ethnography: Turning unplanned moments in the field into data.' *Qualitative Research*, 15, 4, 525–539.

Gagen, E. (2000) 'Playing the Part: Performing Gender in America's Playgrounds.' In S. Holloway and G. Valentine (eds) *Children's Geographies: Playing, Living and Learning*, pp.213–239. London: Routledge.

Gallacher, L.-A. (2005) '"The terrible twos": Gaining control in the nursery?' *Children's Geographies*, 3, 2, 243–264.

Gallagher, M. and Prior, J. (2014) 'Sonic geographies: Exploring phonographic methods.' *Progress in Human Geography*, 38, 2, 267–284.

Gardiner, M. (2000) *Critiques of Everyday Life*. London: Routledge.

Gardiner, M. (2004) 'Everyday utopianism: Lefebvre and his critics.' *Cultural Studies*, 18, 228–254.

Garland-Thomson, R. (2002) 'Integrating disability, transforming feminist theory.' *NWSA Journal*, 14, 3, 1–32.

Garrett, P. (2009) *Transforming Children's Services: Social Work, Neoliberalism and the 'Modern' World*. Maidenhead: Open University Press.

Garvey, C. (1990) *Play*. Cambridge, MA: Harvard University Press.

Gill, T. (2007) *No Fear: Growing up in a Risk-Averse Society*. London: Calouste-Gulbenkian Foundation.

Grosz, E. (2011) *Becoming Undone: Darwinian Reflections on Life, Politics, and Art*. London: Duke University Press.

Grosz, E. (2013) 'Habit today: Ravaisson, Bergson, Deleuze and us.' *Body and Society*, 19, 2/3, 217–239.

Guattari, F. (1996) *Soft Subversions*. New York, NY: Semiotext(e).

Gullov, E. (2003) 'Creating a Natural Place for Children: An Ethnographic Study of Danish Kindergartens.' In K. Fog Olwig and E. Gullov (eds) *Children's Places: Cross-Cultural Perspectives*. London: Routledge.

Gunder, M. (2010) 'Planning as the ideology of (neoliberal) space.' *Planning Theory*, 9, 4, 298–314.

Gyure, D.A. (2006) 'Playgrounds.' In D. Goldfield (ed.) *Encyclopedia of American Urban History*. Thousand Oaks, CA: Sage.

Hannikainen, M. (2001) 'Playful actions as a sign of togetherness in day care centres.' *International Journal of Early Years Education*, 9, 2, 125–134.

Haraway, D. (1991) *Simians, Cyborgs and Women: The Reinvention of Nature*. New York, NY: Routledge.

Haraway, D. (1997) *Modest–Witness@Second–Millennium. FemaleMan–Meets–OncoMouse*. New York, NY: Routledge.

Hardt, M. and Negri, A. (2009) *Commonwealth*. Cambridge, MA: Harvard University Press.

Harrison, P. (2007) 'How shall I say it...? Relating the non-relational.' *Environment and Planning A*, 39, 590–608.

Hart, R. (2002) 'Containing children: Some lessons on planning for play from New York City.' *Environment and Urbanization*, 14, 2, 135–148.

Harvey, D. (1996) *Justice, Nature and the Geography of Difference*. Oxford: Blackwell.

Harvey, D. (2005) *A Brief History of Neoliberalism*. Oxford: Oxford University Press.

Harvey, D. (2009) *Cosmopolitanism and the Geographies of Freedom*. New York, NY: Columbia University Press.

Hayles, N. (2005) 'Computing the human.' *Theory, Culture and Society*, 22, 1, 131–151.

Healy, P. (2004) 'Creativity and urban governance.' *Policy Studies*, 25, 2, 87–102.

Hein, S.F. (2016) 'The New Materialism in Qualitative Inquiry: How compatible are the philosophies of Barad and Deleuze?' *Cultural Studies ↔ Critical Methodologies*, 16, 2, 132–140.

Henricks, T. (2015) *Play and the Human Condition*. Urbana, IL: University of Illinois Press.

Highmore, B. (2011) *Ordinary Lives: Studies in the Everyday*. Abingdon: Routledge.

Hillier, J. (2005) 'Straddling the post-structural abyss: Between transcendence and immanence?' *Planning Theory*, 4, 3, 271–299.

Hillier, J. (2008) 'Plan(e) speaking: A multiplanar theory of spatial planning.' *Planning Theory*, 7, 1, 24–50.

Hillier, J. (2011) 'Encountering Gilles Deleuze in another place.' *European Planning Studies*, 19, 5, 861–885.

Hillier, J. and Abrahams, G. (2013) *Deleuze and Guattari for Planners: Jean Hillier in Conversation with Gareth Abrahams*. Groningen: Aesop Young Academics.

Hinchliffe, S. (2007) *Geographies of Nature*. London: Sage.

Holland, P. (2003) *We Don't Play With Guns Here*. Maidenhead: Open University Press.

Holt, L. and Holloway, S. (2006) 'Theorising other childhoods in a globalised world.' *Children's Geographies*, 4, 2, 135–142.

Horton, J. and Kraftl, P. (2006a) '"What Else"? Some more ways of thinking and doing "children's geographies".' *Children's Geographies*, 4, 1, 61–95.

Horton, J. and Kraftl, P. (2006b) 'Not just growing up, but going on: Materials, spacings, bodies, situations.' *Children's Geographies*, 4, 3, 259–276.

Howell, O. (2008) 'Skatepark as neoliberal playground: Urban governance, recreation, space, and the cultivation of personal responsibility.' *Space and Culture*, 11, 4, 475–496.

Hughes, B. (2001) *Evolutionary Playwork*. London: Routledge.

Ingold, T. (2007) *Lines: A Brief History*. London: Routledge.

Ingold, T. (2011a) *Being Alive: Essays on Movement, Knowledge and Description*. Abingdon: Routledge.

Ingold, T. (2011b) *The Perception of the Environment: Essays on Livelihood, Dwelling and Skills*. London: Routledge.

Ingold, T. (2013) *Making: Anthropology, Archaeology, Art and Architecture*. Abingdon: Routledge.

Ingold, T. (2015) *The Life of Lines*. London: Routledge.

Jablonka, E. and Lamb, M. (2005) *Evolution in Four Dimensions*. Cambridge, MA: MIT Press.

Jackson, A. and Mazzei, L. (2013) 'Plugging one text into another: Thinking with theory in qualitative research.' *Qualitative Inquiry*, 19, 4, 261–271.

James, A. (2010) 'Competition or integration? The next step in childhood studies?' *Childhood*, 17, 4, 485–499.

James, A. and Prout, A. (eds) (1997) *Constructing and Reconstructing Childhood*. London: Falmer Press.

Jenkins, J. (2011) 'Becoming resilient: Overturning common sense – Part 1.' *The Australian and New Zealand Journal of Family Therapy*, 32, 1, 33–42.

Jones, O. (2008) '"True geography [] quickly forgotten, giving away to an imagined universe": Approaching the otherness of children.' *Children's Geographies*, 6, 2, 195–212.

Jung, Y. (2014) 'Mindful walking: The serendipitous journey of community-based ethnography.' *Qualitative Inquiry*, 20, 5, 621–627.

Kallio, K. (2009) 'Between social and political: Children as political selves.' *Childhoods Today*, 3, 2, 1–22.

Karsten, L. and van Vliet, W. (2006) 'Children in the city: Reclaiming the street.' *Children, Youth and Environments*, 6, 1, 151–167.

Katz, C. (2004) *Growing Up Global: Economic Restructuring and Children's Everyday Lives*. Minneapolis, MN: University of Minnesota Press.

Keevers, L., Treleaven, L., Sykes, C. and Darcy, M. (2012) 'Made to measure: Taming practices with results-based accountability.' *Organization Studies*, 33, 1, 97–120.

Klee, P. (1960) *Pedagogical Sketchbook*. New York, NY: Praeger.

Kozlovsky, R. (2008) 'Adventure Playgrounds and Postwar Reconstruction.' In M. Gutman and N. De Coninck-Smith (eds) *History, Space and the Material Culture of Children*. New Brunswick, NJ: Rutgers University Press.

Kraftl, P. (2006) 'Building an idea: The material construction of an ideal childhood.' *Transactions of Institute of British Geographers*, 31, 488–504.

Kraftl, P. (2008) 'Young people, hope, and childhood-hope.' *Space and Culture*, 11, 2, 81–92.

Kraftl, P. (2013) 'Beyond "voice", beyond "agency", beyond "politics"? Hybrid childhoods and some critical reflections on children's emotional geographies.' *Emotion, Space and Society*, 9, 13–23.

Krasnor, L. and Pepler, D. (1980) 'The study of children's play: Some suggested future directions.' *New Directions for Child Development*, 9, 85–94.

Kropotkin, P. (1972) *Mutual Aid: A Factor in Evolution*. New York, NY: New York University Press.

Landauer, G. (1910) 'Weak statesmen, weaker people!' *Der Sozialist*, June.

l'Anson, J. (2013) 'Beyond the child's voice: Towards an ethics for children's participation rights.' *Global Studies of Childhood*, 3, 2, 104–114.

Latham, A. (2003) 'Guest Editorial.' *Environment and Planning A*, 35, 1901–1906.

Latour, B. (2005) *Reassembling the Social: An Introduction to Actor-Network-Theory*. Oxford: Oxford University Press.

Latour, B. and Woolgar, S. (1986) *Laboratory Life: The Construction of Scientific Facts*. Princeton, NJ: Princeton University Press.

Laurier, E. (2013) 'Noticing Talk, Gestures, Movement and Objects in Video Analysis.' In S. Lee, N. Castree, R. Kitchen, V. Lawson, A. Paasi and C. Withers (eds) *The Sage Handbook of Human Geography*. London: Sage.

Laurier, E. and Brown, B. (2008) 'Rotating maps and readers: Praxiological aspects of alignment and orientation.' *Transactions of the Institute of British Geographers*, 33, 201–221.

Laurier, E. and Philo, C. (2006) 'Possible geographies: A passing encounter in a café.' *Area*, 38, 4, 353–363.

Leander, K., Phillips, N. and Taylor, K. (2010) 'The changing social spaces of learning: Mapping new mobilities.' *Review of Research in Education*, 34, 329–394.

Lee, N. (2001) *Childhood and Society: Growing Up in an Age of Uncertainty*. Buckingham: Open University Press.

Lee, N. (2005) *Childhood and Human Value*. Maidenhead: Open University Press.

Lee, N. and Motzkau, J. (2011) 'Navigating the bio-politics of childhood.' *Childhood*, 18, 1, 7–19.

Lefebvre, H. (1991) *The Production of Space*. Oxford: Blackwell.

Lefebvre, H. (1996) *Writings on Cities*. Cambridge, MA: Blackwell.

Lefebvre, H. (2004) *Rhythmanalysis: Space, Time and Everyday Life*. London: Continuum.

Lester, S. (2009) 'Play as Progress.' In R. Carlyle (ed.) *Encyclopedia of Play in Today's Society*. Thousand Oaks, CA: Sage.

Lester, S. (2010) *Play and Ordinary Magic: The Everydayness of Play*. Paper presented at Playwork London Conference, June.

Lester, S. (2011a) 'The Pedagogy of Play, Space and Learning.' In A. Pihlgren (ed.) *Fritidspedagogik*. Lund: Studentlitteratur.

Lester, S. (2011b) *Moments of Nonsense and Signs of Hope: The Everyday 'Political' Nature of Children's Play*. Paper presented at IPA World Conference, Cardiff. Available at: www.ipa2011.org/login/uploaded/tuesday%20papers/Stuart%20Lester.pdf [Accessed 24/01/2016].

Lester, S. (2012) 'We are just playing.' *Shopping Hour*, 7, 16–21.

Lester, S. (2013a) 'Playing in a Deleuzian Playground.' In E. Ryall, W. Russell and M. Maclean (eds) *Philosophy of Play*, pp.130–140. London: Routledge.

Lester, S. (2013b) 'Rethinking children's participation in democratic processes: A right to play.' *Sociological Studies of Children and Youth*, 16, 21–43.

Lester, S. (2014a) 'Play as Protest: Clandestine Moments of Disturbance and Hope.' In C. Burke and K. Jones (eds) *Education, Childhood and Anarchism: Talking Colin Ward*, pp.198–208. London: Routledge.

Lester, S. (2014b) *Thinking About Play*. Evaluation report. Gloucester: University of Gloucestershire.

Lester, S. (2015a) 'Post-Human Nature: Life Beyond the Natural Playground.' In M. Maclean, W. Russell and E. Ryall (eds) *Philosophical Perspectives on Play*. London: Routledge.

Lester, S. (2015b) 'Why Play is Important.' In C. Derry (2015) *Rules for a Playful Museum*. Manchester: Happy Museum.

Lester, S. (2015c) Playful Places. Playwork North West/University of Gloucestershire action research project proposal (unpublished).

Lester, S. (2015d) *LE7005: Play and Space Workbook*. Gloucester: University of Gloucestershire.

Lester, S. (2016a) *The Value of Playwork Provision in Manchester*. Manchester: Playwork North West.

Lester, S. (2016b) Bringing Play to Life and Life to Play: Different Lines of Enquiry. PhD thesis. Gloucester: University of Gloucestershire.

Lester, S. (2017) 'Children's Right to Play: From the Margins to the Middle.' In M. Ruck, M. Peterson-Badali and M. Freeman (eds) *Handbook of Children's Rights: Global and Multidisciplinary Perspectives*. New York, NY: Taylor and Francis.

Lester, S. (2018) 'Playwork and the Co-creation of Play Spaces: The Rhythms and Refrains of a Play Environment.' In F. Brown and B. Hughes (eds) *Aspects of Playwork*. Lanham, MD: University Press of America.

Lester, S., Fitzpatrick, J. and Russell, W. (2014) *Co-creating an Adventure Playground: Reading Playwork Stories, Practices and Artefacts*. Gloucester: University of Gloucestershire.

Lester, S. and Russell, W. (2008a) *Play for a Change – Play, Policy and Practice: A Review of Contemporary Perspectives*. London: National Children's Bureau.

Lester, S. and Russell, W. (2008b) 'Tell your mum I saved your life.' *IPA Play Rights*, 08/02, 4–5.

Lester, S. and Russell, W. (2010a) *Children's Right to Play: An Examination of the Importance of Play in the Lives of Children Worldwide*. Working Paper No. 57. The Hague, The Netherlands: Bernard van Leer Foundation.

Lester, S. and Russell, W. (2010b) *Thinking About Play: Participant's Pack 1*. London: Playwork London.

Lester, S. and Russell, W. (2013a) *Leopard Skin Wellies, a Top Hat and a Vacuum Cleaner Hose: An Analysis of Wales' Play Sufficiency Assessment Duty*. Cardiff: Play Wales.

Lester, S. and Russell, W. (2013b) 'Utopian Visions of Childhood and Play in English Social Policy.' In A. Parker and D. Vinson (eds) *Youth Sport, Physical Activity and Play: Policy, Intervention and Participation.* London: Routledge.

Lester, S. and Russell, W. (2014a) 'Children's Right to Play.' In E. Brooker, M. Blaise and S. Edwards (eds) *The Sage Handbook of Play and Learning in Early Childhood.* London: Sage.

Lester, S. and Russell, W. (2014b) *Towards Securing Sufficient Play Opportunities: A short study into the preparation undertaken for the commencement of the second part of the Welsh Government's Play Sufficiency Duty to secure sufficient play opportunities.* Cardiff: Play Wales.

Lester, S. and Russell, W. (2014c) 'Turning the world upside down: Playing as the deliberate creation of uncertainty.' *Children,* 1, 2, 241–260.

Lester, S., Strachan, A. and Derry, C. (2014) 'A more playful museum: Exploring issues of institutional space, children's play and well-being.' *International Journal of Play,* 3, 1, 24–35.

Lewontin, R. (2000) *The Triple Helix.* Cambridge, MA: Harvard University Press.

Loizou, E., Kyriakides, E. and Hadjicharalambous, M. (2011) 'Constructing stories in kindergarten: Children's knowledge of genre.' *European Early Childhood Education Research Journal,* 19, 1, 63–77.

Lorimer, H. (2005) 'Cultural geography: The busyness of being "more-than-representational".' *Progress in Human Geography,* 29, 1, 83–94.

Louv, R. (2005) *Last Child in the Woods: Saving our Children from Nature-Deficit Disorder.* New York, NY: Algonquin Books of Chapel Hill.

Lyotard, J.-F. (1984) *The Postmodern Condition.* Minneapolis, MN: University of Minnesota Press.

MacKinnon, D. and Derickson, K.D. (2012) 'From resilience to resourcefulness: A critique of resilience policy and activism.' *Progress in Human Geography,* 37, 2, 253–270.

MacLure, M. (2010) 'The offence of theory.' *Journal of Education Policy,* 25, 2, 277–286.

MacLure, M. (2013) 'Classification of Wonder? Coding as an Analytical Practice in Qualitative Research.' In R. Coleman and J. Ringrose (eds) *Deleuze and Research Methodologies.* Edinburgh: Edinburgh University Press.

Malone, K. and Rudner, J. (2011) 'Global perspectives on children's independent mobility: A socio-cultural comparison and theoretical discussion of children's lives in four countries in Asia and Africa.' *Global Studies of Childhood,* 1, 3, 243–259.

Manning, E. (2009) 'What if it didn't all begin and end with containment? Toward a leaky sense of self.' *Body & Society,* 15, 3, 33–45.

Manning, E. (2013) *Always More than One: Individuation's Dance.* Durham, NC: Duke University Press.

Manning, E. (2014) 'Wondering the world directly – or, how movement outruns the Subject.' *Body & Society,* 20, 3/4, 162–186.

Manning, E. (2016) *The Minor Gesture.* Durham, NC: Duke University Press.

Manning, E. and Massumi, B. (2014) *Thought in the Act: Passages in the Ecology of Experience.* Minneapolis, MN: University of Minnesota Press.

Massey, D. (2005) *For Space.* London: Sage.

Massumi, B. (2002) *Parables for the Virtual.* Durham, NC: Duke University Press.

Massumi, B. (2013) 'Prelude.' In E. Manning *Always More than One: Individuation's Dance.* Durham, NC: Duke University Press.

Masten, A. (2001) 'Ordinary magic: Resilience processes in development.' *American Psychologist,* 56, 3, 227–238.

Matthews, H., Taylor, M., Percy-Smith, B. and Limb, M. (2000) 'The unacceptable flaneur: The shopping mall as a teenage hangout.' *Childhood,* 7, 3, 279–294.

May, T. (1994) *The Political Philosophy of Poststructuralist Anarchism.* University Park, PA: Pennsylvania University Press.

May, T. (2005) 'To change the world, to celebrate life.' *Philosophy and Social Criticism,* 31, 5–6, 517–531.

May, T. (2007) 'Jacques Rancière and the ethics of equality.' *SubStance,* 36, 2, 20–36.

May, T. (2010) *Contemporary Political Movements and the Thought of Jacques Rancière: Equality in Action.* Edinburgh: Edinburgh University Press.

Mayall, B. (2002) *Towards a Sociology of Childhood.* Maidenhead: Open University Press.

Mazzei, L. (2014) 'Beyond an easy sense: A diffractive analysis.' *Qualitative Inquiry,* 20, 6, 742–746.

McCormack, D. (2013) *Refrains for Moving Bodies.* Durham, NC: Duke University Press.

Miller, P. and Rose, N. (2008) *Governing the Present.* Cambridge: Polity Press.

Morrow, V. and Mayall, B. (2009) 'What is wrong with children's wellbeing in the UK? Questions of meaning and measurement.' *Journal of Social Welfare and Family Law,* 31, 3, 217–229.

Moss, P. (2007) 'Meetings across the paradigmatic divide.' *Educational Philosophy and Theory,* 39, 3, 229–245.

Moss, S. (2012) *Natural Childhood.* National Trust. Available at: www.nationaltrust.org.uk/document-1355766991839 [Accessed 02/09/2015].

Mozère, L. (2006) 'What's the trouble with identity? Practices and theories from France.' *Contemporary Issues in Early Childhood,* 7, 2, 109–118.

Mozère, L. (2007) 'In early childhood: What's language about?' *Educational Philosophy and Theory,* 39, 3, 291–299.

Myers, K. (2012) 'Marking time: Some methodological and historical perspectives on the "crisis of childhood".' *Research Papers in Education,* 27, 4, 409–422.

Nancy, J.-L. (2008) *Corpus* (trans. R.A. Rand). New York, NY: Fordham University Press.

Olsson, L. (2009) *Movement and Experimentation in Young Children's Learning.* Abingdon: Routledge.

Opie, I. (1993) *The People in the Playground.* Oxford: Oxford University Press.

Opie, P. and Opie, I. (1969) *Children's Games in Street and Playground.* Oxford: Oxford University Press.

O'Shea, K. (2013) *How We Came to Play: The History of Playgrounds.* National Trust for Historic Preservation. Available at: https://savingplaces. org/stories/how-we-came-to-play-the-history-of-playgrounds/#. W29GytU16Uk [Accessed 11/08/2018].

O'Sullivan, S. (2006) *Art Encounters Deleuze and Guattari: Thought Beyond Representation.* Basingstoke: Palgrave Macmillan.

Oyama, S. (2000) *Evolution's Eye: A Systems View of the Biology–Culture Divide.* Durham, NC: Duke University Press.

Paddison, R. and Sharp, J. (2007) 'Questioning the end of public space: Reclaiming control of local banal spaces.' *Scottish Geographical Journal,* 123, 2, 87–106.

Patton, P. (2000) *Deleuze and the Political.* London: Routledge.

Patton, P. (2010) *Deleuzian Concepts: Philosophy, Colonization, Politics.* Stanford, CA: Stanford University Press.

Philo, C. (2000) 'The cornerstones of my world: Editorial introduction to special issue on spaces of childhood.' *Childhood,* 7, 3, 243–256.

Philo, C. (2003) 'To go back up the side hill: Memories, imaginations and reveries of childhood.' *Children's Geographies,* 1, 1, 7–23.

Pile, S. (2010) 'Emotions and affect in recent human geography.' *Transactions of the Institute of British Geographers,* 35, 1, 5–20.

Pinder, D. (2005) 'Arts of urban exploration.' *Cultural Geographies,* 12, 383–411.

Playing Out (1994) BBC2, 1 November.

Playwork Principles Scrutiny Group (2005) *The Playwork Principles.* Cardiff: Play Wales.

Powell, K. (2010) 'Making sense of place: Mapping as a multisensory research method.' *Qualitative Inquiry,* 16, 7, 539–555.

Powell, S. and Wellard, I. (2008) *Policies and Play: The Impact of National Policies on Children's Opportunities for Play.* London: National Children's Bureau.

Prezza, M. and Pacilli, G. (2007) 'Current fear of crime, sense of community, and loneliness in Italian adolescents: The role of autonomous mobility and play during childhood.' *Journal of Community Psychology,* 35, 2, 151–170.

Prout, A. (2005) *The Future of Childhood*. London: Routledge Falmer.

Punch, S. (2003) 'Childhoods in the majority world: Miniature adults or tribal children?' *Sociology*, 37, 2, 277–295.

Purcell, M. (2013) 'A new land: Deleuze and Guattari and planning.' *Planning Theory and Practice*, 14, 1, 20–38.

Ramstetter, C.L., Murray, R. and Garner, A.S. (2010) 'The crucial role of recess in schools.' *Journal of School Health*, 80, 11, 517–526.

Rancière, J. (1999) *Disagreement Politics and Philosophy* (trans. J. Rose). Minneapolis, MN: University of Minnesota Press.

Rancière, J. (2001) 'Ten theses on politics.' *Theory and Event*, 5, 3.

Rancière, J. (2004) *The Politics of Aesthetics: The Distribution of the Sensible*. London: Continuum.

Rancière, J. (2010) *DISSENSUS: On Politics and Aesthetics*. London: Continuum.

Read, J. (2011) 'Gutter to garden: Historical discourses of risk in interventions in working class children's street play.' *Children and Society*, 25, 6, 421–434.

Robinson, K.H. (2013) *Innocence, Knowledge and the Construction of Childhood: The Contradictory Nature of Sexuality and Censorship in Children's Contemporary Lives*. London: Routledge.

Roopnarine, J. (2011) 'Cultural Variations in Beliefs about Play, Parent–Child Play, and Children's Play: Meaning for Child Development.' In A. Pellegrini (ed.) *The Oxford Handbook of the Development of Play*. Oxford: Oxford University Press.

Roosevelt, T. (1907) 'Letter to Cuno H. Rudolph, Washington Playground Association, February 16, 1907.' *Presidential Addresses and State Papers VI*, 1163.

Rose, N. (1999) *Powers of Freedom*. Cambridge: Cambridge University Press.

Rousseau, J.-J. (1762/1979) *Emile* (trans. A. Bloom). New York, NY: Basic Books.

Routledge, P. (2012) 'Sensuous solidarities: Emotion, politics and performance in the clandestine insurgent rebel clown army.' *Antipode*, 44, 2, 428–452.

Rowlands, P. (2011) 'Need, well-being and outcomes: The development of policy-thinking for children's services 1989–2004.' *Child and Family Social Work*, 16, 255–265.

Russell, W., Lester, S. and Smith, H. (2017) *Practice-Based Research in Children's Play*. Bristol: Policy Press.

Ryan, K. (2010) 'Governing the future: Citizenship as technology, empowerment as technique.' *Critical Sociology*, 37, 6, 763–778.

Ryan, K. (2012) 'The new wave of childhood studies: Breaking the grip of bio-social dualism.' *Childhood*, 19, 4, 439–452.

Saldanha, A. (2010) 'Politics and Difference.' In B. Anderson and P. Harrison (eds) *Taking-Place: Non-Representational Theories and Geography*. Farnham: Ashgate.

Schiller, J.C.F von (1909–1914) 'Letters on the Aesthetic Education of Man' ['Über die ästhetische Erziehung des Menschen in einer Reihe von Briefen' 1795]. In C.W. Eliot (ed.) *Literary and Philosophical Essays: French, German and Italian*. Vol. XXXII. The Harvard Classics. New York, NY: P.F. Collier and Son.

Scott, J.C. (1990) *Domination and the Arts of Resistance*. New Haven, CT: Yale University Press.

Seigworth, G.J. and Gregg, M. (2010) 'An Inventory of Shimmers.' In M. Gregg and G.J. Seigworth (eds) *The Affect Reader*. Durham, NC: Duke University Press.

Simondon, G. (1992) 'The Genesis of the Individual.' In J. Crary and S. Kwinter (eds) *Incorporations*. New York, NY: Zone Books.

Smith, P. (2010) *Children and Play*. Chichester: Wiley-Blackwell.

Soja, E.W. (2010) *Seeking Spatial Justice*. Minneapolis, MN: University of Minnesota Press.

Spiller, J. (ed.) (1961) *Paul Klee: The Thinking Eye. The Notebooks of Paul Klee* (trans. Ralph Manheim). London: Lund Humphries.

Spinka, M., Newberry, R.C. and Bekoff, M. (2001) 'Mammalian play: Training for the unexpected.' *The Quarterly Review of Biology*, 76, 2, 141–168.

Springer, S. (2014) 'Spatial delight and the possibilities of childhood.' *Dialogues in Human Geography*, 4, 1, 80–83.

Stagoll, C. (2005) 'Difference.' In A. Parr (ed.) *The Deleuze Dictionary*. Edinburgh: Edinburgh University Press.

Stevens, Q. (2007) *The Ludic City: Exploring the Potential of Public Spaces*. Abingdon: Routledge.

Stewart, K. (2007) *Ordinary Affects*. Durham, NC: Duke University Press.

Stoecklin, V. (2000) Creating Playgrounds Kids Love. Available at: www.whitehutchinson.com/children/articles/playgrndkidslove.shtml [Accessed 12/01/2015].

Strandell, H. (2005) Re-evaluating Difference in Childhood Research. Childhoods: Children and Youth in Emerging and Transforming Societies. International Conference. Oslo, 29 June – 3 July.

Stratford, E. (2002) 'On the edge: A tale of skaters and urban governance.' *Social and Cultural Geography*, 3, 2, 193–206.

Sutton-Smith, B. (1997) *The Ambiguity of Play*. Cambridge, MA: Harvard University Press.

Sutton-Smith, B. (2002) 'Recapitulation Redressed.' In J.L. Roopnarine (ed.) *Conceptual, Social-Cognitive and Contextual Issues in the Fields of Play: Play and Culture Studies Vol 4*. Westport, CT: Ablex Publishing.

Sutton-Smith, B. (2003) 'Play as a Parody of Emotional Vulnerability.' In D.E. Lytle (ed.) *Play and Educational Theory and Practice: Play and Culture Studies*. Westport, CT: Praeger.

Sydnor, S. and Fagen, R. (2012) 'Plotlessness, ethnography, ethology: Play.' *Cultural Studies* ↔ *Critical Methodologies*, 12, 1, 72–81.

Tarulli, D. and Skott-Myhre, H. (2006) 'The immanent rights of the multitude: An ontological framework for conceptualizing the issue of child and youth rights.' *International Journal of Children's Rights*, 14, 187–201.

Taylor, A. (2011) 'Reconceptualizing the "nature" of childhood.' *Childhood*, 18, 4, 420–433.

Taylor, A. (2013) *Reconfiguring the Natures of Childhood*. London: Routledge.

The Lancet (1913) 'Playgrounds in public elementary schools.' *The Lancet*, 11 January, p.124.

The Lancet (1924) 'Salford's remedial playground.' *The Lancet*, 24 May, p.1090.

Thomson, S. (2005) '"Territorialising" the primary school playground: Deconstructing the geography of playtime.' *Children's Geographies*, 3, 1, 63–78.

Thrift, N. (2004) 'Summoning Life', pp.81–103 in P. Cloke, M. Crang and M. Goodwin (eds) *Envisioning Human Geographies*, London: Arnold.

Thrift, N. (2008) *Non-Representational Theory*. Abingdon: Routledge.

Tisdall, E. and Punch, S. (2012) 'Not so "new"? Looking critically at childhood studies.' *Children's Geographies*, 10, 3, 249–264.

Trawick-Smith, J. (2010) 'Drawing back the lens on play: A frame analysis of young children's play in Puerto Rico.' *Early Education and Development*, 27, 4, 536–567.

UNCRC (2013) General Comment 17: The right of the child to rest, leisure, play, recreational activities, cultural life and the arts (Article 31). Available at: www2.ohchr.org/english/bodies/crc/docs/GC/CRC-C-GC-17_en.doc [Accessed 12/01/16].

Ungar, M. (2008) 'Resilience across cultures.' *The British Journal of Social Work*, 38, 218–235.

Ungar, M. (2011) 'The social ecology of resilience: Addressing contextual and cultural ambiguity of a nascent construct.' *American Journal of Orthopsychiatry*, 81, 1, 1–17.

UNICEF Office of Research (2013) 'Child well-being in rich countries: A comparative overview.' *Innocenti Report Card 11*. Florence: UNICEF Office of Research.

Veitch, J., Bagley, S., Ball, K. and Salmon, J. (2006) 'Where do children usually play? A qualitative study of parents' perceptions of influences on children's active free-play.' *Health and Place*, 12, 383–393.

Ward, C. (1979) *The Child in the City*. Harmondsworth: Penguin.

Ward, C. (2008) *Anarchy in Action*. London: Freedom Press.

Welsh Government (2010) Children and Families (Wales) Measure.

Welsh Government (2014) *Wales: A Play-Friendly Country*. Statutory Guidance.

Whatmore, S. (2002) *Hybrid Geographies*. London: Sage.

Williams, T., Russell, W., Lester, S., Smith, H. and MacLean, M. (2016) *Sharing Memories of Adventure Playgrounds*. Gloucester: University of Gloucestershire. Available at: https://issuu.com/wendykrussell/docs/smap_report_131016_for_web_hs [Accessed 02/09/2018].

Woolley, H. (2008) 'Watch this space! Designing for children's play in public open spaces.' *Geography Compass*, 2, 2, 495–512.

Woolley, H., Hazelwood, T. and Simkins, I. (2011) 'Don't skate here: Exclusion of skateboarders from urban civic spaces in three northern cities in England.' *Journal of Urban Design*, 16, 4, 471–487.

Youdell, D. and Armstrong, F. (2011) 'A politics beyond subjects: The affective choreographies and smooth spaces of schooling.' *Emotion, Space and Society*, 4, 144–150.

Subject Index

Sub-headings in *italics* indicate figures.

account-ability 33, 36, 59, 72,
    171–3, 189–90, 191, 216–18
  drawing a line at the zoo 174
  taking account of the everyday 174–6
  see also responsibility
adults 30–1, 32, 36, 76, 220
  perspectives on play 37, 40
  playgrounds 129–30, 139–40
  power of binaries 48–50
  provision of environments for
    children's play 104
  retracing lines 221
adventure playgrounds (APs)
    135–40, 172, 177–8
  the chairs 192–6
affect 46–7, 153, 157–8
  taking account of the everyday 174–6
after-school clubs 96–7, 205, 208
  cushions and childbirth 213–14
  musical worms 153–4
Allen, Lady 135
anarchy 147–8, 157, 158
assemblages 64, 71, 76–8, 85, 111–12
  metastability 107–8
  molar assemblages 16, 112, 145, 201

Barad, Karen 122
behaviours 27, 49, 128, 140
  'becoming-children' 151–2
being well
  see also well-being

Bergson, Henri 22, 29, 123, 224
binaries 48–50
  beyond binary thinking 50–2
bio-politics 46–7, 131, 158
bio-power 45, 100, 134, 156, 165, 216
bodies in movement 70–2, 85, 92–3, 153
  becoming trees in the art
    gallery 118–21, 160, 166
  bodies without organs' 71,
    76, 81, 92, 95, 158
  moving lines at the bus stop 78–84
boundaries 52, 62, 104
  pushing at boundaries 151–2

Caroll, Lewis *Alice in Wonderland
    and Through the Looking-
    Glass* 11–12, 13, 62
Cartesian dualism 43
cartography 33, 176
  towards a cartography of play 181–2
  see also critical cartography
Chess 72
Chester Zoo 172
childhood 40–1
  cultural practices 37–8
  natural playgrounds 130–5
  neoliberalism 44–8
  participation rights 105–6
  power of binaries 48–50
children 30–1, 76, 220
  becoming dogs 61, 109
  becoming trees in the art
    gallery 118–21, 160, 166

children *cont.*
  bedroom scenario 26–9,
    65–7, 69, 99, 151
  behaviour in public 108–9, 124
  children's well-being 89–92
  circle time 214–15
  cushions and childbirth 213
  drawing a line at the zoo 174
  drawing lines at the nursery 180–1
  I didn't go anywhere, I was
    on the coach 137
  leopard skin wellies 178–9, 222
  moving lines at the bus stop 78–84
  musical worms 153–4
  negotiating playing at the park 161
  no going on the field 149–50
  observation of a teddy bear 183
  perspectives on play 37–41
  playing on the benches in
    the plaza 166–7
  protection 105–6, 129–30
  retracing lines 221
  strawberry mermaids 59–60, 77, 99
  tag on a tango swing as
    choreography 116–17, 118
  tell your mum I saved your life 94–8
  the dangerous river 143–4
  the frozen food cabinet 167–8
  walking blindfold 60
  walking the lines at the museum
    70–3, 79, 82, 93, 118, 82
  worlds made of poo 55–7, 62, 71,
    77, 92, 99, 101, 123, 156, 160
Children and Families (Wales)
  Measure 2010 178
children as future citizens 32, 38–40
  adventure playgrounds 135–6
children's geographies 29, 31, 166
children's rights 105–6, 203–5
  children's right to play 106–11
circuses 99
cities *see* good city
critical cartography 28, 30, 33,
  190, 191–2, 216–18
  Amin's four registers of the
    good city 199–208
  lessons from resilience
    scholarship 199
  planning for play 209–16

the chairs 192–6
  theory, research and practice 197–9
  towards a critical cartography
    of play 192–7
  see also cartography

Deleuze, Gilles 11–12, 22, 28, 29, 31,
  33–4, 63, 70–1, 73, 109, 123, 220, 221
  mapping 171–2, 179–80
  new land 163–4
  ontology 65–8, 145, 222
  plugging in 33–4, 198–9, 222
  political philosophy 156–7
delinquency 46, 135
democracy 158–60, 170
  play, spatial justice and a right
    to the city 163–8
Denmark 135
Derrida, Jacques 13–14
Derrida, Pierre 13
desires 57–8, 92, 93
  life 85
  lines of desire 71
deterritorialisation and
  reterritorialisation 15–16,
    33, 76–7, 162
  adventure playgrounds 136, 139–40
  new land 163–4
development 38, 40, 68
  playtime 128
developmental psychology 30, 41–3, 128
  A line of development 42
  A self-enclosed organism 43
differentiation 68, 136
dualism 43, 50, 221
Dubuffet, Jean 21

education 100, 103–4
  educational achievement 89–90
Emerson, Ralph Waldo 130
emotional regulation 99–101
enchantment 216, 224
  re-enchantment 206–8
English Heritage 172
entanglements 31, 62, 63–4,
    65–6, 76, 223
  account-ability and response-
    ability 33, 191

entanglements in movements 67, 71, 93, 95, 97
everyday acts of playing 57
space 115–16
well-being 91, 111
ethics 109–11
Eureka Museum 172
everyday acts of playing 57–61
becoming dogs 61, 109
strawberry mermaids 59–60, 77, 99
walking blindfold 60

Ferlinghetti, Lawrence 157
Foucault, Michel 156
France, Linda 22

Galeano, Eduardo 23
games 12–13
Germany 127
Go 72
good city 33, 199–200
re-enchantment 206–8
relatedness 202–3
repair and maintenance 200–2
rights 203–5
Guattari, Félix 11, 22, 28, 63, 70–1, 123
new land 163–4
political philosophy 156–7

habits 175, 192
health 32
children's well-being 89–92
Hockney, David 118
humanism 51

immanence 52, 64
plane of immanence 67, 178, 207, 216
individualisation of life 41–3, 100, 112
Ingold, Tim 22–3
International Council for Children's Play 214
International Play Association 222

Jack and the Beanstalk 50–2, 75
Jackson, Rebekah 60

Kandinsky, Wassily 21
Kearsley, Mel 61
Klee, Paul 23
Burdened Children (1930) 21–2

Labour Party Play Strategy 125–6, 139
learning 38, 40
Lefebvre, Henri 142
Lester, Stuart 9–16, 21–2
life 85, 115, 219–20
individualisation of life 41–3, 100, 112
life and play 63–9
lines of flight 16, 74, 86, 103, 112, 136
Lines of flight on a plane of organisation 103
lines of movement 29, 73–8
A (life)line of movement 74
A child's drawing of a body 74
Moving lines at the bus stop 78
moving lines at the bus stop 78–84
local authorities 126–7, 172, 178, 222–3

Manchester Museum 172
mapping 33, 75–8, 171–2
diagrams and mappings 186
drawing lines at the nursery 180–1
leopard skin wellies 178–9, 222
mapping as process 176–81
towards a cartography of play 181–2
see also tracing
material-discursive effects 39, 48, 62, 101, 103, 106, 121, 124, 142, 164–5, 173, 184, 187, 201–2, 220
Matisse, Henri 21
May, Todd 157
messing about 27, 39–40
metastability 78, 83, 93, 96, 107–8, 122
micro-politics 33, 147–8, 169–70
play, spatial justice and a right to the city 163–8
playing and 'becoming democratic' 156–62
playing as political action 148–56
milieux 95–6, 114, 117, 153, 180, 221
Miró, Joan 21
molar assemblages 16, 112, 145, 201
molecular see lines

movements 25, 27–34, 56–9,
    62, 85, 99–100
    bodies in movement 70–2, 85, 92–3
    bringing play to life 63–4, 66–9
    lines of movement 29, 73–8
    moving lines at the bus stop 78–84

National Playing Fields Association 127
National Trust 131
National Trust for Historic
    Preservation 125
natural playgrounds 130–5
navigation and negotiation 33, 191, 199
negotiation 96–7, 104, 109, 152, 204
    navigation and negotiation
        33, 191, 199
    negotiating playing at the park 161
neoliberalism 30, 32, 44–8, 100–1, 112
    democracy 158–60
    neoliberal economics 163–5
new land 163–4, 169
Nietzsche, Friedrich 29
nomadic approach 15, 22, 75
    audio and visual methods 184–6
    diagrams and mappings 186
    mobile methods 182–9
    observation 186–9
    observation of a teddy bear 183
    storytelling 189
Non-Representational Theory (NRT) 58
normativity 49, 90, 122, 136,
    140–1, 169, 201

observation 186–9
    audio and visual methods 184–6
    diagrams and mappings 186
    observation of a teddy bear 183

participation rights 105–6
philosophy 64–9
Physical Training and Recreation
    Act 1937 (UK) 127
Picasso, Pablo 21
plane of immanence 67, 178, 207, 216
planes of organisation 32, 46,
    74, 82, 86, 103, 112
    A plane of organisation 45

Lines of flight on a plane of
    organisation 103
playgrounds 128
playgrounds on a plane of
    organisation 140–5
space 122
planning for play 32, 34, 209–16
    circle time 214–15
    cushions and childbirth 213
Playground Association of America 127
playgrounds 32, 125–7
    adventure playgrounds (APs)
        135–40, 172, 177–8
    brief genealogy of children's
        playgrounds 127–30
    I didn't go anywhere, I was
        on the coach 137
    natural playgrounds 130–5
    playgrounds on a plane of
        organisation 140–5
    The dangerous river 143–4
playing 9–10, 15–16, 25–6, 29–34,
    52–3, 55, 84–6, 115, 219–20
    bedroom scenario 26–9,
        65–7, 69, 99, 151
    everyday acts of playing 57–61
    moments and movements
        of hope 224–5
    perspectives on play 37–41
    playing as process 36
    playtime 128
    retracing lines 221
    setting the scene 35–6
    tell your mum I saved your life 94–8
    value of the example 61–3
    walking the lines at the museum
        70–3, 79, 82, 93, 118, 82
    worlds made of poo 55–7, 62, 71,
        77, 92, 99, 101, 123, 156, 160
playing as political action 148–56
    musical worms 153–4
    negotiating playing at the park 161
    no going on the field 149–50
    play, spatial justice and a right
        to the city 163–8
    playing on the benches in
        the plaza 166–7
    the frozen food cabinet 167–8

playing as progress 38, 40
    individualisation of life 41–3, 100, 112
Playing Out 94, 97
playworkers 138–9, 153, 205, 217
    the chairs 192–6
plugging in 33–4, 198–9, 221–3
policy-making 88–9
    resilience 100–2
posthumanism 51–2, 63, 148, 171
power (*potentia* and *potestas*) 158, 165
practice 33–4, 198–9
practitioners 27, 31, 35–6, 39
Professional Studies in Children's Play,
    University of Gloucestershire 223
psychogeography 9

Rancière, Jacques 148, 164
Recreation Grounds Act 1859 (UK) 127
research 33–4, 198–9
resilience 31–2
    lessons from resilience
        scholarship 199
    playing and resilience 99–104
response-ability 33, 36, 72,
    171–3, 191, 216–18
    circle time 214–15
    cushions and childbirth 213
    four registers of the good
        city 199–208
    navigation and negotiation 199
    planning for play 209–16
    plugging in 198–9
    the chairs 192–6
    towards a critical cartography
        of play 192–7
    see also account-ability
reterritorialisation *see* determination
rhizomatic approach 15, 75
risk aversion 129–30
road use 165–6
Rousseau, Jean-Jacques 130, 131

sand gardens 127
schools 103, 128
Simpson, Emma-Louise 55
Situationism 9
social constructivism 49–50
Sørensen, Thomas 135

spaces for play 32–3, 115–16,
    145, 199–200
    adventure playgrounds 135–40
    Becoming trees 119
    becoming trees in the art
        gallery 118–21, 160, 166
    brief genealogy of children's
        playgrounds 127–30
    co-creating play spaces 118–21
    Cutting play from movement 121
    natural playgrounds 130–5
    planning for play 32, 34, 209–16
    playgrounds 125–7
    playgrounds on a plane of
        organisation 140–5
    production of children's
        'play spaces' 125–7
    re-enchantment 206–8
    relatedness 202–3
    repair and maintenance 200–2
    rights 203–5
    tag on a tango swing as
        choreography 116–17, 118
    what is space? 121–5
spatial justice 33–4, 72, 145
    play, spatial justice and a right
        to the city 163–8
Spinoza, Baruch 13, 29, 71, 92, 98, 124
Springer, Simon 157
storytelling 189
subversion 10, 40, 104, 151–2, 155–6

theory 33–4, 198–9
Thoreau, Henry 130
timespace 18, 32, 33, 49,
    57, 124, 141, 145
    adventure playgrounds 136–7
    becoming trees in the art
        gallery 119, 160, 166
    worlds made of poo 123
tracing 75–6, 176–7
    see also mapping

UK 127, 135, 153
UNCRC (United Nations Convention
    on the Rights of the Child)
    32, 105–6, 113, 155, 222
University of Gloucestershire 223

urban environment *see* good city
US 127, 128

walking 82–3, 184
Ward, Colin 10, 157
Washington Playground
    Association 128
well-being 31–2, 87–8, 111–14, 115, 224
    children's right to play 105–11

children's well-being 89–92
playing and being well 94–8
playing and resilience 99–104
well-being and policy 88–9
Welsh Government's Play Sufficiency
    Duty 172, 178, 179, 222, 223
four registers of the good
    city 199–208
World War II 135

Author Index

Abrahams, G. 206, 207
Aitken, S. 130, 132, 156, 203, 208
Alaimo, S. 63, 134
Alexander, S. 91
Allen, M. 139
Amin, A. 33, 45, 142, 191, 200,
	202, 203, 206, 208, 210, 218
Anderson, B. 45, 46, 158, 203
Ansell, N. 37
Armstrong, F. 155, 205

Banerjee, B. 182
Barad, K. 39, 49, 50, 51, 53, 62,
	63, 64, 69, 71, 77, 108, 111,
	157, 174, 177, 187, 222, 225
Bednar, R. 138
Bekoff, M. 97
Benjamin, W. 9, 156
Bennett, J. 57, 58, 59, 60, 63, 81,
	93, 175, 206, 220, 224
Beunderman, J. 210
Blaise, M. 182, 187
Bloch, E. 224
Bonta, M. 76, 77, 124
Borden, I. 201
Borges, J.L. 14
Borgnon, L. 188
Bradshaw, J. 88
Bradwell, P. 210
Braidotti, R. 63, 109
Brenner, N. 45
Brewer, T. 133
Brown, B. 77
Brown, W. 45
Bundy, A.C. 129

Burghardt, G. 25, 38, 64, 70
Burkitt, I. 203
Burman, E. 41, 42, 44

Callard, F. 181
Camfield, L. 88
Carroll, L. 9, 10
Carver, A. 202
Childers, S. 182
Cilliers, P. 73
Clegg, S. 134
Cloke, P. 109, 206
Colebrook, C. 68
Crampton, J. 76
Cranwell, K. 139
Crossa, V. 163, 164
Crouch, D. 183
Cunningham, H. 130
Curti, G. 59

Dahlbeck, J. 48
Dahlberg, G. 44
Damasio, A. 43
Darwish, M. 11
De Freitas, E. 186
Degen, M. 184
DeLanda, M. 50, 70
Deleuze, G. 10, 12, 13, 15, 28, 30,
	46, 49, 62, 64, 65, 67, 69, 71, 72,
	73, 74, 75, 76, 77, 79, 82, 92, 98,
	110, 112, 136, 137, 140, 141, 142,
	153, 156, 160, 162, 163, 177,
	181, 190, 198, 204, 221, 224

Department for Children, Schools and Families (DCSF) 125–6, 139
Derickson, K.D. 101–2
Derrida, J. 13, 73
Derry, C. 172, 182, 208
Devine, D. 214
Dewsbury, J.-D. 76, 187, 188, 194
Duff, C. 93, 95, 203, 205

Edensor, T. 180

Facer, K. 90
Fagen, R. 28–9, 52, 58
Fenech, M. 48
Ferrell, J. 169
Fitzgerald, D. 181
Fitzpatrick, J. 33, 172, 177, 184, 192, 208, 218
Foucault, M. 44–5, 47, 127, 169, 204–5, 209
Fox, N. 91, 112
France, L. 22
Frohlich, K. 91
Frost, J. 127
Fujii, L. 187
Fusco, C. 91

Gagen, E. 127
Gallacher, L.-A. 103–4
Gallagher, M. 184
Gardiner, M. 58, 155
Garland-Thomson, R. 46
Garner, A.S. 128
Garrett, P. 45
Garvey, C. 70
Gill, T. 202
Gregg, M. 82
Grosz, E. 71, 175, 180, 192
Guattari, F. 15, 30, 46, 49, 64, 65, 67, 69, 71, 72, 74, 75, 76, 77, 79, 82, 92, 110, 112, 136, 140, 141, 142, 153, 156, 160, 162, 163, 177, 181, 190, 198, 204, 224
Gullov, E. 134
Gunder, M. 210
Gyure, D.A. 128

Hadjicharalambous, M. 64
Hannikainen, M. 214, 216
Hannon, C. 210
Haraway, D. 63, 188
Hardt, M. 98, 156, 165, 168, 216
Harrison, P. 174
Hart, R. 128, 141
Harvey, D. 44, 121, 122, 123, 132, 141
Hayles, N. 52
Hazelwood, T. 201
Healy, P. 207, 211
Hein, S.F. 64
Henricks, T. 41
Highmore, B. 112
Hillier, J. 207, 210–11, 211–12
Hinchliffe, S. 49, 50, 63, 132
Holland, P. 205
Holloway, S. 41
Holmes, R. 90
Holt, L. 41
Horton, J. 47, 97, 137
Howell, O. 127, 201
Hughes, B. 213

Ingold, T. 23, 36, 42–3, 57, 63, 73–4, 82, 119, 122, 157, 186, 217, 220

Jablonka, E. 41
Jackson, A. 91, 198
James, A. 37, 40
Jenkins, J. 112
Jones, O. 109, 188, 205, 206
Jung, Y. 184

Kallio, K. 152
Karsten, L. 202
Katz, C. 37, 41. 151, 163
Keevers, L. 197
Klee, P. 78, 181
Kozlovsky, R. 135, 140
Kraftl, P. 47, 52, 97, 137, 156, 214
Krasnor, L. 70
Kropotkin, P. 147
Kyriakides, E. 64

Lamb, M. 41
Lancet, The 130
Landauer, G. 150
l'Anson, J. 76
Latham, A. 59, 188
Latour, B. 188, 210
Laurier, E. 73, 77, 175
Leander, K. 214
Lee, N. 40, 45, 48, 90, 203, 210
Lefebvre, H. 124, 141, 142,
    187, 207, 210, 214
Lester, S. 10, 31, 32, 33, 38, 39, 40, 41,
    43, 48, 49, 50, 51, 55, 59, 64, 70,
    78-9, 81, 83-4, 94, 95, 96-7, 99, 100,
    104, 105, 106, 107, 110, 113, 118,
    132, 137, 140, 141, 153-4, 155, 172,
    173, 177, 178-9, 181, 182, 183, 184,
    185, 190, 192, 197, 198, 199-200,
    201, 202, 204, 205, 206, 207, 207-8,
    208, 214, 215, 218, 221, 222
Lewontin, R. 41
Loizou, E. 64
Lorimer, H. 58
Louv, R. 132
Lyotard, J.-F. 40

MacKinnon, D. 101-2
MacLure, M. 62, 187, 188, 197
Malone, K. 202
Manning, E. 46, 67, 68, 69, 70, 71-2, 81,
    82-3, 108, 107, 119-20, 153, 160
Massey, D. 122-3, 203, 207
Massumi, B. 46, 50, 51, 61, 62, 64, 85,
    95, 117, 119-20, 126, 197, 222
Masten, A. 96, 175
Matthews, H. 166
May, T. 148, 157, 170, 222
Mayall, B. 40, 41, 88-9, 90, 202
Mazzei, L. 91, 192, 198, 200
McCormack, D. 62, 123, 124,
    138, 174, 180, 181, 186
Miller, P. 47
Moreno, C. 59
Morrow, V. 88-9, 90, 202
Moss, P. 44, 141, 173
Moss, S. 131
Motzkau, J. 45, 210
Mozère, L. 46, 47, 151, 204

Murray, R. 128
Myers, K. 202

Negri, A. 98, 156, 165, 168, 216
Newberry, R.C. 97

Olsson, L. 36, 46
Opie, I. 32, 35, 152
Opie, P. 32, 35
O'Shea, K. 125
O'Sullivan, S. 177
Oyama, S. 41, 49

Pacilli, G. 202
Paddison, R. 207
Parnet, C. 28, 30, 46, 73, 221
Patton, P. 85, 157, 159, 169
Peck, J. 45
Pence, A. 44
Pepler, D. 70
Phillips, N. 214
Philo, C. 37, 73, 144
Pile, S. 158
Pinder, D. 163
BBC 94, 97
Playwork Principles Scrutiny Group 70
Plows, V. 156
Powell, K. 186
Powell, S. 173
Prezza, M. 202
Prior, J. 184
Protevi, J. 76, 77, 124
Prout, A. 40, 50, 52, 63, 155
Punch, S. 41
Purcell, M. 164

Ramstetter, C.L. 128
Rancière, J. 157, 158-9, 163, 166
Read, J. 131
Robinson, K.H. 90
Roopnarine, J. 37-8
Roosevelt, T. 128
Rose, G. 184
Rose, N. 47, 152, 210
Routledge, P. 163
Rowlands, P. 88

Rudner, J. 202
Russell, W. 31, 33, 40, 41, 48, 49, 55,
    94, 95, 96, 97, 99, 100, 105, 113,
    118, 137, 155, 172, 173, 177, 178–9,
    181, 184, 192, 197, 199–200, 202,
    206, 207–8, 208, 218, 222, 223
Ryan, K. 50, 52, 108, 134, 140

Saldanha, A. 142
Schiller, J.C.F von 9
Scott, J.C. 151
Seigworth, G.J. 82
Sharp, J. 207
Simkins, I. 201
Simondon, G. 67, 153
Skott-Myhre, H. 75, 204
Smith, H. 197
Smith, P. 40
Soja, E.W. 165, 168
Spiller, J. 21
Spinka, M. 97
Springer, S. 169
Stagoll, C. 69
Stevens, Q. 209, 212
Stewart, K. 57, 174, 175
Stoecklin, V. 133
Strachan, A. 172, 182, 208
Strandell, H. 50
Stratford, E. 201
Streuli, N. 88
Sumsion, J. 48
Sutton-Smith, B. 38, 40, 44, 58, 86,
    87, 97, 98, 99, 104, 133, 150–1

Sydnor, S. 58

Tarulli, D. 75, 204
Taylor, A. 131, 132–3
Taylor, K. 214
Theodore, N. 45
Thomson, S. 130
Thrift, N. 45, 46, 58, 142, 177, 201, 216
Tisdall, E. 41
Trawick-Smith, J. 98

UNCRC 33, 113, 126
Ungar, M. 33. 91, 101, 102,
    104, 126, 191, 199
UNICEF Office of Research 88

van Vliet, W. 202
Veitch, J. 202

Ward, C. 136, 141, 147, 150, 169, 171
Wellard, I. 173
Welsh Government 126, 178, 179
Whatmore, S. 63
Williams, T. 137, 172
Woodhead, M. 88
Woolgar, S. 210
Woolley, H. 127, 201

Youdell, D. 155, 205

notes—

playing creates joy — but only when it is child centered, unplanned — & joy is what makes life worth living — how is civic engagement then related to joy — & here are the non-restrictive play behaviors demonstrating what we might see in a civically engaged person

civic behavior — can we see these behaviors in the coercive classroom? This is why we don't have civically engaged young people.

p. 37—
Being civically engaged
provides for a sense of
accomplishment &
well being —
play does the same